FASHIONABLE
CHILDHOOD

FASHIONABLE CHILDHOOD

Children in Advertising

ANNAMARI VÄNSKÄ

TRANSLATED BY EVA MALKKI

FILI FINNISH LITERATURE EXCHANGE

Bloomsbury Academic
An imprint of Bloomsbury Publishing Plc

BLOOMSBURY
LONDON · OXFORD · NEW YORK · NEW DELHI · SYDNEY

Bloomsbury Academic

An imprint of Bloomsbury Publishing Plc

50 Bedford Square
London
WC1B 3DP
UK

1385 Broadway
New York
NY 10018
USA

www.bloomsbury.com

BLOOMSBURY and the Diana logo are trademarks of Bloomsbury Publishing Plc

First published 2017

© Annamari Vänskä, 2017
Translated by Eva Malkki, 2017

British Library Cataloguing-in-Publication Data
A catalogue record for this book is available from the British Library.

ISBN:	HB:	978-1-4725-6845-8
	PB:	978-1-4725-6844-1
	ePDF:	978-1-4725-6846-5
	ePub:	978-1-4725-6847-2

Library of Congress Cataloging-in-Publication Data
Names: Vänskä, Annamari, author. | Malkki, Eva, translator. |
Translation of: Vänskä, Annamari. Muodikas lapsuus.
Title: Fashionable childhood : children in advertising / Annamari
Vänskä ; translated by Eva Malkki.
Other titles: Muodikas lapsuus. English
Description: New York : Bloomsbury Academic, 2017.
Identifiers: LCCN 2016043565 | ISBN 9781472568441 (paperback) |
ISBN 9781472568458 (hardback)
Subjects: LCSH: Children in advertising. | Advertising–Psychological
aspects. | Advertising–Children's clothing. | Mass media and children. |
BISAC: SOCIAL SCIENCE / Gender Studies. | SOCIAL SCIENCE /
Children's Studies. | DESIGN / Fashion.
Classification: LCC HF5822 .V3613 2017 | DDC 659.19/74692–dc23
LC record available at https://lccn.loc.gov/2016043565

Cover design: Clare Turner
Cover image: Heidi Lunabba from the series "Twins" © Heidi Lunabba

Typeset by Integra Software Services Pvt. Ltd.
Printed and bound in India

CONTENTS

LIST OF ILLUSTRATIONS

ACKNOWLEDGMENTS

As we all know, carrying out research and writing books is not a solitary endeavor, let alone getting that work translated into English, revised, edited, and finally published with a prestigious publishing house. Professor Caroline Evans was key in this process—without her, I would not be writing these acknowledgments. My editors at Bloomsbury have also been vital to the project. Emily Ardizzone's enthusiasm opened the doors to Bloomsbury, and Hannah Crump's patience, belief in my work, and kind support throughout the whole process from translation to publication have been simply invaluable.

I also want to give my sincere thanks to colleagues who have supported me in different phases of this project. Thank you Minna Autio, Claudia Castañeda, Hazel Clark, Ulrika Dahl, Tim Edwards, R. Danielle Egan, Pia Livia Hekanaho, Harri Kalha, Mary Jane Kehily, Anu Koivunen, Tora Korsvold, Katariina Kyrölä, Eva Malkki, Peter McNeil, Susanna Paasonen, Marco Pecocari, Jessica Ringrose, Leena-Maija Rossi, Maria Sell, Anna Sparrman, Louise Wallenberg, and Jan Wickman. Your comments and encouraging words have helped me believe in what I am trying to say. Very special thanks go to the two external reviewers of the manuscript. Your careful reading and precise comments helped me tremendously in revising, rewriting, and editing the manuscript. You helped me make this a much better version than the original manuscript ever was.

I like to conduct research in dialogue with artists and designers. It is a very fruitful way of expanding one's academic analysis. Each chapter of this book opens with a photograph from a series entitled *Twins* by the incredibly talented visual artist Heidi Lunabba. I was so pleased that she immediately replied "yes" when I suggested that she make an artistic research project about children, fashion, and advertising. Without her input, the book would not be as multifaceted as it is. All other images and advertisements in this work have been used by me, the author, and the publisher on the basis of fair dealing for the purpose of criticism and review.

I am too well aware that family and friends are often neglected when research calls. My eternal gratitude for putting up with me and my absence during the writing process goes to you, Jenni. You give me space when I need it, support me when I need it, and take me away from my work when I need it but don't know it myself. I can always count on you. I have also many lovely children in my life—you have been, and continue to be, an important window to the world of children's fashion.

Research also needs financial support. Thanks go to the Kone Foundation, Riksbankens Jubileumsfond, the Academy of Finland, the Finnish Association of Non-fiction Writers, School of History, Culture and Arts Studies at the University of Turku and FILI—Finnish Literary Exchange.

INTRODUCTION: CHILDHOOD AS MEDIA SPECTACLE

On June 5, 2012, the Finnish tabloid *Ilta-Sanomat* reported on a "scandal over teen girls' clothing." The first media sensation of the summer was about the way girls dressed. The article reported that a school in Southwest Finland had banned students from wearing shorts that "revealed bare buttocks." Apparently, the school had had to ask its students to cover up after too many teen girls had attended in excessively tight and revealing summer clothes. The school's cited reason was "propriety": that a place of learning called for "respectable," non-revealing clothing rather than "half-nakedness."[1] Interviewed by the paper, the head of the local council's Education and Culture Department drew a link between proper clothing and conscientious, good behavior:

> Students must complete their tasks conscientiously and behave properly. In my opinion, proper behavior also implies proper dress.

The same head of department also suggested that school pupils must not be "provocative," but behave "sensibly," taking others into account in their choices of clothing. Soon a women's magazine reported that the school's principal had stressed the needs of other pupils in banning the shorts. However, unlike the head of the Education and Culture Department, the principal was not referring to the needs of all students, but specifically male ones.[2] In the principal's view, short shorts caused problems for boys in particular:

> If there is so much bare skin that buttocks can be seen and everything is in plain sight, it can make a lot of boys quite uncomfortable.

The principal felt that short shorts should be banned because teenage boys might be unable to control their sex drives and behavior on seeing them. In other words, instead of working to prevent possible uncontrolled behavior on the part

Figure I.1 From the series *Twins*, Helsinki, 2010. © Heidi Lunabba.

of boys, the principal focused on girls and decided to solve the problem by restricting their choices of clothing. Teens interviewed by the tabloid considered the intervention to be unfair, saying that shorts are basic summer attire and that clothing is a matter of personal choice. The grown-ups, on the other hand, said they were only looking after the children's best interests. They claimed that adults have to intervene in the way girls dress if the girls themselves fail to understand what is best for them. The school also assured the paper that it did not intend to ban skirts and shorts completely; it just wanted to make sure that the students' "trouser legs and skirt hems were of a decorous length."

This clothing-related furor relates to many of the central themes of this book. Firstly, it revealed that articles of clothing—shorts in this case—are more than simply innocent items of attire. They are connected to stereotyped conceptions regarding girlhood, boyhood, adulthood, behavior, values, and sexuality. Secondly, it shows how easily children's clothing will cause concern and awaken diverse feelings in adults, and what an integral part of today's media content clothing has become. Scandals and outcries related to children and their appearance are an important theme of this book. Controversies related to allegedly unacceptable children's attire bring to light how fundamental a part clothing and images of children play when we construct the idea of a proper or improper childhood. At the heart of the clothing scandal lay the fear of corrupting innocence and oversexualizing children. Innocence is a theme that runs through this book. The innocence we uphold today as the natural and indisputable model of proper childhood has, in fact, only become established fairly recently. This book shows how innocence is constructed through children's clothing and certain ways of visual representation in fashion advertising. Innocence is very fragile and seen as constantly running the risk of being spoiled. Sexuality is often considered to be the opposite of innocence and something from which children should unquestionably be protected. Often this protection takes the form of control and censorship of clothes that are deemed harmful for children—such as too-short shorts—and images that represent children in the wrong way. There appears to be a powerful concept, particularly in everyday discourse and the media, of the sexualizing impact of certain garments, gestures, and images. This book also presents views on the complex history of childhood and sexuality, and sheds light on the links between sexuality and innocence. Fashion advertising has espoused the conflict between these two supposed opposites and makes effective use of it in attracting attention and building the identities of fashion brands.

Several successful reality television programs have been produced in recent years that focus on children and their looks. One very popular program is *Generation XXL*, shown by Channel 4 in Britain, which follows the lives of seven children for a decade to discover what it is like to grow up as an obese child in Britain. The US cable channel TLC, meanwhile, airs the show *Toddlers & Tiaras*, which is about child beauty pageants. In the series, which started in 2009, children—mostly girls but also a handful of boys—aged three to nine compete for the titles of Beauty Queen and Pageant Prince. The contestants are first filmed getting ready at home, where the (often unwilling) toddlers are plied with makeup and fake tans, taken to beauty salons, and dressed up in finery. The little girls' hair is crimped, backcombed, and extended into a mound of curls twice the size of their heads. In the pageant, every child performs before a jury of grown-ups. The jury assesses the contestants' appearance and performance, and eventually picks the winners who will receive merchandise and around one thousand dollars in prize money.[3]

In January 2012, Sweden's TV 3 began airing the reality show *Mammor & Minimodeller* ("Mummies and Mini Models"); in it, experts from the modeling world train mothers and their six- to ten-year-old girls in dressing, being made up and posing right to become successful models. The show caused a lot of controversy and the Swedish national broadcaster's debating program, *Debatt*, dedicated an entire episode to it.[4] In the studio various experts, including a child psychologist, described how detrimental the program was to the development of little girls, as it led them to believe that they can cope in the world with looks alone. One of the mothers who had been criticized for her particular thoughtlessness in the press and in online discussion forums defended herself in the debate. It made no difference that she claimed always to think of what was best for her daughter: the experts' condemnation of the series and of that mother in particular was unyielding.

Today's children are born into a reality that is filtered through the media. They surf expertly through virtual worlds, meet their friends in online chat rooms, and play World of Warcraft. Images flood their consciousness from every angle: smartphones, the Internet, magazines, TV, films, and computer games. They grow up in an age in which the body is an avatar to be modified and decorated with clothes and accessories. Various virtual environments and the idea of the editability of the body have to be accepted as elements of the reality in which children now live. In the case of girls, for example, playing with dolls has shifted from the playroom to online Barbie and Bratz websites, where they can dress up the dolls while also learning to style themselves with makeup and fashionable clothes.[5]

In our commercial culture, children are increasingly also used as models for advertising products or services. Child figures are used to sell everything under the sun, from Pampers nappies to ready meals, and from home insurance to cars and holidays. Additionally, children are advertising toys, branded clothes, and beauty products aimed at themselves more and more often. It shows the progression of consumerism to become an increasingly ineluctable part of their lives. Many made-up characters—Peppa Pig, Barbies, Bratz, Moomins, and so on—are used for selling clothes, while famous fashion brands such as Dior, Armani, Diesel, and Guess have their own lines of expensive attire for the youngest family members.

Today's Looks-Obsessed Children

In 2008, the Finnish teen magazine *Demi* conducted a survey on the importance of appearance among its readers. The results indicated how important looks have become for today's children and preteens.[6] Some of the questions posed to the *Demi* readership related to the significance of beauty. Even though the concept of beauty was not specifically defined, it was understood to refer to outward appearance rather than "inner beauty." According to the survey's results, looks were very important to 85 percent of the magazine's readers, while 69 percent considered fashionable clothes to be a vehicle for self-expression. Although these answers cannot be extrapolated to apply generally to all teens (or, rather, teen girls), they do indicate that looking after one's appearance and styling oneself using fashion are an integral part of the lives of modern children and adolescents. According to the responses, today's youth increasingly believes that the secret to success is on the body rather than in the mind. The respondents' ideals were beautiful, acne-free skin, well-styled hair, fashionable clothes, and a well-proportioned, slim figure. These were mentioned as the foundations for success and self-confidence. The people that the respondents named as most beautiful were (American) celebrities with a major media presence—models, actresses, and pop stars.

The *Demi* survey was directed at the readers of a magazine that focuses on looks and lifestyle, so it is unsurprising that the responses should stress the significance of beauty. Researchers have made similar observations, however. The links between images in the media and the body-consciousness of children, as well as the idea of the body as a modifiable element in identity-building, are strongly emphasized in many researchers' works. Naomi Klein, Alissa Quart, and Juliet B. Schor, among others, have written about the ways in which the lives of American children and adolescents revolve around looks, fashionable products, and brand consumption.[7] The bodies of preteens and teens have become public items that are modified and styled using clothes, makeup, and even plastic surgery. In other words, consumption is not limited to clothes and other design items. Quart, for example, writes about American girls who have after-school jobs for the purpose of earning enough money to pay for breast enlargements.[8] Schor, for her part, mentions children who are able to recognize hundreds of brands by the age of two. Among other things, this is due to commercial companies having wrapped their tentacles around children's TV programs: they not only fund the production of the programs but turn their brands into main characters. In this way they prep children from an early age to become active consumers with an increasing amount of power when it comes to making purchase decisions in the family.[9] The objective of corporate marketing and advertising is to get young consumers to buy themselves an identity out of the selection of characters they offer (and often present in a very sexy way).

The results indicate that body image pressure is common among Western children. Even primary school children are very aware of their appearance and feel stress related to it.[10] Girls want to be pretty and popular, while for boys the aim is to dress "cool" without standing out too much.[11] The ideals for girls are thinness, fashionable attire, and flawless skin, while for boys body image is related to athleticism and the chances of getting a girlfriend: both highly masculine reasons for looking after one's appearance. The difference between girls and boys reflects the still-current idea that it is a woman's duty to make herself beautiful, whereas excessive preening is inappropriate in a man. Although British studies on masculinity, for example, spoke already in the late 1980s about the "new man"—the consumerist man who looks after himself and is interested in fashion—and although the concept of the urban and fashion-conscious "metrosexual" was launched in the United States in the late 1990s, young boys still seem to feel that male grooming serves a purely functional purpose.[12] It is acceptable when related to athleticism or to finding a girlfriend, but beautifying for its own sake is not for boys.

Healthy Mind in a Beautiful Body

Children and adolescents raised in today's thoroughly visual culture have learnt to see their physical appearance as a tool for creating and managing impressions. High fashion plays an important role in this: it forms part of a luxurious lifestyle directed at children, which is represented by "fashion toys" such as Barbie dolls, lifestyle magazines, pop stars, and Hollywood actors in their trendy clothes. The links between the worlds of children and high fashion became especially evident in 2008 when the toy giant Mattel announced Barbie's very own fashion show. The next year was Barbie's fiftieth anniversary, and it was celebrated by fifty top designers creating stylish clothes for her. Since the beginning of the twenty-first century, Barbie has had competitors in the form of globally marketed, fashion-conscious, and provocatively dressed Bratz dolls made by MGA Entertainment, Inc. From the very beginning, a whole ecosystem of products has been built around the Bratz doll: children's clothes, accessories, movies, cartoons, a magazine, and music, among other things. Although Barbie has also become a clothes brand, Bratz dolls were the first toys that were marketed in openly consumerist fashion, with the slogan "Girls with a passion for fashion!"[13]

Fashion also trickles down to the world of children through various publications. One example is the magazine *Top Model*, directed at six- to twelve-year-old girls who are interested in fashion, which is published in Europe by the German company Depesche Vertrieb. When the magazine was launched in Finland in the spring of 2011, many adults were concerned: online debates raged on whether a magazine focusing on fashion and beauty tips would expose girls under the age of ten to normative beauty standards too early. The actual content of the magazine was somewhat forgotten amid the uproar: it mainly consists of paper dolls, for which the reader draws—or, as the magazine puts it, designs—the clothes. The magazine claims to nourish creativity in order to bring out the next generation of imaginative designers.

The magazine's aim is already being fulfilled. The twenty-first century has seen children being molded into fashion trendsetters. In the winter of 2011, the fashion magazine *Elle* reported on celebrity kids who had become "fashion icons." According to the article, children were increasingly setting the pace of the fashion world. It told the reader that Suri Cruise, 4, Willow Smith, 10, and Lourdes Ciccone, 14, among others, had good taste and dressed fashionably. It also mentioned that eleven-year-old Cecilia Cassini had been the head designer for her own fashion label since the age of six. In May 2011, even the broadsheets picked up the story: Sweden's daily newspaper *Dagens Nyheter* reported that "girls are the latest fashion icons."[14] In early 2012, the Swedish gossip magazine *Bild* ran a piece on supermodels from the 1980s and 1990s, whose daughters had followed in their career footsteps.

Fashion toys and websites based on styling, articles in the press about children-turned-fashion icons, and designer lines aimed at kids indicate that it is no longer enough in life for children to be clean and healthy. They also have to look good and understand that their bodies are important tools for communication. The twentieth century turned people into individuals who are supremely self-conscious, concerned about their health, constantly seeking objects of self-improvement, and ever reshaping their personalities as if they were commodities. Now, the twenty-first century has started injecting this way of thinking into childhood.[15]

Although we want to keep children out of the world of grown-ups, we transfer our looks-centric culture into their world. Under the adult gaze, children are expected to express their selfhood and their status in life; looks have become important to the degree that they are used to judge how well children are cared for. Many people are quick to determine a child's upbringing, diet, degree of exercise, and personal hygiene from his or her appearance. Children are expected to pass a certain "validity test" on sight: a child with the "wrong" looks is a sign of (the parents') moral laxity and sloth, whereas a physically cared-for child is thought to demonstrate a healthy attitude from the parents.

Vogue Bambini: A Window into Fashionable Childhood

This book examines representations of childhood in fashion advertising. The fashion researcher Jennifer Craik links the rising status of children in the fashion industry to population aging and low birth rates in the West.[16] As family sizes shrink, parents have begun investing more and more in their children—both financially and psychologically. This has increased both demand for and the supply of designer clothes and luxury products for children. Many high-fashion houses, including Dior, Versace, Calvin Klein, Burberry, Armani, Alberta Ferretti, and Gucci, have kids' collections.[17] Some market analysts say that children themselves direct fashion trends; others see it as wealthy parents creating miniature versions of themselves in their offspring.[18] Parents interested in children's fashion have also found their way into the social media. A growing number of fashion-conscious toddlers can be followed on Instagram. Facebook hosts groups built around top fashion brands, where thousands of users—mostly mothers who are fans of the brand in question—exchange information about the clothes and buy and sell them, sometimes at exorbitant prices. They also upload pictures of their children wearing the clothes.

Although this book is about more than just fashion photography, most of its visual material was collected from the Italian kids' fashion magazine *Vogue Bambini*. It is a member of the *Vogue* family of products, which represents the elite among fashion magazines. It has been issued since 1973, originally monthly, and then six times a year since the late 1980s. Additionally, the magazine prints catalogues containing catwalk images from children's fashion shows in spring and autumn, as well as special issues on themes such as sportswear. In other words, just one year's issues of the magazine contain huge amounts of visual material that displays childhood in different ways. It is fair to say that *Vogue Bambini* does not just present the latest in children's fashion but also acts as a guide for fashion professionals and parents alike in how to turn small children into fashion gurus.

The magazine illustrates how depictions of childhood have changed and evolved over the last forty years, and how closely childhood is linked to clothes, visual culture, and consumerism. Large images and visual elements on the whole have always played a central role in *Vogue Bambini*; in that sense, the magazine reflects an era in which photography has become an inseparable part of the world of fashion. This was not always the case: in the nineteenth century, women's magazines were illustrated by hand, if at all. Photographs of clothes became more common as the twentieth century wore on, but in 1950s' *Vogue*, for example, there was still more text than images. Now the balance has been reversed. *Vogue Bambini*, in particular, looks more like a thick picture book. Thomas Condé Nast, publisher of the *Vogue* family of magazines, was, in fact, one of the first to start using photography instead of artwork. Initially, photographs of clothes served a documentary purpose, being intended to show the apparel as objectively as possible.[19] Quite soon, however, fashion photography broke free of any restrictions imposed by objectivity and more emphasis was placed on artistic expression. Today's fashion advertising strives to create narratives and diverse moods. It is more than descriptive; it builds an image of the brand, as well as of the consumer and his or her identity.

Besides advertisements from *Vogue Bambini*, this book's materials include media coverage of debates related to children's clothing, as well as recent fashion advertising campaigns. Young girls, in particular, have started to be involved in advertising clothes together with, or instead of, adults. The chosen examples are included because they complement the fashion magazine materials and help in forming a bigger picture of the issue. They also attest to the way the world has changed: children are no longer confined to their own publications or to advertisements intended for their age segment. They have entered the grown-up advertising world and help to sell fashion items intended also for grown-ups.

Even though *Vogue Bambini* is not read in every household, it is a widely issued coffee-table magazine and a kind of Bible of children's fashion, particularly for those in the profession. It is often used for inspiration when designing "ordinary" kids' clothes. The circulation of *Vogue Bambini* is 70,000 per issue with a readership of 200,000.[20] This is humble in comparison with the main *Vogue*, for example, which is around two million, but that does not make it any less visible a part of the world of children's fashion. Sometimes the magazine is sold as a package with other magazines. Additionally, it is delivered to high-fashion boutiques, exhibition spaces, and hotels, where it is seen by their respective clienteles. *Vogue Bambini* also has a presence at fashion fairs all around the Western world.

Vogue Bambini is fascinating because the thousands of fashion photographs printed on its pages form a narrative that tells us that by the beginning of the twenty-first century, children had become fully fledged and highly visible participants of consumer culture.[21] They dress fashionably, pose for photographs like grown-up models, and embody the fashion industry's conception of the ideal childhood. *Vogue Bambini* provides front-row access to see how the outlines of modern childhood are defined and branded. Children's fashion has also started playing an increasingly important role in high-street brands' advertising. In 2010, for example, the Swedish edition of *Metro* magazine published several full-page spreads advertising kids' clothes. The use of children as models—that is, as concrete builders of ideals—has increased in recent years. More and more popular articles are written on children who are interested in fashion or who work in fashion as models or style icons. This is an explicit example of ways in which fashion and couture have entered the everyday lives of young children and their parents.

Fashion as Idealized Imagery

The fashion designer duo Viktor & Rolf are said to have asserted that "fashion doesn't have to be something people wear; fashion is also an image."[22] This statement crystallizes the idea that fashion consists of more than just producing new consumables for people to buy. Fashion is closely tied to imagery: it is divulged to consumers through the use of diverse visual media, and looking at images of fashion is at least as important an aspect of fashion consumption as buying expensive clothes—if not more so.[23] In fact, the transformation of fashion into images and other visual symbols on the global market has brought haute couture closer to the ordinary consumer. Most consumers do not buy high-fashion brands or visit their stores. Their contact with the world of couture is mostly through fashion magazines and other media built for viewing, browsing, skimming, or surfing. This makes spectacularity a fundamental element of fashion. One could even say that fashion is a universe of images and symbols.

Visuality defines every aspect of fashion: not only the products but also the décor and displays of the stores that sell them, the appearance of the salespeople, the brands' advertising and logos, and so on. The sumptuous imagery related to fashion is mostly the outcome of highly calculated product development, and its aim is to create a feel of exclusivity and luxury around specific brands. The marriage of fashion, spectacle, and commercialism is directed at maximizing financial gain by making a brand, and its products stand out from their competitors through a unique visual world. While the pictorial spectacle around fashion does entice consumers to buy products, fashion imagery is also consumed by itself, independently of the clothes. It is not necessarily linked to buying or using the advertised products. Fashion advertisements do more than just objectively describe garments for the purpose of selling them: they are part of a broader visual culture. Their function is to build independent worlds in which goods and brands play a significant role but are not the only thing that matters.[24]

Fashion images are also crucial tools in building the consumers' identity. Among other things, they mold our conceptions of what makes an ideal childhood. Children's fashion and the related advertising are a perfect example of how inseparably the real, the virtual, the imagined, and the pictorial are woven together in the definition of contemporary childhood. Although fashion images feature child models, they are not about real children. Childhood is represented in them symbolically as a way of bestowing various meanings upon the clothes, the brand, and the consumer.[25] The idea of the symbolic nature of childhood is crucial to my research, because it links together consumerism and visuality. Child models give their faces and bodies to a product and brand, and thereby represent them. The story told by fashion images is that in the early days of this millennium, childhood is seen pretty much as a thoroughly commercial phenomenon.

Because imagery has become such an essential part of consumption, it is particularly important to discuss how, where, and by whom its meanings are constructed, and how these meanings could be challenged. In starting out my research, I was often asked why I was basing it on marginal high-fashion images. Many fellow researchers felt it would be "more sensible" to study "ordinary" children's clothes instead of designer ones. I feel that high fashion provides visual material that stands not for everyday life but for ideals.[26] It shows how childhood should be, rather than what it is. Fashion images are interesting to study because they both express and challenge the prevailing conception of the ideal childhood.

Ultimately, fashion images reflect the values and visions of our whole society, not just of the companies that produce them. In this respect they should be seen as visually encoded wholes with meanings that extend beyond the surface of the image or the brands' marketing departments. By analyzing fashion imagery representing children, we may get an idea of the values, estimations, and ideals that are linked to childhood and adulthood.

Multiple Meanings of Fashion

The meanings of fashion images are constructed in many ways. On the one hand, they are contrasted to other, comparable images and the companies that produce them. On the other hand, the meanings are constructed in analyzing the images. The ways in which the images are interpreted are regulated by many factors, which means that our interpretations are never completely arbitrary. They arise from the viewer and from the context in which the images are interpreted.

When childhood is considered as part of a visually oriented consumer culture, many meanings are unavoidably ignored. For example, we may fail to consider how advertising that represents young people might affect children. The chosen perspective narrows down the possibilities and diversity of interpretations. Researchers may, however, expand on the constructed meanings through creative use of concepts and symbols, and by placing the images in new interpretive contexts. When successful, such creative readings can add new, unexpected meanings onto the familiar layers of significance that arise from visual texts. This means that images have more meanings than those that are retrieved from a stock of existing meanings. They arise from active and creative doing, a kind of recycling of interpretations coming from individual processing.

Prior studies have looked quite extensively at the active roles of children as consumers and skilled media users.[27] Conversely, there is very little research on the construction of childhood in advertising and other visual materials.[28] Certain inroads have been made, for instance, in analyzing the breakdown of the concept of childhood innocence in late-twentieth-century media imagery and art.[29] Research has also been conducted on the representations of ideal childhood in older paintings and early-twentieth-century photography, as well as on the fetishizing and eroticizing of innocence as the complete opposite of idealization.[30] In contrast, there has been no research at all on children who work as models and take part in creating the fictional narratives of fashion advertising and their diverse affective and emotional interpretations.

Learning Visual Literacy

This book tackles the trinity of consumerism, childhood, and the visual representation of children in fashion advertising. Recently, visual culture, consumption, and critical gender studies have examined images, goods, clothes, and gender using methods adopted particularly from linguistics and semiotics. This book continues in this tradition, studying—that is, interpreting and reading—advertising and fashion images as visual texts. Obviously, images do not literally consist of text; their textuality is metaphorical and constructed out of pictorial elements such as colors, model poses, clothes, and styles.

By studying these elements, I demonstrate how certain interpretations are formed. At the same time I show how interpretations that are thought to be unquestionable can be challenged. One of the important premises behind this book is the development of visual literacy, that is, the ability to read images. This skill is increasingly important in our image-filled world. It is good to be aware of how the meanings about images and clothes are formed; it is equally important to know how established meanings can be challenged. Each chapter of this book provides examples of this.

The first and second chapters look at research on childhood and the position of fashion and fashion images in defining childhood in today's media-oriented culture. One of the fundamental concepts in this is innocence, which has been the crucial determinant of childhood in recent centuries. The third chapter examines the history of childhood innocence and how it has become a construct that is built through specific forms of imagining and dressing.

Innocence has always been defined in contrast to its opposite: children who know too much, do not do as they are told, and are sexual. This theme is tackled in the fourth chapter. We look at it historically by examining some of the discourse that became popular in the nineteenth century, in which innocence began to refer specifically to sexual innocence, thereby differentiating the innocent—that is, asexual—child from the sexual child. Although the concept of childhood sexuality was formed in parallel with that of childhood innocence, it has not gained a similar acceptance in Western culture. Innocence has mostly become the ideal, whereas a sexual child is seen as a problem requiring drastic measures. The pictorial analysis conducted in this chapter shows that childhood innocence is no absolute or even natural state for a child. In fact, the opposite is true: innocence is a symbol for a middle-class childhood, created in contrast to notions of a working-class, non-Caucasian, non-Western, and sexualized childhood. The chapter proves that innocence equals whiteness in many senses. Whiteness here refers to mental and physical cleanliness, to ethnicity and to the concrete color of children's clothes. Advertising today recycles and repeats the historical constructs of innocence and sexuality, while also bringing in new levels of interpretation in order to reach new consumer groups.

The fifth chapter considers media discourse generated by fashion advertising, which is usually permeated by concern and worry. The most common claims in this discourse are that childhood is in crisis and that children are prematurely sexualized. Just over one hundred years ago, the Swedish women's rights activist Ellen Key described the 1900s as the Century of Childhood.[31] The start of the ongoing century, on the other hand, could well be called the era that turned childhood into a media spectacle. This shift has generated a new kind of interpretation, in which images are seen as genuine proof of childhood sexualization and sexual exploitation, against which children should be shielded. The chapter considers the historical roots of this exploitation/protection idea through examples.[32] Do the images exploit children? Is the presumed sexualization of children a sign of the "over-sexualized" nature of our culture, or even of "corporate paedophilia," as some would have it?[33] Or is it more likely that this concerned discourse stems from a certain historic background of which the advertising world makes conscious use in its brand-building? The chapter also questions the idea that an image should have the ability to exploit anyone. When discussing the interpretation of images, it is impossible to speak of genuine exploitation, because an advertising image is never directly connected with reality.

The sixth chapter takes a step away from the discourses of sexualisation and abuse and analyses images that are like wallpaper—in other words, it analyses images that do not bother anyone—and to which the "disturbing images" are compared. The chapter shows that innocence is an ideologically charged concept. Even though it is represented as asexuality, a closer analysis of representations of innocence expose that it actually means heterosexuality. The examples of the chapter indicate that fashion advertisements imagine children as already heterosexual: girls dressed in pink frilly dresses are represented as feminine and passive counterparts of active and masculine boys, dressed in blue. The chapter shows how this applies already to babies and how they are positioned, in various and imaginative ways inside the romantic confines of heterosexual intimacy and future relationships.

The seventh chapter starts from a notion of the absence of certain kinds of images when it comes to imagining relationships between little children. While advertising is filled with representations of little girls and boys hugging and kissing each other, there are only a handful of images where two girls almost kiss each other, and no images of kissing boys. This absence opens up a possibility to rethink innocence: the chapter brings forth examples that offer ways of fantasising childhood as a time which is not defined by heterosexual innocence posing as asexuality but rather, as a time that is defined by a plethora of different sexual potentialities. This chapter also takes advantage of constructivist approach: it aims at thinking about childhood beyond the ideology of childhood innocence. The chapter shows that fashion advertising offers good material for this; there are examples of active tomboys, girls almost kissing each other and boys hugging each other.

1
HISTORICALLY CONSTRUCTED CHILDHOOD

Although many social and cultural phenomena are today believed to be socially constructed, childhood is still thought of as a time when a person is directly connected with reality.[1] Adulthood is seen as a rational period, weighed down by moral responsibilities, whereas childhood is connected with all the things that later life is not. A child is commonly understood as a spontaneous and wild creature with a tendency to use his or her imagination. Childhood innocence refers to the idea that a child is still free of the corruption and depravity that are inevitably linked with growing up. Children are thought not yet responsible for their actions; they do not know about sexuality and are especially removed from man's inexorable fate—death.

This book critically examines everyday conceptions of childhood. The starting point is that childhood and its related innocence are social and historical constructs and that children's fashion and visual representations are emblematic of this sociohistorical constructedness. Such an approach is not necessarily agreeable for researchers or for our everyday understanding of childhood. For a researcher, it may be easier to hide behind the cloak of objectivity and to avoid open discussion on the actual motivation behind the research. And in everyday experience, childhood rarely presents itself as constructed—it just is. The constructionist approach analyzes the processes and forces that are fundamental in producing the everyday experience of children and childhood. It explores how values and worldviews—including those of the researcher— influence the kinds of questions that are asked and the answers that are found in the research, and how they influence the way in which we are able to present the world. It also shows that research results do not correspond to any real or natural order: they are just one way of understanding things. This implies that

Figure 1.1 From the series *Twins*, Helsinki, 2010. © Heidi Lunabba.

meanings about childhood are not set in stone. They can—and I hope to show in the course of this book that they should—change, even radically.[2]

The constructionist approach stresses the status of language and other systems of symbols—such as children's visual representations and their clothing—in constructing and interpreting childhood and its meanings. For example, the word "child" does not just signify a physical child, but can also symbolize concepts such as happiness, the future, or a burden, depending on the situation and the interpreter. Symbols may seem to exist outside of our human activity, but in reality they are ways of understanding and seeing the world that are born as a result of it.

Of course each individual does not start constructing the world from scratch. We are all born into a social reality fashioned by our predecessors; we learn a language and the prevailing way of communicating in our culture. Becoming socialized in relation to our culture's mind-sets and understanding them is a prerequisite for meaningful social intercourse, but also if we want to change these mind-sets. Our conceptions of children and childhood are molded by social communities that take a certain place within hierarchical systems: for example, the world of science or fashion catalogues. Although the view presented on childhood by the scientific community might be considered more true than that given by fashion photographs, both are inadequate and stereotyped. This is why we must strive to specify and modify the existing definition of childhood.

Images of children and their clothes do not just appear out of thin air. Images do not merely describe a child; nor do clothes simply dress them. Ways of representing and dressing children have respective histories and are entangled with knowledge and an understanding about childhood from a given moment in time. Every single advertisement and piece of clothing that we encounter are informed by a long history and set against a background of specific ideas regarding the nature of childhood.

Let's look at an example. Figure 1.2 is an advertisement for the clothing brand Maripier from 1982. It features two girls who, typical for that time, are dressed in tones of beige and off-white, colors which are also repeated in the background. We may ask: What stages have been completed before this photograph ended up as an advertisement for the brand on the pages of the fashion magazine *Vogue Bambini*? Excluding the production process of the clothes themselves, it went through at least the following stages: the fashion label decided to market its products (dresses and skirts for little girls); then a whole platoon of people took part in producing the image that does that: the company whose product is being advertised; the ad agency that came up with the visual narrative surrounding the product; the model agency that, together with a representative of the company, selected suitable child models for the ad; a stylist who has styled the models in an appropriate way for the product and the narrative; a costumier who dressed the children; a set designer who created the background; the photographer, who interpreted and visualized the narrative; and the medium or context in which the image was published (the fashion magazine).

Figure 1.2 Fashion images do not often reveal their constructedness, unlike this ad by Maripier from 1982. © Maripier 1982. Photograph by Danilo Frontinini.

The example shows that once the photograph is finished, so many factors have been involved that it clearly cannot have just one meaning. An advertisement is the result of a complex collaboration, whose participants—not to mention their intentions—do not always reach the viewer. Those looking at the advertisement always add their own meanings, as well. These depend, for instance, on the viewer's educational background and conceptions of childhood, and the context in which the image is viewed. If the context is that of a glossy magazine specializing in displaying fashion photographs, the viewer will see the image in relation to other similar images. If the context is a constructionist study on childhood, different meanings will arise in that direction.

As viewers of advertising, we usually see only the end result: in this case an advertisement for children's clothes from the 1980s, featuring two anonymous girls. We can only guess that at the time of the photo being taken they were around ten years old and fitted the company's assumptions of how potential buyers saw ideal childhood and fashionable girlhood. This image is a particularly good example of the constructedness of an advertisement, which becomes evident in the setting.[3] The girls are placed in poses that are in no way natural or easy: one stands with hands on hips and the other one sits bolt upright. Both are staring into the camera. The stiff poses make it clear that the image was staged, rather than trying to capture a fleeting moment. The photograph has been taken indoors, most probably in a photographer's studio; this is evident from the untidily hanging, creased hessian-like fabric in the background, and the studio spotlights, which are not cropped out of the frame. The advertisement clearly exposes its constructedness—a feature that connects the photograph to the 1980s, which is often defined as a time of deconstruction. In fashion, this meant making visible the construction of a garment,[4] while in visual representation, it referred to the construction of image-making, as in the Maripier advertisement.

The layout on the page of *Vogue Bambini* emphasizes the constructedness of the image even further. The company's logo is beneath the photograph, while the top left-hand corner has the names of the hair stylist and the photographer. The latter is the well-known Italian fashion photographer Danilo Frontinini. All the details hint at a lot of preparation and post-editing work on the photograph.

Fashion images, like images in general, are always constructed and carefully considered entities. Their language is not subject to the rules of grammar, but they do follow certain criteria—a kind of visual rhetoric.[5] The crucial components in high-fashion photographs depicting childhood are not only the colors, composition, setting, lighting, brightness, and depth but also the children's apparel, hairstyles, and accessories, the colors and materials of the clothes, the models' poses, and the directions of their gazes. Girls are usually attired in dresses, skirts, and dainty leather shoes, just as they are in the Maripier ad. Contemporary boys never wear skirts or dresses; instead they are casually dressed in trousers, T-shirts, and sporty trainers, or more formally in button-down shirts, blazers, and leather shoes. Today's girls' clothes are often light or pastel in color—tones which are unheard-of for boys, who usually wear blue, brown, and primary colors. The actions of the children in the photographs are also significant. Girls are often portrayed in model-like poses, while boys are mostly shown in action: cycling, jumping, painting, and so forth. A clear change has been evident in recent years in this respect, though: the closer we get to the modern day, the more professional and adult-like the child models of both sexes are. This change is also visible in children's clothing: today, they do not necessarily differ much from adult clothes.

(Ad)dressing Childhood: New Childhood Studies

One of the interpretive starting points in this book for fashion advertising featuring children lies in constructionist childhood studies, which emphasize the historic and social constructedness of childhood and analyze how clothes and visual representations contribute to its construction.

For cultural studies of fashion, social constructionism offers a highly suitable methodology for examining human reality and how fashion and its visual representations shape it. It challenges the positivistic idea that a single truth can be found and emphasizes knowledge as something historical, contextual, and culturally specific, built through interpersonal communication and undergoing continuous change.[6] The changing ways of depicting and dressing children bring out the fact that knowledge about childhood is localized and processual; that is, that children have no predetermined being. Instead, the ways that they are seen, dressed, and understood are the product of diverse social processes.[7]

The constructionist approach does not define childhood as a natural state or age but as a conception of what passes for childhood in our culture, formed as a result of continuous struggle and negotiation, and mediated by various visual/material representations. This philosophy became established in studies of childhood in the early 1990s and came to be known as "new childhood studies." One of its main achievements is to have brought children into the sphere of research as active agents and meaning producers. It looked for support from disciplines including anthropology, which in postwar times turned its attention to children's nursery rhymes, fairy tales, games, jokes, and spells, asking whether they should be studied as examples of the immaturity of children or as their own culture.[8] Researchers concluded that the latter was true, and today there is plenty of research in which children are seen as active agents and meaning producers.[9] University degrees are now available that study children's culture: the University of Stockholm, for example, has had a specific Centre for the Studies of Children's Culture since 1980.

New childhood studies do not focus only on analyzing children's agency, childhood cultures, or their prerequisites, however. Children are still not always present as speaking and acting agents in research. Here is another achievement of new childhood studies: differentiating between the concepts of children and childhood(s). Although the children who are born into the world live and act as children and then leave childhood behind them, childhood is permanent. Children grow up to be adults, but childhood is a permanent social structure that is formulated and changes in time with historical periods and social situations. In this sense, although childhood is permanent, it is not unchanging. Childhood is a social state that receives all the children who are born and keeps them for a certain period of time. Then, "when the child grows up and becomes an adult, his or her childhood comes to an end but childhood as a form does not go away and will stay there to receive new generations of children."[10]

One of the main impulses behind new childhood studies, arising mostly in the field of social sciences, was the observation that childhood had never been considered a pertinent subject of research in social studies and had instead been overshadowed by adulthood.[11] New childhood studies also posed a challenge for the period-based thinking that prevailed in developmental psychology: the idea that childhood is a period with a clear beginning and end, during which a child develops toward adulthood via various stages or according to a predefined curve.[12] Because new childhood studies observe not just individual children but social, scientific, economic, and political factors, they form a kind of opposite for the analyses carried out by developmental psychology.

What this means for the study of fashion and visual representation is that when visual representation and children's clothing are discussed, they are seen as material and visual objects which visualize and materialize understandings about the permanent, yet changing, structure of childhood. Images and clothes make visible that which is invisible to the eye and is otherwise forgotten over time: ideas and ideologies that have framed—and that continue to frame—how children are seen and understood. Visual representations and children's clothes are evidence of the cultural values we attribute to childhood. In contemporary culture, children's clothing suggests, for example, that children are capable consumers, and capable subjects who have the ability to style themselves from an early age. The visual representations and clothing also construct children as individuals who have a right to be fashionable, just like adults.

The field of new childhood studies—much like the fashions on offer to children today—has also cast a highly critical eye over the assumption that childhood, youth, adulthood, and other age categories used to define human life are actual, separate periods in our lives. It emphasizes the overlapping nature of these periods and the fact that none of them has any specifically defined content.[13] This is often particularly clear in children's fashion and its visual representations: while children may be photographed as children, they are also shown with characteristics typical of teenagers or even self-conscious adults, which blurs the boundary between children and adults. Generally the child models do not have adult bodies, but they are purposefully made to look like adults through clothing, poses, and makeup. The reverse also applies; especially in recent years there have been many advertisements in which grown women and men are portrayed as childish characters.[14]

Besides traditional age category, new childhood studies employ social categories used as descriptors of people of various ages. In this sense constructionist childhood studies have questioned the categorical divide between adults and children—or at least attempted to bridge the gap by formulating diverse concepts that exist somewhere between childhood and adulthood. These include "preteen," "teenager," "adolescent," and "young adult"—concepts that are thought to be more descriptive of the personalities of people belonging to a certain age category than simple "child" or "adult," and that are used regularly in kids' fashion stores.

The aforementioned categories are discursive structures, however, whose contents vary over time.[15] For example, what we mean by the words "child" or "preteen" depends on context and is continuously debated. The Maripier advertisement is an apt example here, because it blends the categories of childhood, teenhood, and adulthood. On the one hand, the girls are dressed in opaque tights and ballet flats or Mary Janes, which are clear signals of childhood, as are the standing girl's facial expression and resolute posture. Conversely, the sitting girl's bored, world-weary expression hints at adulthood, as do both girls' on-trend back-combed hair and head scarves. On the other hand, again, the cut and patterns of the girls' attire are typical of 1980s' clothing for middle-class girls. These visual elements and poses place the girls on the borderline between girlishness and miniature womanhood. They are children, but at the same time they are preteens on their way toward adulthood.

The preceding visual literacy exercise gives an idea of what it is like to pick out the meanings of visual imagery. The analysis considers what elements an image is composed of and what established meanings these elements already carry with them. The overall interpretation of an advertisement is built out of the sum of these meanings, but not exclusively. It is also affected by the context in which the image is found. In the early 1980s, the Maripier ad would have been seen in relation to other advertisements for the brand and to children's clothing by other similar brands, whereas in the 2010s, its interpretation is affected by our awareness of more recent history. In the context of this book, the meanings of this fashion advertisement adapt to the theoretical framework of the book, when the ad is cited as an example of how images and clothes will be analyzed.

In the Footsteps of Enlightenment Philosophers: Dressing Modern Childhood

New childhood studies show us that developmental psychology, which is used, for example, to define the "natural development curve" of childhood, derives from modern evolution theory and its ways of seeing the world. This means that childhood does not exist as a natural phenomenon outside of discourse.[16] In fact, the development curve is a very recent way of understanding childhood and its ideological foundations. In it, a child is seen as different from an adult in many ways: where adults are mature, independent, rational and able, children are the opposite, that is, a passive human "seed" who is incomplete, irrational, and dependent on others.[17] The idea of the development curve was not born in a vacuum, however. It has echoes of considerably older conceptions of childhood. Sigmund Freud's theories are an important historical milestone, but layers are present that predate those by a significant amount. The earliest can be dated back to the beginning of the modern age—the turn of the seventeenth into the eighteenth centuries—and the work of one of the first conceptualizers of "new childhood," the British philosopher John Locke. He defined the mind of a child as a *tabula rasa*, a blank slate. In other words, Locke said that a child had no mind of her own, and only became a thinking being after undergoing carefully regulated education and schooling.[18]

Both boys and girls were dressed in long shirts when they were born and continued to wear long dresses through childhood, as demonstrated by Figure 1.3, a painting by Anthony van Dyck from 1634 depicting the children of Charles I. On the left, Prince Charles at the age of four wears a long skirt with a full-length coat, with a waistline marked by ornaments and a fashionable white collar. On the right, the one-year-old Prince James is dressed in a low-necked bodice. In the middle, Princess Mary, aged three, also has a long skirt and a fashionably shaped bodice. Children's clothes were miniature versions of women's dress, which indicates that children were not regarded as individuals in the sense that we regard them today. They were seen as a part of the world of women. This would change at the age of six or seven: boys started wearing breeches and thus were visibly removed from the women's world. Girls, on the other hand, stayed in long skirts. For the contemporary viewer, children's dress as it is represented in the van Dyck painting may seem ungendered or unisex. However, there were subtle gender differences in the details of the dress. Both girls and boys wore skirts and back-fastening bodices in their infancy; however, boys were given front-fastening bodices to accompany their skirts at the age of two, while girls continued to wear back-fastening bodices. When boys abandoned their skirts at the age of six or seven, it was a ceremonial occasion: the change in dress marked the boy's next coming-of-age phase.[19]

The opposite of Locke's view of childhood was held by his contemporary the French philosopher Jean-Jacques Rousseau in his classic work *Émile, or On Education*.[20] Whereas Locke did not even quite see children as human, Rousseau defined the child as good by nature. Like Locke, Rousseau emphasized the importance of the child's upbringing, but in contrast he encouraged parents to raise their children with tenderness. Rousseau's philosophy was based on the idea that a child's upbringing determined what he would become like as an adult. Rousseau's worry was that grown-ups did not treat children as children— as reflected in the miniature adults we see posing in van Dyck's painting—but considered them from their own point of view, that is, as future adults:

Figure 1.3 Seen it all—experienced it all. Children were represented as miniature adults in seventeenth-century paintings. Anthony van Dyck, *The Children of Charles I of England*. © Getty Images. Photograph by De Agostini/Turin, Galleria Sabauda (Picture Gallery).

> We know nothing of childhood; and with our mistaken notions the further we advance the further we go astray. The wisest writers devote themselves to what a man ought to know, without asking what a child is capable of learning. They are always looking for the man in the child, without considering what he is before he becomes a man.[21]

Locke and Rousseau both took a significant step away from earlier thoughts on children and childhood. Previously, children had been seen as weak, immature versions of adults.[22] The ideas of Locke and Rousseau made way for new conceptualizations of childhood. Gradually, children began to be seen as separate individuals who grow into adulthood with education and guidance. Another crucial harbinger of change was Erasmus of Rotterdam, sometimes known as the "Prince of the Humanists," who wrote about the importance of early childhood education. He believed that the best possible adulthood was guaranteed by early instruction and the establishment of good manners at the soonest opportunity. When the writings of Erasmus were translated from Latin into modern European languages, he became one of the most influential thinkers in Protestant and Catholic child-rearing alike, even though the main model for education was still for a long time the Bible, especially in the Protestant world. Thanks to the influence of Locke, Rousseau, and Erasmus, various books on manners and other child-rearing guides gradually began to appear in Europe.[23] All this demonstrates that children became an important part of the family and of social reality.

The writings of Locke and Rousseau, as well as those of many eighteenth-century poets, indicate that childhood was understood in a new way. It was no longer necessarily a preparation period for something else (adulthood or Heaven), but its own, inherently valuable period. "Children can be classed alongside slaves and animals as the recipients of the sentimentalism and humanitarianism that characterized the latter part of the eighteenth century," the historian Hugh Cunningham writes, describing the shift in the status of childhood.[24] The key to the shift lay in secularization. The hold that religion had on various aspects of life weakened, and many worldly phenomena began to be explained through the new natural sciences. Scientific methods were used for explaining and manipulating human behavior, and youth education was seen as a way of fighting "against nature." A romantic view of childhood was formed in the 1800s and 1900s. It criticized Rousseau for believing that children only became virtuous through education. The Romantics described children as "creatures of deeper wisdom, finer aesthetic sensitivity and a more profound awareness of enduring moral truths."[25]

This change in understanding of childhood as a separate phase in life also brought about a significantly new way of dressing children. Even though infants still wore long dresses, boys took on a new style of dress at the age of three: trousers. Girls continued to wear the infancy style, emphasizing the idea of childhood as the symbol of original innocence.[26]

The meanings of childhood have continually changed. The social historian Harry Hendrick, who has examined the history of conceptions of childhood in the United Kingdom, has pointed out that "childhood" as we know it is entirely the product of Western culture and thinking.[27] There is no and never has been a single, universal childhood; instead there are many different, competing versions. Childhood is a social construct created by adults, and its formation has always been influenced by the discourses of history, sociology, science, law, education, medicine, economics, psychology, and family policy, among others.[28] Childhood is also a thoroughly gendered concept. Rousseau, for example, mainly referred to boys when he wrote about childhood and only briefly mentions his "counterpart," the girl named Sophie, in the fifth book of his treaties. While Émile is described as a child who will become a physically strong and alert man through education—

and whose difference from girls is also visible in his dress—Sophie is merely described as the ideal woman and a wife-to-be: a weak and passive creature who should not resist the will of a man and always be ready to please him. She is a creature who continues to wear long skirts throughout her life. Childhood is a web of various concepts and values, visual representations and symbolic meanings. How we see it and conceptualize it is strongly linked to the historical and cultural context within which we speak of it and represent it textually, visually and through the materiality of garments.

Branded Childhood

The constructionist perspective offers researchers of fashion and advertising the tools for examining the kinds of impressions and interpretations of childhood that contemporary fashion brands seek to build about themselves through the symbolic figure of the child. It is evident that they do not look for the objective reality—that is, the child—behind the image that might be presented in any authentic or unbiased fashion. Instead, attention focuses on the interpretation of childhood created by advertising. The way a brand represents children in its advertising and the kinds of clothes it designs for them is interesting because it is ultimately most revealing about the brand itself.

What is particularly crucial is the major role that visual representations and the human figures contained therein play in building brand identities in today's consumer culture. For a brand, it is very important that the human figure, the figure of the child in this case, corresponds with the values that the brand sets out to embody. It is worth considering the original meaning of the word "brand" here: the mark burned onto cattle with a hot iron to distinguish them from other farmers' cattle.[29] This agrarian meaning has faded, but the idea of the cattle iron lives on in the ability of a brand to imprint a memory on a consumer's mind. Brands stand out by altering consumers' ways of seeing the world, and they do this, among other ways, by using advertising which weaves together the brand's products with a visual narrative about the imagined consumer and his or her lifestyle. A brand consists of a company's name, but above all of a visual logo and a world of visual representations that bring together all the (positive) connotations that the company wants to have associated with itself.

The symbolic value of the luxury brand Versace, for example, is constructed with the help of images created by the company's marketing machinery. Advertising for the brand's adult clothes often emphasizes active sexuality and a cosmopolitan air, but its children's wear marketing has a more androgynous and natural feel, as we can see in Figure 1.4. This image dates from 1996 and features two children dressed identically in a white cotton shirt and blue jeans. In contrast to previous centuries, these children wear not skirts but trousers, regardless of

Figure 1.4 Childhood androgyny is a recurring theme in fashion advertising. Here the brand is constructed as a promoter of androgynous and natural childhood. © Versace 1996.

their gender. Children in jeans is a rather new phenomenon, dating back to the 1930s, when parents started looking for hard-wearing play clothes.[30] Jeans have a particularly interesting history in that they have always been associated with that which is natural, wild, innocent, and authentic.[31] The Versace image adds "androgynous" to this list, implying that jeans are suitable for girls and boys alike.

The brand uses advertisements and clothes to create a notion of the original sameness of children and its own authenticity. What is paradoxical is that while attempting to raise itself above consumerism and commercialism by emphasizing naturalness and other ideals, the brand does this by styling and dressing child models to look natural. The purpose of the Versace ad is to advertise specific clothes, but at the same time it draws attention to some of the immaterial properties of the brand. An advertising image awakens associations in consumers' minds. It attaches them to the brand and may encourage them to buy the products, especially if they identify with the values and meanings the brand mediates through its visual representations of children.[32]

Brands cannot generate just any associations they like, however. Usually their marketing machinery strives to create positive rather than negative connotations. They must not be disjointed, either; there should be cohesion to the impressions linked to a brand in consumers' minds. Therefore, advertising must offer a consistent theme around which the other images related to the brand arise. In marketing speak, this is the "brand promise."

A convincing brand promise is the foundation upon which marketers can build the brand's beguiling world.[33] Globally renowned brands such as Coca-Cola, for example, are known for having built their identities around a myth, such as freedom. Children's wear brands operate on the same principle; like the painting by van Dyck, and the advertisements by Maripier and Versace also rely on the myths related to childhood and on visualization methods that have developed through history. On the surface, both Maripier and Versace reflect the eighteenth-century conception of childhood innocence in their advertising, but they also contain a more modern idea of children as capable consumers.[34] While our consumer culture maintains the concept of the innocent childhood, the rest of society wonders whether childhood is in crisis[35] or has even completely disappeared.[36] Various extreme negative examples keep coming up in social debates—child murderers, school shootings, and children on drugs.

Studying Brand Associations: A Brief History of Representation

Childhood and brands have one common denominator: both are representations that are constructed and externally imbued with meaning. The concept of representation is seldom used in brand studies, whereas in cultural studies of fashion it has become one of the major analytical tools in recent decades. It is a highly useful concept also when examining the construction of meanings related to brands and their advertising. Broadly speaking, representation is related to considerations of the degree to which an experience is transmitted, authentic or typical—themes which are essential in the construction of brand identities. While it is important for the makers of advertisements to produce images of childhood that feel real and genuine, the researchers who study those images pay attention to how that feeling of reality and genuineness was achieved. Mostly advertisements featuring children do not come up with anything new, but recycle familiar beliefs—such as, for example, the one pertaining to childhood innocence. Simultaneously, the accepted meanings are of course constantly and deliberately challenged as, for example, mixing childhood innocence with sexuality.

"Representation" has two main, parallel meanings: that of presenting or reproducing something, and that of acting on behalf of someone or something. Etymologically the term comes from the Latin *representare*, which means "making something present" or "re-presenting something."[37] In classical Latin, the term was almost exclusively linked to inanimate objects, whereas today we also use it for people. *Representare* originally meant literally giving something a presence or, alternatively, making one's audience aware of something abstract (such as innocence: one of the virtues) through certain means (e.g., an image of a child or a piece of clothing). In this sense, *representare* also referred to the replacement of an abstract concept with a concrete object, such as an image.[38]

The purpose of advertising images is to make the brand visible, to concretize its identity, and to imprint a certain set of images into the viewers' consciousness. Visual representations are a link between the consumer and the company whose products are being marketed. When advertising presents products belonging to brands, it also represents the brand's ideals in relation to life and people. Advertisements do not only provide product information to consumers; they also invite viewers to enter the ideal world built by the brand.

When brand advertising is seen from the perspective of representation, the focus is not on evaluating how well or realistically the brand manages to depict its products. Instead, we look at what kinds of ideals the advertising creates; what is the idealized childhood marketed to consumers by the brand? What kinds of children are depicted? What is the mythical story of childhood that advertisements recycle? Is something left out completely? Used in this way, the concept of representation is a critical and analytical tool.[39] It is used to assess how presentation and representation are interwoven, what kinds of information the advertising images generate, and what that information is used for.

Applied thus, representation refers primarily to public and collective significance-building and to the critical analysis of the meanings that are created.[40] Because representation emphasizes shared meanings, it is clear that fashion brands do not build their concepts of childhood in isolation from the rest of culture; instead, they make use of culturally distilled information on childhood. By consuming a specific brand, people communicate to their peers about their own values, their egos, their income level, and their social status. In other words, we use brands to build images of our own identities. Information that has been polished over time is easy to use in increasing our own and the brand's credibility. On the global market, the brand stands not only for the company's products but also for the values supported by the company. This culturally approved information provides the brand with an aura of authenticity and, in return, a believable brand offers consumers a tool for building their own credibility.

Authentic and Natural Childhood at the Heart of a Brand

In recent years, researchers of visual culture have come to believe that images construct meanings in the same way as language, even though images lack a clear grammatical structure. This theory also applies to clothing: clothes produce meanings even though their "grammar" is arguably even more concealed than that of visual representations. These ideas connect to the British linguist J. L. Austin's theory of language as a builder of reality.[41] Austin defines various utterances (such as "I christen you X," "I pronounce you man and wife," "I promise you this," "I bet you that," "I bequeath X to Y," and so on) as performative, that is, as "speech acts." According to Austin's theory, language does not just describe the surrounding reality but also constructs it. Austin went against his contemporaries in maintaining that language has the ability to change the world.[42]

Since then, Austin's speech act theory has been refined and criticized by numerous philosophers,[43] while in cultural studies of fashion it has become a very popular analytical tool. In our visually oriented culture, and especially in the world of fashion and advertising, reality is increasingly constructed by images and clothes, maybe even more so than by text. The innocent childhood depicted in the Versace ad in Figure 1.4 is a good example of how advertising brings to life the idea of the "authentic" child, and how the brand utilizes this idea of authenticity to give itself a genuine and timeless image. In this sense the power of performativity, which is based on repetition, has declared certain representations of childhood to be real and authentic.

For example Figure 1.5, which is a fashion advertisement from 1996 by the clothing brand Arthur, depicts a summery lawn with a paved path passing through it. A barefooted child with a bobbed haircut, facing away from the camera, is dancing or skipping in the foreground. The child's gender is accentuated through clothing, which consists of a dress with an opaque bodice and a bell-shaped chiffon skirt as ethereal as a summer breeze. The bodice is white while the skirt is delicately flowery. The image looks like a snapshot, capturing a fleeting moment of an innocent childhood not yet beset by worries.

The Arthur ad represents one of the most typical ways of representing children and their clothes. In it, the child, a little girl, is shown as a small creature that is clearly distinguished from an adult, and whose most evident characteristic is innocence. Innocence is constructed in many ways in this image. Firstly, the photograph has the appearance of an action shot, with the girl not posing for a camera but seemingly engrossed in play and unaware of the camera. Secondly, the child is styled with clothes that are clearly different from contemporary grown-up clothes. Arthur, a well-known French children's wear company, describes

LAPIDO · 15228 BERTAMIRANS · SANTIAGO DE COMPOSTELA · SPAIN · TEL. 34.81/883329 · FAX 34.81/890305

Figure 1.5 Innocence as understood by the French children's fashion brand Arthur. © Arthur 1996.

itself as a brand built around "the authentic, timeless values associated with the family."[44] The image of a barefooted child skipping in a breezy dress on a summery lawn draws from the discourse related to natural, authentic, and timeless childhood, on which the brand's image is built. Her clothing, a white T-shirt-like bodice attached to a long light skirt with an Empire waist, echoes late eighteenth- and early nineteenth-century children's dress, which emphasized freedom of movement. The girl's pose underlines the idea that the child is free to explore the world before beginning to prepare seriously for adult life.

The image comes across as momentary and impulsive, yet it is the outcome of a carefully considered but well-concealed plan. Instead of a virgin forest, for example, nature is represented by a manicured lawn split in half by a sandstone path. This brings the setting to a man-made, stately garden. In other words, the child's innocent ingenuity is not just any child's natural state but the natural state belonging to a certain social class—white, upper-class—although it is presented as timeless.

Why does the innocence depicted here seem so real? Why do we read naturalness and timelessness from the image so evidently? One answer lies in the history of childhood innocence, whose traces are clear in the ads by Maripier, Versace, and Arthur. They mediate meanings that have formed over a much longer time than at the moment of the image being taken. Rather than a window on reality, these advertising images offer a vantage point over the history of childhood, children's clothes, ways of depicting children, and the innocence constructed therein. The mythical story behind these images reaches back to the origins of modern childhood—the time when childhood started to be seen as distinct from adulthood.

At the same time, there are also differences between the images. Of the three examples, Arthur's advertisement is clearly the most classical and has an upper-class air about it, contrasted with a hint of modernity. While the style of the girl's dress is Empire with a fitted bodice and a long, gathered, and loosely fitting skirt, the bobbed haircut refers to the 1920s and the modern new woman—the flapper, who has come to be known as an independent and empowered woman, and her style the emblem of modernity. While the image is nostalgic, its modernity is symbolized in the girl's haircut. The other advertisements are much more contemporary in their treatment of childhood. The Versace ad depicts contemporary innocence: children dressed in trousers and an understated, casual, and gender-neutral style, whose difference from adult clothes is unclear. Jeans and cotton shirts are the uniform of any contemporary casual grown-up. The difference between child and adult is achieved in the Versace ad through the children's poses: kneeling is particularly associated with childhood. The girls in the Maripier advertisement are most removed from childhood, which is accentuated by their poses and hairstyles, as well as their miniature-adult clothing.

Unlocalized Images

In recent decades, our culture has become visualized, which in a nutshell means that people communicate increasingly via diverse visual symbols.[45] In our consumer culture, commercial images have achieved special status as visualizers and disseminators of information related to childhood.

The British art historian Norman Bryson has referred to the recent cultural changes as "the imperative to visualize."[46] He claims that our time is characterized by an ethos of having to turn everything into visually appealing and attractive design. This does not apply only to objects but also, for example, to children: both are styled because they are intended to communicate a message, either on the object's owner or the child's parents. Especially in the hands of well-off Western parents, children are treated like a highly malleable material to represent their parents' values and worldview. The fashion brands, in turn, manipulate and style children to suit their own brand identities.

One advertisement by Armani in Figure 1.6 depicts a somewhat scared-looking child dressed in a white cotton turtleneck, white stockings, a denim frock with a low waistband, and flat black patent-leather booties. The image clearly draws from the history of the innocent child that is distinct from adulthood, recycling the story of children needing adult protection. The girl's childishness is also underlined by her white shirt and stockings, the flat shoes, and the style of the frock, which dates back to the simple and loose dresses of the late nineteenth century, all of which mediate her innocence.[47] Additionally the ad strives to mold our impressions of the brand and its values as genuine and authentic. At this point it would be good to remember the thought expressed by the media philosopher Jean Baudrillard, that capitalist societies no longer consume goods but signs and symbols.[48] As fashion becomes increasingly pictorial, representations of children achieve symbolic status: advertisements draw from the history of childhood, but their ultimate purpose is to describe the brand and construct its identity, not only that of children. The function of the seemingly authentic childish figure, staring at the viewer while apparently upset, is to build a history for the brand and to tell us something essential about it: Armani protects children, not only against the weather but also from the evils of the world.

The idea of the symbolization and pictorialization of childhood can be deepened further by a look at the history of technology. Although images were, naturally, produced long before today's communication technology was available, a huge revolution came about thanks to the invention of modern lens-based image reproduction techniques in the late nineteenth and early twentieth centuries. The mass production of images led to the erosion of text as the supreme means of communication and gave rise to the pictorialization that is still going on today. Consequently it contributed to globalization, which has allegedly "shrunk" the world by providing us with real-time information on events—such as fashion shows—happening on the other side of the globe.[49] Today's world is characterized by this kind of closeness and interweaving, almost interdependence. The same, usually Anglo-American, advertisements are spread around the world and non-Western images are assimilated into Western pictorial culture.[50] This makes far-away things, people, and phenomena approachable and near to us, so that we are touched by them, while it also strives to transform Western ideas such as childhood innocence into universal truths about childhood.[51] From the point of view of fashion, globalization also means that adults and children alike wear clothes designed by the same Western brands but produced in Asia and other regions with cheap (child) labor. A fundamental aspect of globalization is that many non-Western economic areas are entirely dependent on the production of consumables for the Western market.

The global dissemination of fashion images reflects a fairly recent but constantly growing phenomenon for brands. The trend is clear: the objective for brands is to increase their footprints, find new consumers, and identify new

Figure 1.6 Armani's advertisement draws from the visual history of childhood innocence and suggests that innocent children need adult protection. © Armani Junior 2008.

opportunities for turning a profit. Images play an important role in that they not only impart information on brands effectively but also are thought to have the ability to bypass linguistic and cultural barriers. The triumphal march of brands and the pictorialization of consumer culture have changed the relationship between images, clothing, and reality. When images of fashion are shared from one side of the world to another, it is impossible to pinpoint their origins. For example, if an ad for the Italian fashion brand Armani is published in *Vogue Bambini* and viewed in Finland, what is the origin of the image? Is it Italy, the home of the brand, or Finland, where the advertisement is seen, or Britain, where the style of the advertised dress originated? Is it the magazine's coverage area? Or perhaps a book, in which the ad is used as an example in discussing representations of childhood? It is usually difficult to determine any single point of origin for images disseminated by the global fashion industry. As borders between nations become more fluid, people, corporations, products, and images have started moving from one culture to another. It makes sense to consider advertising images depicting children, for example, as having several interpretive contexts, in which the local blends with global visual culture.

Glocal or Global Meanings of Fashion and Images?

The ubiquitous tentacles of the global media culture have turned Western fashion into a global playing field, in which fashion absorbs influences from other cultures like a sponge and fuses together many of their features to form new fashion culture hybrids.[52] Critics of the concept of global culture see the idea of global fashion mostly as a syncretist construction without history, engendered by recent media culture and aimed at maximizing profits.[53] Additionally, critics are concerned that in reality global culture means Western culture invading and permeating everything. This would lead to mono- rather than multiculturalism.[54]

Some have also pointed out that rather than global culture, we should speak of glocal culture. This adds the perspective of locality to globality. As fashion is disseminated around the world thanks to magazines, films, the Internet, social media, and other information systems, ideas that are generated in a certain cultural context become a part of the global culture. At the same time, however, images are endowed with different meanings depending on the local culture. Images are always interpreted against a specific cultural background: there is no such thing as a single, globally understood meaning or identically shared image literacy. Simultaneously, meanings can also cross cultures. This is especially true of the moral debates that surround children's fashion images. A worry that has been generated in one part of the globe will easily transmit to another part and become the "truth" about the representation. As the world "shrinks" through globalization, so does the array of meanings of the globally transmitted and debated images, while stereotypical meanings take up more space.

In fashion, the blending of global and local culture has turned certain local characteristics into clearly distinguishable signs and symbols. For example, when the fashion industry uses the concepts of "African," "Scandinavian," or "Latino," it is referring to certain stereotypical properties from which that culture can be recognized.

Vogue Bambini provides excellent examples of how fashion advertising has taken part in the blending of global and local cultures and their meanings in recent decades. The Benetton brand, for instance, has brought together children from diverse ethnic backgrounds in its advertising since the 1980s. The brand's advertising imagery, which brings together children from different cultural backgrounds, is a concrete indication of the cultural changes that started taking place in fashion advertising in the pre-Internet age. In the 1980s, *Vogue Bambini* also published special "ethnic issues": *Vogue Bambini* in China, India, Latin America, the Nordic region, Ireland, the UK, Brazil, Scandinavia, and so on. These special feature issues are particularly interesting to study in order to see what national distinguishing characteristics the magazine decides to feature in its articles and cover photographs. When the magazine is set in China, the child models are Chinese and they are dressed in Mao jackets and Chinese work clothes—although of course these garments are produced by European high-fashion brands. Similarly, in India the children are Indian, adorned with *bindis* and dressed in colorful saris and jewelry (again of European design). Images set in Central America feature a girl who looks a bit like Frida Kahlo, whereas Nordic children are portrayed as blond, blue-eyed, and rosy-cheeked. In an article set in Austria, the models are light-haired and pictured wearing lederhosen in an Alpine setting. In Ireland they are freckled redheads posing on moist green moorland.

This method of nationally identifying and ethnicizing children using certain stereotyped symbols disappeared from the magazine entirely in the 1990s, after which the ethnicity of children per se has no longer been emphasized. Figure 1.7, an advertisement by Benetton, illustrates how fashion transits from ethnic special issues to fashion imagery as the global melting pot. In this ad, we can see how the nationality of the child models is denoted by a national signifier—a flag—held in the hand or painted on a cheek. After these kinds of examples, ethnicity would only be brought in by arranging children of different skin colors in images. The way in which the children are dressed is also of interest here: they all wear similar clothes, either a knitted jumper or a cardigan in red or blue and a knitted scarf. While the children's upper bodies are unisex, their gender is accentuated in their lower parts: girls wear stockings, boys, trousers. The advertisement's message seems to be that, despite our cultural differences, we all wear the same (Benetton) clothes.

In global media and fashion culture, local characteristics such as race, ethnicity, or nationality are distilled into symbols: skin color, clothes that hint at specific cultures, or landscapes that are recognizable from tourism ads. These symbols become tools for distinction.[55] In fashion advertising, race, ethnicity, and nationality are not shown as biological or unchangeable categories, let alone facts; they are given as choices between equivalent options. In fashion culture, global communities are created by like-minded people. Some speak of "affective communities" that transcend national boundaries.[56] Those who share mutual interests or opinions, or who are interested in similar styles, gather around certain brands or blogs that report on top fashion, for example.[57]

New Tribes and Brand Communities

Children's fashion forms a seamless part of a broader high-fashion culture and is a good example of shared, global, and virtual cultures. Fashion and its related imagery, in print and in electronic media, bring people together regardless of their

Figure 1.7 We are the world—multiculturalism as understood by Benetton. Photograph by Oliviero Toscani. © Benetton 1985.

language, culture, or home background. Fashion consumers are forming diverse new tribes and brand communities. The concept of "new tribe" was launched by the French sociologist Michel Maffesoli,[58] to signify a group that shares similar lifestyles and tastes, rather than a tribe in its traditional anthropological sense. The members of the group interact even if they are not usually found in the same place at the same time. The concept of the "brand community" is a further refinement of the new tribe: it, too, refers to a specialized and geographically unlimited grouping brought together by admiration for a specific brand, as well as its values and related rituals.[59] The Benetton advertisement illustrates the theoretical ideas presented by Maffesoli: since the 1980s, the brand has strived to construct itself as a community through its slogan, "United Colors of Benetton," to underline its importance for the members of the brand community. While a brand such as Benetton can represent personal and local values, it also promises to bring together supporters of those values from all around the world. These are the kinds of values that global brands want to encapsulate in their advertisements.

The concepts of global culture, new tribes, and brand communities are closely linked to the idea of modern consumerism, toward which today's children are heavily directed. Besides products, it centers on virtual tribes or communities consisting of people joined together, not by geographical location or language but by their interest for a certain visual style, lifestyle, or brand. In this way, the concept of global culture as engendered by our late capitalist consumer culture

2
CHILDREN THROUGH FASHION

Until recently, there has been little academic research on children's fashion and children's representation in fashion advertising. Many of the accounts that exist either describe the historical development of children's dress or discuss the harmfulness of fashion and its representation to children—little girls in particular. The negative view of fashion connects to the still largely prevailing understanding of fashion as feminine, irrational, ugly, or merely decorative, a wasteful culture that creates delusional and distorted body ideals, particularly in women and little girls.

But what exactly is fashion? While there is little agreement over the cultural importance of fashion, neither is there a single definition or meaning of fashion. One quite common way of understanding fashion is as adornment: clothing, dress, and costume, as well as other ways of styling and modifying the body.[1] In everyday speech, however, the terms "fashion," "dress," and "clothing" are often used synonymously, even though the former refers to a hugely diverse cluster of phenomena, whereas the two latter terms can just be what people wear on a daily basis, without constituting fashion. Even though fashion would not exist without material objects, they are not the only elements that constitute it.

The multiple meanings of fashion are evident in the etymology of the concept. Fashion was first alluded to in the English language around the year 1300, with the terms "style" and "manner." In French, the term *la mode* appeared first in 1482, referring to the collectively accepted way of dressing. The word "fashion" derives from the Latin *facio* or *factio*, which refers to making and production, whereas the French comes from the Latin *modus*, meaning "manner." Over time, both terms have absorbed diverse meanings and become linked to a whole network of terms that refer to making, manners, style, design, and specific ways of individual and collective dress. "Fashion" as a concept does refer to the actual production of garments, but it is also a term that defines the usage of these garments. As such, it is one significant way

---

Figure 2.1 From the series *Twins*, Paris, 2012. © Heidi Lunabba.

of constructing, experiencing, and understanding individuals and the social relations between people. This is tangible in the history of fashion: until the twentieth century, fashion was determined by those belonging to the upper classes, and understood as a means of showing social status. But as mass-production of clothes developed and fabrics and clothing became cheaper in this process, being fashionable has become available to almost anyone, regardless of their social status or class.[2]

Another important definition of fashion relates to time and change. The French essayist and art critic Charles Baudelaire defined fashion as a phenomenon of the modern urban world, characterized by transience and continuous change.[3] John Carl Flügel, on the other hand, differentiated fashion or "modish" dress from "fixed" or unchanging types of dress. He concluded that fashion and that which is not fashion are opposites in their relationships to space and time. While fashion changes rapidly, non-fashion remains unchanged or changes very slowly. The value of fashion lies in its ability to change, while non-fashion is valued precisely for its permanence.[4] In fashion studies, this dichotomy is often illustrated by the contradiction between folk dress and fashionable dress, but it can equally be demonstrated through children's dress versus adult dress prior to the late 1800s. While adult clothing has undergone changing styles for centuries, children's clothing remained largely unchanged until the late nineteenth century. Daniel Thomas Cook argues in *The Commodification of Childhood* (2004) that the idea of the "consuming child" was constructed by the industry as late as between 1910 and 1940. This transformed children into a special marketing niche and constructed childhood as the fashion-driven period we know it as today.

In contemporary culture, children's dress has become a central part of the "fashion system,"[5] which is rooted in late nineteenth-century Europe and the United States. The American economist Thorstein Veblen and the German sociologist Georg Simmel, for example, connect fashion to political struggle and to the birth of modern nation-states and democracies in the aftermath of the French Revolution in 1879. They see fashion as an effect of the demise of the feudal class system and the development through mass immigration of big metropolises such as Paris, Berlin, and New York. For Veblen and Simmel, and contemporary researchers such as Diana Crane in her *Fashion and Its Social Agendas* (2000), fashion is a lens through which history's political and societal changes can be viewed. This is reflected in the history of children's fashion: as we saw in the previous chapter, it remained more or less unchanged for a long period of time, reflecting children's marginalized status as human beings.

Fashion as Change

The fact that contemporary children's fashion changes seasonally suggests that children are acknowledged as fashion-oriented individuals and consumers from early on. Georg Simmel, as most fashion researchers since, has also suggested that fashion is a way to express one's individuality in anonymous urban surroundings.[6] This is evident when strolling through the streets of any contemporary metropolis: the fashionable child is easy to spot and incites ideas about the child's personality and individuality.

Another important aspect of fashion relates to class. This was first examined by Thorstein Veblen and developed by many sociologists of fashion after him, such as Pierre Bourdieu, Diana Crane, and Fred Davis. Veblen observed immigration in New England and described fashion as a phenomenon defined by people in the wealthier echelons of society. His observations led him to develop a theory about how people strive for a certain social class through consumption.[7] He argued that once the lower classes have obtained the things that the wealthy considered fashionable, the fashion will change. In other words, fashion trickles down from the elite to the masses.[8] This trickle-down theory has been widely criticized since the blooming of mass production and the so-called democratization of fashion[9]. However, what is important to note here is the position of children in these theories. While neither Simmel nor Veblen—or later theorists of fashion, for that matter— was particularly interested in children's fashions or children as fashion consumers, Veblen did mention them in his discussion of fashion and status, emphasizing that consumption and status were particularly evident in women and children. In fact, he considered both as "surrogate consumers": it was the duty of women and children to create the image of the family's social life and financial position by showing off conspicuous fashions. This underlines fashion's function as social regulator: a means through which social status can be displayed. These ideas have been further developed by sociologists such as René König in his study *The Restless Image: A Sociology of Fashion* (1973), Pierre Bourdieu in *Distinction* (1984), and Diana Crane in *Fashion and Its Social Agendas* (2000).

But the idea of fashion as display also paves the way to an understanding of fashion as an institutionalized system, removing it from the material garments to the world of language, abstract ideas and meanings. One of the earliest definitions comes from the French philosopher Roland Barthes, who understood fashion as a linguistic system and analyzed how texts that surround clothing in fashion magazines produce "the myth of fashion."[10] After Barthes, the distinction between clothing and fashion and fashion as a system has been thoroughly analyzed. For the sociologist Fred Davis, the fashion system is a complex institution made up of different elements: design, display, manufacturing, distribution, and sales.[11] For another sociologist, Yuniya Kawamura, it is a network of specialized and interdependent actors, each with a role in accomplishing the design, production, distribution, and consumption of dress.[12] Like Davis, Kawamura separates clothing from fashion and defines fashion as a collective endeavor.

This means that that which is acknowledged as fashion and fashionable at each time comes from a wide group of people involved in the industry. In other words, fashion designers do not have an exclusive say in what makes up fashion. They are surrounded by an entire industry that specializes in "fashion forecasting." This refers to specialist companies sending their employees to various corners of the world to sniff out the trends taking place on the streets, in urban fashion, in films, and in the mass media. Fashion forecasters also look at old fashion magazines and other historical material.[13] Their observations are used as a basis for making catalogues that can cost up to tens of thousands of euros. Brand and fashion designers buy these catalogues to support their own inspiration and to decide what colors, patterns, and styles should be in fashion in the next season. Other agents who decide what is "in" in fashion include fashion editors, boutique and department store buyers, bloggers, stylists, pop stars, and actors.[14] In recent years, this group of influential fashionistas has expanded to include celebrity children: designers, models, and performers.

The Added Value of Fashion

The many definitions of fashion indicate that fashion is neither an internal nor a descriptive property of an object. It is a web of human and non-human actors: a permanent social structure which persists even though individual trends come and go, and vary depending on time and place. Ultimately, fashion is the institution that controls what is fashionable, fostering change and generating novelties at regular intervals.[15] Fashion is performative in that the actors make an object or a phenomenon trendy by giving it a special status and added value. These qualities can be enhanced, for example, if the said object belongs to a well-known brand, comes from a famous designer, or is used by a child celebrity. Status and added value are immaterial attributes; they are an indefinable quality that can turn goods into desirable fashion items.

The idea of the status and added value of fashion is at its most concrete in well-known brands. Clothes can become fashionable when they are included under a certain brand name, even if the garment itself is no different from its non-branded counterpart. The added value percolates from the object into its wearer and makes him or her fashionable. Status and added value lie in the impressions, beliefs, and associations that are linked to the item. In many ways, the invisible value of fashion—be it created through a brand or through association to a celebrity—can be considered the most important characteristic of contemporary fashion.[16] It attracts consumers, who feel that they can become a part of fashion by buying things that contain it. Another crucial aspect of added value is that it can disappear as quickly as it appeared. That is what happens when trends change.[17]

Additionally, a trendy garment has the ability to raise the wearer's social status. The fact that a child is wearing jeans and a shirt from an expensive brand, for example, may derive from the parents' desire to dress the child in high-quality clothes, but it is more likely to be interpreted by the surrounding world as a sign of the child's social status and family wealth. This means that children's fashion is never intended purely to dress a child. It also symbolizes and signifies the status of the child's parents or guardians in comparison with others. The clothes are meant for interpretation, and in this sense they are like an argument or a text.[18]

The Individual Clothes of the Modern Child

The connection between fashion and social status is one of the first extensive areas of discussion and research in fashion theory.[19] The classic fashion writers discussed the fact that consumption of luxury items expresses not only the consumers' style but also their tastes and their inclusion in a certain social class. Additionally, fashionable clothes can express the desire to enter a certain class. As the fashion historians Giorgio Riello and Peter McNeil have aptly stated, fashion is "a passive receiver of historical transformation and an active shaper of change," meaning that fashion precedes many, if not most, sociocultural changes.[20]

One milestone of fashion history and a symbol of transformation that materialized through fashion is the French Revolution (1789–1799). It is defined as a turning point that had a crucial impact on the status of fashion and produced the "first modern individual," the dandy: "A Man whose trade, office and existence consists in the wearing of clothes," as Thomas Carlyle put it.[21] Before the revolution, people's clothing was strictly tied to their social status and reflected the class to which they belonged, but after the revolution, the purposes of clothing started to change. For the first time, society shifted from a highly class-bound fashion system to a society of impressions, in which clothing and looks no longer gave facts but rather helped to form an impression of the wearer.[22] Carlyle described the dandy as a man who created an image for himself through the clothes he wore.[23] Charles Baudelaire, on the other hand, came very close to the constructionist philosophy by stating that (especially women's) fashion and cosmetics were important building blocks of modern individuality.[24] Later theorists such as Joanne Entwistle in *The Fashioned Body* (2000) have examined the crucial role of fashion in the formation of modern identity through its articulation of the body, gender, and sexuality.

These definitions of modern fashionable women and men did not apply to children, however. While adults were seen as individual dressers, the change in children's dress was slower. For a long time, children's wear followed the centuries-long tradition of tunics, robes, and skirted garments, which were worn by boys and girls regardless of their gender.[25]

It may seem to the contemporary eye that little boys who were attired in skirts or dresses were dressed "like girls." However, clothing that we consider feminine today simply represented the infants' dependency on adults; skirted boys and girls were dressed like this to separate them from adults. In other words, they were dressed age-appropriately.

The Fashionable Mini-Me

Today, dressing children individually and according to gender begins right after the child is born. Gendered clothing started to appear in the late nineteenth century: as Jo Paoletti remarks, parents started dressing their children in more gendered ways between 1890 and 1910.[26] At that time, the French fashion magazines *Journal des Demoiselles, Journal des Jeunes Personnes*, and *La Mode illustrée* started to print children's fashions alongside those of women,[27] as we can see in Figure 2.2, showing a fashionable woman with four children circa 1878. The "father of haute couture," Charles Fredrick Worth, had used his own children as models for his fashion photographs in the late 1860s. Although Worth is usually credited as being the first couturier to use women as fashion models and to professionalize the practice,[28] Figure 2.3 indicates that his sons also modeled alongside their mother, Marie Vernet. The late nineteenth century was thus also the time when child modeling first appeared and the affluent were educated to dress their children fashionably—a practice that has continued ever since.

The reasons for dressing young children in fine fashion are not unambiguous. Firstly, it is about recognizing the child as an individual; secondly, it can be used to show caring and concern for the child; and thirdly, buying the clothes may give satisfaction to the adult in question. It may also be that the adult wants to give the child something that he or she did not have as a child. If a child is bought branded clothing several times a year, it evidently has to do with something other than caring for the child or satisfying the adult's desires. The idea of the Veblenian surrogate consumer seems to apply when examining purchases of children's high fashion. Growing children provide a fine opportunity for demonstrating how much money their parents can afford to spend on their children.

At the same time, children's fashions are used to educate and refine children's taste—hence the phenomenon of the fashionable mini-me.[29] The French sociologist Pierre Bourdieu considers fashion to be related to two types of capital: financial and cultural. Whereas financial capital refers to money and monetary value, cultural capital is linked to status and social value. Cultural capital is built and maintained through lifestyle choices, of which buying luxury consumables is one. For example, a parent's decision to dress a child in a specific brand is, from Bourdieu's perspective, a clear symbol of possessing financial capital and wanting to build and foster cultural capital by educating

Figure 2.2 A French vintage fashion illustration featuring a stylish lady with four young children in a comfortable interior, published in Paris, circa November 1878. Photograph by Popperfoto. © Getty Images.

and refining the child's taste. Children's fashion consumption thus plays an important role in lifestyle-building, or, as Bourdieu puts it, socializing the child into a certain style of life.[30]

This idea is useful when considering how images featuring children or children's clothing are used in establishing lifestyles. Fashion magazines featuring fashionably dressed child models contribute to instilling normative ideas about

MME. C. F. WORTH IN 1863 WITH
HER TWO CHILDREN

Figure 2.3 Mme C. Fredrick Worth with her two sons in 1863. In Jean Philippe Worth, *A Century of Fashion* (1928) © The British Library.

childhood. Children's high fashion is part of the process by which people's minds become indoctrinated with the ideals of middle-class life and childhood-appropriate dress. Bourdieu's Veblenian tendency is evident in that he, too, emphasizes that consumption does not follow on from a specific social class, but rather that class can be constructed through the consumption of specific goods.

The idea of fashion as a tool for group formation and class construction lived on through the latter part of the twentieth century, but the closer we get to contemporary times, the more fashion is considered to be about individuality. This relates to the emergence of youth fashions in the 1950s and 1960s, when fashion was found on the streets and among youth subcultures with their own specific styles. The British cultural theorist Dick Hebdige, for example, described the fashions of rockers, teddies, mods, skinheads, and punks,[31] while Ted Polhemus has written about the various street styles from 1940s' zooters and zazous to the late-millennium goths, hip-hoppers, riot grrrls, and cyberpunks: styles that "bubble up" from the sidewalk to the catwalk.[32]

The thoughts of Veblen, Simmel, Bourdieu, Crane, and Entwistle, as well as those of Hebdige and Polhemus, concerning consumption (of fashion) as a visual and material expression and builder of a certain social class, lifestyle, or subcultural identity are discernible in advertising for children's (high) fashion. While parents may aspire to mediate impressions about themselves as good and caring parents through their children's expensive brand clothing, advertising and the whole fashion culture that represents children as miniature adults certainly aspires to educate and refine the tastes and styles of the future adults. Children should not only be seen as surrogate consumers or even co-consumers, but consumers in their own right: active agents who have a say in what kinds of clothes they want to wear and how they want their bodies to be styled.

Upper-Class Fantasies of Childhood

Fashion magazines have acted as important adapters and mediators of fashion since the late nineteenth and early twentieth centuries. One of the earliest disseminators and gatekeepers of fashion was today's fashion Bible, *Vogue*, which started off as a society magazine in 1892.[33] The *Vogue* family grew steadily in the twentieth century, and in 1973 it was joined by *Vogue Bambini*, which focuses solely on presenting and conveying children's fashion. It was long the only fashion magazine disseminating children's fashion, but in the course of the research for this book, new magazines reminiscent of the glossy *Vogue Bambini* have regularly popped up on newsstands. These include, for example, the French magazine *Milk*, published since 2003, the Polish *Kikimora* (since 2010), and the Finnish *Kiddo* (since 2013). *Vogue Bambini* is a bilingual international children's fashion magazine that was initially issued monthly. The magazine's issuing frequency slowed down in the late 1980s, and it now appears six times a year.

Although *Vogue Bambini* claims to cover everything related to childhood, it no longer has any text articles. It is like a (children's) picture book, mostly consisting of images displaying children's fashion (in the form of advertisements, fashion editorials, and photojournalism) and text in the form of descriptive image captions. The images provide an almost cinematic narrative of the development of childhood either side of the turn of the millennium. The advertisements in the magazine form a continuum with the fashion journalism: the advertised products are included in the reports, blurring the line between product advertising and idealized childhood. In the *Vogue Bambini* world, childhood ideals are always tied to fashionable clothes and, as it is possible to see from the covers of the magazine in Figures 2.4–2.7, to the kind of photography that creates an interplay between childhood innocence and grown-up sexiness.

Like the other publications in the *Vogue* family, *Vogue Bambini* has an upper-class look and feel, not least because it is printed onto expensive glossy paper and contains images of top fashion items from expensive brands. The magazine's high print quality and exclusive photography invite the reader to spend time with the magazine and to step inside the luxurious world therein. The magazine is not aimed at a single social group, that is, those who can afford to buy the clothes and other goods displayed in it; in actual fact, the readership of high-fashion magazines includes many people who cannot.[34] A majority of the magazine's readers fall into the working middle-class category rather than the upper class, which means that there is a deep chasm between the readers' financial assets and the luxurious lifestyle that is displayed.

Although *Vogue Bambini* and the fashion and other consumer goods advertised in it never directly claim to belong to any specific social class, it doesn't mean that the luxury ads do not contain subtle visual hints of a desirable upper-middle-class lifestyle. The readers are able to partake of fantasies of high society life even if in reality they cannot afford it. Peter Corrigan, who has studied the sociology of fashion, describes how advertisements generate class meanings, on the one hand, and blur them, on the other, by suggesting that fashion consumption is a natural part of the human civilization process.[35] He also points out that the original aim of advertising was to transcend class boundaries, which it achieved by creating the concept of the mass consumer. The purpose of advertising was to turn the class society into a mass society in which the needs, desires, and frustrations of the individual were channeled into consumption, and the self was turned into a sellable consumable. To become a good American, for example, you had to drink Coca-Cola and buy other appropriate products.[36]

Vogue Bambini's pages contain excellent examples of fantasies concerning the civilizing effect of high fashion, as described by Corrigan. Fashion consumption is displayed as a function that leads to a better and more civilized life. In the world of children's fashion, the ideal is a harmonious middle-class existence. It involves clothes in understated, matching colors, as well as a careful hairdo, cleanliness, freshness, and a restrained sensuality.

Figure 2.6 *Vogue Bambini* cover from March–April 2007. © Vogue Bambini/Condé Nast. Photograph by Avi Meroz.

In other words, clothes explain—or so we believe—something about a person's internal properties. The idea of clothing as language was further developed by the sociologist Fred Davis in *Fashion, Culture and Identity*.[41] He claimed that clothing has a grammatical structure,[42] composed of certain key elements: fabric, texture, color, pattern, size, cut, shape, volume, and silhouette. This generates, shapes, and entrenches concepts related to childhood. For example, straight lines and primary colors are associated with activeness and boyhood, whereas roundness, curves, frills, and pastel colors are seen as clearly girlish properties. Jeans, T-shirts, and sneakers, on the other hand, communicate a more androgynous image of the child. The gendered grammar of clothing implies that in fashion, girls and boys are not discussed as anatomical beings. Instead, we speak of the gender-specific meanings that are materialized in the colors, patterns, shapes, cuts, and textures of clothes.[43]

Figure 2.7 *Vogue Bambini* cover from March–April 2009. © Vogue Bambini/Condé Nast.

The theory of fashion as communication is very popular nowadays and it is not uncommon to refer to it as "non-verbal communication."[44] However, the grammar of fashion is not like that of written language.[45] It is not as strict, but rather ambivalent and fickle, despite the fact that our understanding of the meanings of clothing is based on commonly shared definitions, rules, codes, and conventions.[46]

Barthes's work relied on Ferdinand de Saussure's linguistic philosophy, on the basis of which he defined fashion as an abstract language (*langue*) and individual garments as individual utterances (*paroles*). Various rituals, such as weddings, funerals, and christenings, with their strict dress codes, demonstrate that fashion is regulated by norms and stereotypes. We are accustomed to thinking that fashion is the opposite of ritualistic dressing, which has very little room for individual freedom of choice. We like to think that clothing shapes the self and constructs a personal narrative. It is true that the symbols generated by clothes are interpreted in much the same way as images, and clothes are associated with a person's identity. When it comes to children, individuality is suddenly less important than ritualistic dressing. This applies specifically to the ritual of dressing the child according to gender norms. For many adults, it is unthinkable to dress a boy in a pink dress while a girl may even be encouraged to do so. This has not always been the case, as we shall see in Chapter 3.

Gender-Coded Clothes for Children

When fashion is understood as communication, research on the subject must look at the processes by which meanings are constructed by clothes. This principle is rooted in cultural studies, for example, the ideas of the cultural theorist Stuart Hall. He proposes that decoding of messages is based on an understanding of acquired codes, that is, conventional meanings.[47] We learn these codes in the same way that children learn: through repetition. In this way the meaning of the code becomes so well established that we don't have to think about where it comes from: it just is.

The interpretation of visual representations containing clothes and children requires that we have access to pre-decoded signs and symbols.[48] Although children's separate wardrobes have much to do with ideas about children's nature, it is also true that the birth of industrialism plays a role here: it makes economical sense to produce separate clothing for each sex. The separation of women's and men's wardrobes became more visible in the late eighteenth and nineteenth centuries, with the emergence of mass-produced and factory-made fabrics and garments. This was aided by the invention of the spinning machine and the rise of the textile industry and the more affordable machine-made fabrics in Britain. In line with the decline of the silks and satins worn by royalty and the aristocracy came the emergence of cotton, which made clothes cheaper. The French historian Philippe Perrot has explained how new technological advances not only changed and modernized clothing but how small details became the crucial signifiers of gender and fashionableness.[49] Men started to dress more simply and the colors they wore became darker, hand in hand with working in modern factories—hence the claim for "great masculine renunciation."[50] Men were not expected to make a spectacle of their bodies, while decorativeness became a code linked to fashionable women and femininity.

The more rationally oriented dress code for men communicated characteristics linked to masculinity: reason, control, and social activity. Meanwhile, the more decorative styles intended for women reflected women's submissiveness and their duties as expressions of their husbands' wealth.[51] The same coding applies to children's fashions historically: their gender codes followed those of the adult world. Girls never gave up wearing skirts and dresses—the only difference that ensued was that their dresses were eventually cut along the same lines as those of grown women. Boys, on the other hand, had several phases of dressing, which also separated them gradually from girls and women and associated them with men and masculinity. After boys gave up dresses and skirts, they started wearing breeches, skeleton suits, and, finally, trousers.[52]

In other words, the understanding of social reality and gender materializes through clothes. This is also at the root of today's fashion images of children and their way of constantly reminding us of the importance of proving a child's gender. Feminine girls' clothes help to construct a girl's future sexiness, because the feminine attire of grown women is one of the most important sexual symbols of our culture.[53] Boys' clothes do not usually carry such connotations.

Gender dichotomy is apparent in the majority of fashion advertising, including adverts featuring babies and infants. For example, Figure 2.8, which is an advertisement for Dolce & Gabbana from spring 2010, shows two babies who at first sight seem identical; it is difficult to discern their gender. A closer look makes subtle gender-specific signs evident, however. The baby on the left is wearing a dress, the one on the right, shorts. Already this opposition is enough to create an interpretation of a boy and a girl. Further details stress this. The one on the right has a serious and assertive expression, while the one on the left is looking at the camera excitedly, open-mouthed and wide-eyed. The child on the left has longer hair, clothes with a heart pattern, and red shoes, while the baby on the right wears a white polo shirt, dark-blue dungarees, and shoes. Comparing these details, we can fairly confidently conclude that the one on the right is a boy and the left is a girl. The child dressed in trousers could possibly be a young tomboy but the one wearing a skirt is definitely a girl: a skirt is such a strongly feminized garment in our Western contemporary culture that it would never be worn by a boy in an advertisement.[54]

It is the viewer's task to derive meanings from the object at hand (in this case the advertisements for an Italian clothing brand). There are two alternatives for our interpretation. Firstly, we can read the image according to the prevailing code, such that "skirt" and "dungarees" are considered signs of stereotypical gender roles. Hall calls this a reading of the primary meaning. Secondly, we can interpret them in contravention of the prevailing code, meaning that the child coded as a boy is actually understood to be a girl.

Meanings are not constructed in relation to reality and facts, but to a certain ideological structure. In the case of interpreting the Dolce & Gabbana ad, the ideology is either accepting or questioning the traditional split into male and female genders.[55] Although the primary interpretation is that the babies represent a girl and a boy, there is no reason to assume that other interpretations shouldn't be possible. They could just as well be seen as two girls or two boys, because they are both fairly gender-neutral and even their clothes are not as evidently gender-specific as most. Although the meanings of clothes and images are linked to a specific context, there will always be a surplus of meanings, that is, areas that could leave the images and clothes open to alternative readings.

Figure 2.8 Traditional gender codes can be read through clothing. Dolce & Gabbana aim to erase dichotomous gender differences in this *Vogue Bambini* advertisement. © Dolce & Gabbana 2010.

Even if the designer or wearer of a garment wants to express a certain meaning, there is no guarantee that the message will be understood according to their intention.[56] Communication is never about transmitting and receiving predefined meanings; instead the meanings are formed as a result of interplay between the transmitter, the receiver, and the surrounding culture. Meanings are a result of a constant negotiation. For example, people from different cultural backgrounds form different interpretations of clothes and related visual representations of children. A contemporary Western consumer most likely sees the advertisement as a representation of a boy/girl couple and understands it as marketing somewhat gender-neutral clothing while still maintaining gender division.

Children's Fashion: A Battlefield of Meanings

Social constructionism is an excellent framework for the kind of research of fashion imagery that analyzes different levels of design, ranging from the content of the images to the structures and contexts within which they are situated. The information garnered from images is formulated through social interaction and interpersonal communication, and the same applies to clothes. Both play a crucial role in communication between people. This perspective is fruitful in that it permits a researcher to bestow her or his own meanings on images and clothes in order to open new routes for seeing and understanding things. The new meanings appear in parallel to the existing ones, often in a creative conflict with them. This clash is usually described in bellicose terms, as the "struggle over definition" or the "politics of meaning."[57] In the case of images and clothes related to children, it really is about battles and politics. The struggle or negotiation usually appears in situations where two opposing interpretations face each other, and it is related to figuring out which interpretation should be given primary status and which is secondary.[58] Although the ultimate interpretive truth is actually impossible to reach, due to the openness of the interpretation process, some interpretations usually achieve prevalence over others—like the interpretation of the babies as a girl and a boy in the Dolce & Gabbana advertisement. In relation to childhood, the concept of innocence is one of the most established interpretations, and it has an affinity with the unquestioned gender roles ascribed to children. Its opposite is the idea of children's sexuality, which is also kept at bay through stereotypical gender roles. In actual fact, childhood innocence is not even understood as an interpretation, because it has become so well established over the centuries that it is a truism. In contrast, childhood sexuality is known as something from which to distance oneself. Debates are wrought over questions such as whether innocence is "spoiled" if a girl is attired in a body-hugging dress or a boy in a pink skirt. Instead of accepting different garments as items with which to create all kinds of meanings, we endow them with interpretations centered on innocence and its corruption, or even the purposeful sexualization of children. Usually there is no room for negotiation in the debate because "innocence," understood as asexuality, is linked to children as some sort of universal truth rather than one possible interpretation, as we shall see in Chapter three.

3

INNOCENT CHILDREN

A fashion ad for the clothing brand Silvia (Figure 3.2) features a girl who poses in a sun hat and a slightly too-large dress. The white dress has puff sleeves, a lace-adorned collar, a bell-shaped skirt, and a belt tied into a bow at the hip. The barefooted girl stands, with her arms crossed, staring somewhat apathetically down toward the bottom of the image, as if she had been dragged away from some fun outdoor activity (located outside of the camera's reach) to come and have her picture taken. This setting is familiar from family events: when it is time to have the children photographed in their Sunday best, they don't want to come and start to pout. This picture's genre lies somewhere between a portrait and a snapshot. In the world of fashion photography it has a specific duty, which is to make the image believable. The chosen style makes the advertisement natural.

Analysts of advertising have pointed out that while advertisements try to sell us products, they are also used to peddle and mold diverse identities.[1] The sociologist Erving Goffman, for example, wrote in his classic work *Gender Advertisements* (1979) that few of us consider advertising images to be strange or unnatural, even though they are carefully planned and constructed entities (i.e., particularly strange and unnatural). With a careful semiotic analysis of advertisements Goffman demonstrated that the relationship between women and men in 1970s' advertising corresponded to that between adults and children. He achieved this by focusing on certain details within the images, including hands. He showed how women's hands often only stroke, feel, or caress objects, while male hands are more self-assured, assertively grabbing things. Women are also very often placed in a reclining position, while men stand up and are usually actively doing something. While the women pose childishly with a finger between their lips, looking vacant, the men are mentally present.

This asymmetrical presentation reflects the still prevailing gender inequality in the world. This is also why the advertisements do not look strange to us. The way advertising works is by generalizing and caricaturing existing and well-established models of behavior and existence. Goffman called this

---

Figure 3.1 From the series *Twins*, Helsinki, 2010. © Heidi Lunabba.

Figure 3.2 Large dress—small child. A too-big dress accentuates the smallness and incorporeality of the girl. © Silvia 1987. Photograph by Calliope.

strategy "hyper-ritualization."[2] Paradoxically, these kinds of ritualized gender representations help us to interpret our social reality.

While advertising underscores and intensifies established gender conceptions, it also normalizes them by further stylizing what is already stylized. Goffman's hyper-ritualization is evident in the Silvia advertisement in the way that it caricatures the style of the snapshot. The image does not look strange or stand out to us because it draws from other, similar representations. Instead, it seems pretty natural. The natural feel of the image comes from its use of a very specific form of visual descriptions of childhood. In it, it is typical for children to pose in white dresses that cover the curves of their body, and not to meet the viewer's gaze. This archetype is derived from the visual paradigm of innocence, popularized from the 1700s onward, in which children are depicted in loose clothing that is clearly distinct from adult attire, and shown as small creatures who are unaware of the photographer or artist. The slightly-too-big dress with its puff sleeves and frilly collar repeat the canon of the child as a small, innocent creature. These symbols have become established as a part of the representation of natural, innocent little girls.

However, when the Silvia advertisement is placed in its proper context, that is, a fashion magazine and the fashion industry, it is evident that there is nothing natural about the image, the dress, or the girl's apathy at all. The setting is carefully planned and it reflects the brand's views on festive clothing for little girls—and on a certain kind of girlhood as well. The ad is derived from a countless number of representations of fairy tales and popular culture, in which little girls wear dresses with puff sleeves. Just think of Disney's classic animations or Lewis Carroll's *Alice in Wonderland*: their well-behaved little girls have neatly combed, often braided hair, and they wear dresses similar to that in the Silvia ad. Once this archetypal representation of a child has been recycled often enough, we may come to think of this kind of girlhood as natural.

The reality-enhancing effect of the ad is emphasized by the fact that photographs are assumed to have a more direct relationship with their objects than animations or written stories. Photographs are thought to show their objects authentically, because they have many elements that remind us of the real child outside of the image. This visual correspondence can easily make us believe that the image is a direct reproduction of reality. Of course, this is not the case. Despite a certain concurrence with reality (there was a little girl dressed in white standing in front of the camera at the time of shooting), a photograph is not a literal reproduction. Just like a written text or a drawing, it is an interpretation of the object. An advertisement in particular is a purposeful construction made to transmit a specific idea to consumers. In Silvia's case, the ad transmits the image of the brand as a provider of clothing to natural children. By making use of the historically layered meanings related to childhood innocence, both the brand and its advertisement seek to erase their commercial and constructed nature.

A Brief History of Innocence

In our Western culture, adults have for centuries been trained to see innocence as an indelible part of childhood. Many will recognize the Aristotelian idea of potentiality: we admire a newborn because we don't yet know what the child will become. A small, innocent child also personifies Plato's idea of the Ideal Form, as well as the thought of a child's inner goodness. Purity, virtue, and innocence are often attributed to little children.[3]

For a long time, Christianity held a more skeptical view of the innocence of the newborn. Saint Augustine, one of the most important Church Fathers, for example, reveals his beliefs on childhood innocence in his *Confessions*.[4] Firstly he proposes that children are not to be trusted, because they value the life of a pet more highly than that of a man; secondly, that there is no reason to assume innocence at birth, because children are selfish and greedy and only haven't sinned yet because they have not had the chance.[5] The Christian notion of a child as a pure and unsullied creature started to develop in the fifteenth and sixteenth centuries in contravention of Augustine's teachings, and children began to be treated with a growing ambiguity.[6] The controversial questions were not only whether children were born in sin, that is, were they good or evil, but also at what age they were to enter the society of adults.

By the seventeenth century, the Infant Jesus had become the model for childhood. This radically changed the prevailing conception of childhood, implying it should be viewed as a period characterized by innocence, incorporeality, and asexuality. Contrary to Saint Augustine's beliefs, children began to be seen as creatures with no understanding of evil.[7] "Childish" gradually started to take on the meaning of "Christ-like"; it was believed that Jesus had redeemed his followers' innocence through his own sacrifice. The followers of Christ were called Children of God, and it was believed that they had access to Heaven. The paradox lay in the fact that while children were at the bottom of the social hierarchy and were not considered equally conscious or demanding as adults, they were also viewed with admiration and wonder.

In medieval folklore, children could be depicted as such virtuous creatures that even lions would not attack them.[8] Children and childhood were connected with the idea of the angelic, and started to be seen as a force of good in an evil world. Their innocence, in particular, gradually began to stand for hope and the promise of a better world, and these are notions that still prevail. The concept of childhood virtue and the hope of a better future are at the heart of the modern concept of childhood. A more secularized theory of innocence was developed by the French Enlightenment philosopher Jean-Jacques Rousseau, whose radical idea was that the best way to good adulthood was in letting children grow in connection with nature, without forcing them to learn or adopt moral rules.[9] Rousseau's child–nature link became an important premise for childhood and a cornerstone of education in the eighteenth and nineteenth centuries. This history can be discerned in the Silvia fashion ad, as in many other fashion images featuring barefooted children.

From Depravity to Innocence

The French historian Philippe Ariès dates the establishment of the concepts of the naturalness and innocence of children to the late seventeenth century and early eighteenth century.[10] That centurial shift is for him a milestone separating two opposing attitudes. Before it, children were hardly cared for and were mistreated, whereas after it, they became the target of caring and love.[11] Previously, children were carnal, sexual beings, while afterward they were considered incorporeal.

According to Ariès, the difference is evident in how the figure of the child was depicted in paintings before and after the seventeenth and eighteenth centuries. Whereas before the 1600s, children were painted as "mini-mes" or miniature adults, from the 1700s onward images in which children clearly stood out from their grown-up counterparts began to emerge. With this dichotomy of childhood concepts, Ariès reflects a paradigm shift that could be described as the switch from depravity to innocence. Before the time of innocence, there wasn't really a division between childhood and adulthood. Children slept with adults in the same rooms and beds; they listened to grown-ups talking and saw them having intercourse—something which today would be considered a sexual offence against an innocent child.

Although Ariès is mainly talking of the French royal courts, that is, the highest social class in that country, he says that the child and adult worlds were similarly mixed also among the peasantry. The difference was that while high-society people were expected to clean up their speech and deeds when they grew up, this was not true in the lower classes. The future King Louis XIII of France (1601–1643), for example, is reported to have played sexual games with adults and his peers when he was under seven years of age. He heard and told pornographic jokes and his morning erections were carefully observed by the whole court. Adults also fondled the prince's genitals and showed him theirs. These jokes and acts were completely eradicated once the future ruler turned seven. This was because that age was the watershed at which young Louis became a young man, that is, entered adulthood. The shift meant that the boy must adopt the codes for decent speech and behavior expected of a grown man of his rank. Although only a few years before he had been shown the bed in which he was conceived, after the age of seven he was no longer told how children are made. The question might be answered, for example, by saying that children are born through the ear—which is not that far-fetched compared to today's story of the stork. The future king would be chastised if he made the mistake of showing his penis in public. "The boy of ten was forced to behave with a modesty which nobody had thought of expecting of the boy of five," Ariès writes.[12] The same did not apply to small children or peasants—and Ariès makes no mention of girls.

For a modern reader, the descriptions of the straight sex talk and, particularly, of the intimacy between children and adults may seem shocking, even abusive. This was not true in seventeenth-century European culture. It was normal then for parents—or for the nurses of upper-class children—to play with their children's genitals. This has been explained in at least two ways. Firstly, because children did not understand anything about sex, actions of a sexual nature were not thought to hold the same meaning for them as for adults. Secondly, there was no fear that sexual actions or works might sully a child's innocent mind, because the general view was that there was no such thing as real innocence.[13]

Bringing up a Chaste Child

Ideas like today's concerning the fact that certain things are acceptable and permissible for children while others are not started to take shape around the end of the sixteenth century and beginning of the seventeenth century. Children should be brought up to be chaste, and they should be spoken to in different tones than adults, using only decent and modest expressions.[14] When children played together, adults must watch that girls and boys did not kiss, look at, or touch each other. A rule also appeared against anything immoral taking place between adults and children, at least in bed. It was recommended that they should sleep apart. In the early seventeenth century, children's books were separated out into their own category. Where previously high-society children had been educated by reading the classics, now books started to be edited and cleaned up to suit young readers. There was a new principle for good behavior: any words or expressions that were indecorous or possibly offensive for children must be avoided. These changes gradually formed a new concept of childhood innocence, which would become established as the determining characteristic of childhood around one hundred years later. With the shift, a large number of good behavior and etiquette guides started to be published, in parallel with education guides for parents and teachers.[15]

The new educational ideology soon began to heavily regulate the upbringing of children in the upper classes especially. They should not be left alone for one moment, and their thoughts should be kept pure by teaching them to read thoroughly chaste books. Self-control and seriousness were demanded of children at a very early stage, and the modern school system supported this plan.[16] All of today's research on childhood dates the establishment of childhood innocence to the seventeenth and eighteenth centuries, particularly highlighting the roles of John Locke and Jean-Jacques Rousseau.[17] The modern era, which reclassified all things and phenomena, simultaneously resulted in the definitions of adulthood and childhood. The main dividing factor between the two was innocence: while a child was still an unspoiled human bud, an adult was defined as a creature that had lost that paradisiacal state. Childhood innocence, which meant honesty, spontaneity, and freedom, was lost to grown-ups for good.

Future Hopes

Recent childhood studies generally credit Ariès with having pinpointed the time of the paradigm shift in conceptions of childhood.[18] As the ideal for adulthood started to consist of rationality, awareness, and independence, childhood took on the meanings of innocence, irrationality, and dependence. And as adults began to be seen as independent actors and workers, children were defined as non-competent players who depended on others and needed protection. Even now, we cannot define childhood except in relation to adulthood—and vice versa.[19] The fact that children are defined as dependents has made childhood easy to manipulate. It is thought that in the wrong circumstances, a child may grow up to be a bad adult. This is why there is still such an emphasis on providing guidance, education, and discipline.

Childhood innocence has played a role in society since the eighteenth century. In the early 1900s, the British doctor Theophilus Nicholas Kelynack proclaimed that children hold the keys to tomorrow, because the responsibility for leading and defending the nation, as well as looking after its education and civilization, will rest on their shoulders.[20] Similar thoughts can still be heard daily. In these cases, children are not seen so much as flesh-and-blood beings but condensed into symbols or signs for the future. Childhood is seen from the perspective of the future, for example, when considering the prerequisites for the operation and maintenance of the Scandinavian welfare state. It might be that now more than ever before we look at and bring up our children with the future in mind.[21]

From Miniature Adulthood to Innocent Childhood

The concept of innocence has always been closely linked with the ways in which children and childhood are portrayed.[22] Before the eighteenth century, children were depicted as adults of small stature; the biggest difference in art between children and adults was their size. In every other respect, the child figures were adult-like. In older paintings, the aim was not to portray individuals or children so much as a social class as a whole (predominantly royals or aristocrats). As we can see from Figures 3.3 and 3.4, the impression of miniature adulthood comes from the fact that the paintings reimagine children—in this case King Louis XIV of France and Queen Kristina of Sweden—with all the signs and social status of adults.[23]

Our understanding of childhood connects closely to visual and material cultures: to how children are depicted visually and how they are dressed. While children, regardless of gender, had worn long dresses up until six or seven years of age until the late eighteenth century, they still wore skirts until age three or four until 1910.[24] At this mythical four-year milestone, boys' dress codes changed radically as they started to wear trousers, sailor suits, Eton suits, or Norfolk jackets with shorts, knickers, or long trousers. Meanwhile, girls only experienced a small change in their clothing; although in the seventeenth century they acquired corsets and hoop skirts and in the early twentieth century lingerie dresses cut with waistlines low on the hip or slightly above the anatomical waist, with full-bloused bodices similar to

Figure 3.3 Is it a boy, a girl, a woman, or a man? The Sun King Louis XIV holding the hand of his mother, Anne, Queen of France. Unknown French painter, *Portrait of Anne of Austria, Queen of France, with Louis XIV as a Child* (seventeenth century). © Getty Images. Photograph by DEA/G. DAGLI ORTI/De Agostini.

those of the adult women, the change was but a nuance. The emphasis was not only on gender differences but on the hierarchy between genders: women were seen as only slightly more developed than small children, and boys were removed from this hierarchically lower status through a change of clothing.

Figure 3.4 The childhood portrait of Kristina, Queen of Sweden, shows the social standing associated with becoming an adult monarch. Jacob Heinrich Elbfas, *Queen Christina as a Child* (seventeenth century). © Getty Images. Photograph by Universal History Archive/UIG.

The shift from miniature adulthood to childhood innocence in the eighteenth century redefined children and led to new ways of visually depicting them. Educational guides contained dress codes. Rousseau, for example, advised that children should be brought up gently, directing them to play with toys and dressing them in simple, diaphanous clothes.[25] The philosopher was opposed to women's hoop skirts and claimed that excessively tight and close-fitting clothes were bad for the spiritual growth of a child. In Rousseau's words:

> The limbs of a growing child should be free to move easily in his clothing; nothing should cramp their growth or movement; there should be nothing tight, nothing fitting closely to the body, no belts of any kind. The French style of dress, uncomfortable and unhealthy for a man, is especially bad for children. The stagnant humours, whose circulation is interrupted, putrify in a state of inaction, and this process proceeds more rapidly in an inactive and sedentary life; they become corrupt and give rise to scurvy; this disease, which is continually on the increase among us, was almost unknown to the ancients, whose way of dressing and living protected them from it....The best plan is to keep children in frocks as long as possible and then to provide them with loose clothing, without trying to define the shape which is only another way of deforming it. Their defects of body and mind may all be traced to the same source, the desire to make men of them before their time.[26]

The interesting thing about this excerpt is that Rousseau seeks the model for a good and natural life from the closeness to nature of ancient peoples. He puts forth the still valid idea that excessively tight clothing is damaging to a child's body and mind. Apparently, close-fitting, adult-like garments were even a threat to physical and mental health, while the right kind of attire could help in raising healthy citizens. Loose clothes also gave room for the mind and soul, and helped to keep the child in a natural state as long as possible, outside of the tight clutches of the corset of civilization. These days few would claim clothing to cause mental health issues, but the idea of a link between tight-fitting clothes and spiritual corruption remains. Today the fear is that adult-like clothing may expose the child to "adultification" and sexual abuse, therefore primarily spoiling the body rather than the mind.

Visual Grammar of the Natural Child

Through textual, visual, and material changes, childhood gradually became socially visible. Children evolved into the targets of a critical adult gaze, and childhood came to be the battlefield for a number of ethical and moral dilemmas. The shift also rooted the prevailing vision of childhood innocence. Although

Rousseau's philosophies were not widely supported in his time, they became the norm in the next century.

The shift in the conceptualization of childhood became clearly evident in eighteenth-century art. Suddenly children were no longer shown as miniature adults but as sensitive tiny beings.[27] Details of their bodies, such as their faces, shapes, and postures, were now depicted in child-like fashion.[28] The fundamental symbols of innocence were the roundness of the body, pale skin, light, curly hair, blue eyes, and pearly teeth. In older paintings, this kind of angelic or Christ-like child or putto was mostly shown naked, reflecting the idea of the purity and innocence of the body. Soon, however, innocent children were, even in paintings, dressed in loose-fitting lightweight clothes that hid their figures.

The 1700s saw the rise of many painters who synthesized innocence or the Romantic idea of childhood.[29] They included the Britons Sir Joshua Reynolds, Thomas Gainsborough, Sir Thomas Lawrence, William Raeburn, and John Hoppner. They created a highly standardized way of depicting childhood innocence. One paradigmatic example is seen in Figure 3.5, Reynolds's *The Age of Innocence* (c. 1788). Unlike Rousseau's book, the painting portrays a little girl in the foreground, placed in a natural setting. The frothy style accentuates the figure's softness and roundness—the large eyes, downy cheeks, and chubby hands and feet. The child is depicted in profile and seems to be engrossed in her own childhood, as if unaware of the painter.

The painting's landscape and the girl's loose white dress give no straightforward indication of social status, unlike details such as the clothes, jewelry, corsets, and crowns of royal children in paintings like Elbfas's depiction of Queen Kristina's childhood and the portrait of Louis XIV in Figures 3.3 and 3.4. Reynolds and Gainsborough broke out of the tradition of painting royals and noble children, in which the main point was to denote future power and wealth. They focused on showing the immaturity of youth, which drew attention to the gap between the adult and childhood worlds.

The new way of portraying children underlined naturalness by placing the child in nature, away from the built environment and its associations with social class. They painted children wearing simple white smocks, without jewelry.[30] This does not mean, however, that signs of class would be altogether absent. On the contrary, they are understated, visible in the details of clothing—the fine fabrics, the shoes, or the cleanliness of the child's body—but not in any impressive signs of wealth. This means that the innocent child "trickled down" from the higher social strata to become a sign of middle-class childhood.

The Age of Innocence by Reynolds managed to capture the Western visual fantasy of childhood innocence typical of the eighteenth and nineteenth centuries. It became a paragon or crystallization of innocence, influencing visual representations for centuries to come. One noteworthy development in paintings depicting only children was that unlike the 1600s, when the main message of

Figure 3.5 The archetype of childhood innocence. Sir Joshua Reynolds, *The Age of Innocence* (c. 1788). © Getty Images. Photograph by The Print Collector.

the painting was linked to the child's future social status, in the 1700s the future is no longer present. The paintings make no references backward or forward but present the child here and now, forever frozen in her innocence. Another novelty is that the painting lets the viewer believe that childhood innocence is universal.

From the 1700 onward, children began to be distinguished from adults also in their dress. The choice of clothing was particularly tied to the child's freedom of movement. Immobilizing corsets were given up in the late eighteenth century in favor of simpler, more comfortable, and lightweight clothing: ankle-length dresses for girls and short jackets and shorts or long trousers for boys. Their shoes became low-heeled and their hair was simply cut rather than being covered with powdered wigs. The change is evident, for example, in Figure 3.6, John Hoppner's *The Douglas Children (or Juvenile Retirement)* from 1795.

The interesting thing about these centuries-old paintings is their reflection of how visual representations are tied to concepts and to changes taking place on the conceptual level. Just like Christian ideas concerning the purity of childhood were reflected in the nudity of child figures, the teachings of Enlightenment philosophers started to be seen in the form of carefully raised children, certain kinds of clothing, and certain ways of visualizing the body. Their innocence was clothed, because during the nineteenth century nakedness came to be associated with sexuality. In the same way as theological teachings on divine incarnation in the Middle Ages were reflected in representations of the Christ Child, modern paintings of childhood seek to fade out the child's corporality.[31] Images have always had a special power in how we envision a child's body and its innocence or sexuality.

Commodified Innocence

The image of childhood innocence ingrained by eighteenth-century paintings spread through mass-produced images in the following century. Illustrators adopted the painterly style, and the visual grammar of the innocent child became entrenched in children's books, posters, and cards, among other things. The English children's book illustrator and writer Kate Greenaway is known as one of the most famous portrayers of innocence. Her style of drawing child figures is described as consciously childlike.[32] Greenaway's drawings stand out in the visual history of childhood because she turned the symbols previously connected with innocent children into a whole visual style, as we can see in Figure 3.7, *Ring-a-ring-a-roses* from 1846.[33]

Greenaway's illustrations are examples of the commercialization of innocence. They turn the gaze away from the child's body and emphasize the clothes. Thanks to mass production and wide distribution, they promoted the development of certain kinds of clothes into symbols of innocence. The loose and light girls' dresses are still seen as symbols of innocence, which is evident in many high-fashion brands. An example is Figure 3.8, a Baby Dior advertisement from 1999. The infant is dressed in white, connoting youth and innocence, and bends over in front of the viewer, suggesting the child's innocent immersion in childhood. Especially in high fashion, children's nostalgic party clothing still draws heavily from the visual and sartorial history of innocence.[34]

Figure 3.6 Children were visually separated from adults from the eighteenth century onward. Girls and boys are differentiated from one another through details in dress. John Hoppner, *The Douglas Children* (or *"Juvenile Retirement"*) from 1795. © Getty Images. Photograph by The Print Collector.

Besides Greenaway's drawings, there were many other characters, too, such as Lewis Carroll's Alice, Shirley Temple, and Swiss Heidi and many of Walt Disney's animated heroines, who helped to turn innocence into one of the most desirable assets in modern culture. In contemporary fashion advertising, innocence is thoroughly commercialized. It is constructed as an aesthetically backward-looking and gender- and class-specific childhood. An image of an innocent child immersed in its childhood and posing alone in an anonymous

Figure 3.7 Kate Greenaway's drawings created mass-produced visual codes about childhood. Kate Greenaway, *Ring-a-ring-a-roses* (1846). © Getty Images. Photograph by The Culture Club.

environment, such as a garden, turns the child into a prototype or an ideal. Many adverts recycle the truism of the universal innocence of childhood. In reality the fact is, of course, that the ad only creates the effect of naturalness and innocence by dressing and photographing the child in certain ways. In the contemporary fashion industry, innocence seems to fulfill the same function as the outfits of the

Figure 3.8 Contemporary fashion advertising utilizes the visual codes of childhood innocence: the baby is placed in nature, dressed in a white dress, and bends over in front of the camera accentuating the child's unawareness of the photographer. © Baby-Dior 1999.

miniature adults in premodern painting—that is, to draw attention to the wealth and social status of the family—and innocent garments by high-end fashion brands are among the most expensive children's clothes.

Pink Innocence

Looking at contemporary visual representations of innocence, it is surprising to think that until the 1800s boys were used as the model for childhood. Prior to that, girls were rather invisible, especially in literature. When authors wrote about childhood in the Middle Ages, for example, they were usually thinking of boys. Girls are mentioned in some German texts, but in general boys' lives were considered more interesting.[35] Educational literature, including Rousseau's *Émile* (1762), only or mostly refers to boys when speaking of childhood and children. In other words, the first attempts to distinguish children from adults in the seventeenth century related to boys.[36]

It wasn't until the Romantic movement of the late eighteenth century that attention was drawn to girls. That was the moment at which the archetypal images of innocence began to appear. The 1800s saw the birth of female literary figures such as Charles Dickens's pretty, angelically virtuous orphan girl Nell Trent, who taught adults to learn from their mistakes.[37] In Victorian Britain, there was even a brief attempt to minimize gender differences: for example, it was thought that playing together would help to diminish the weakness of girls and soften the hardness of boys. A certain level of androgyny also took over as the childhood ideal in the early 1800s, of which there are traces, for instance, in the hairstyles and ways of depicting the faces of children in paintings by Hoppner—even if the clothes did indicate gender differences. Later examples can be found in many issues, images, and covers of *Vogue Bambini*, where androgynously styled children pose unsmilingly to the viewer. Within literature, androgyny was crystallized in Goethe's Mignon, the strange young acrobat without a clear-cut gender. It should be pointed out, however, that Victorians only approached non-gender-specific instructions concerning children's clothing, diet, and outdoor activities so nonchalantly because they stoutly believed in the essential difference between girls and boys.[38] This belief lives on and is incredibly vital still in children's fashion images. Even fashion brands such as the Italian Moschino, which is known for its avant-gardist, experimental, and cutting-edge designs and images, turns conservative when it advertises children's clothing. In Figure 3.9, an advertisement from 2001, the brand has a boy dressed in a black-and-red motorcycle jacket, sitting on a black, masculine motorcycle, while a little girl is dressed in lighter shades of the same colors (gray and pink) and only gets to wonder at the world and at the motorcycle-riding boy from a seat made of pillows.

Like Hoppner's painting, the Moschino Bambino advertisement emphasizes gender differences through clothing and its coloring, as well as through the children's poses and activities. Although the children in Hoppner's painting seem androgynous when judged by their hairstyles and facial and physical features, gender is announced through their dress and poses: the boy stands up, dressed in a skeleton suit, while the girls are sitting down wearing white dresses with pink sashes. In Moschino's advertisement, the boy is on a motorcycle, while the girl is sitting on pillows. Neither fashion ads nor paintings that visualize innocence manage to erase indications of social class, either. Status symbols may be lacking from the background setting, but they are discernible in the garments and in the children's slim and cared-for bodies, and, in the contemporary advertisement, in the brand logos printed on their clothes. Even today, a middle-class child is expected to dress in figure-concealing, simple clothes. This norm appeared gradually hand in hand with the development of the new, growing bourgeoisie in the nineteenth century.[39] Since then, the bourgeois identity and personality have been determined through careful control over the body and its clothing.

Figure 3.9 Subtle gender difference is a recurrent theme in children's fashion advertising. The active boy rides a motorbike, while a girl sits passively on a stack of pillows. © Moschino Bambino 2001.

The gender affiliation of innocence is self-evident in Hoppner's painting and in the Moschino Bambino advertisement. In the latter, the boy seated on a Harley Davidson is dressed in biker-like black leather trousers and a black-and-red baseball jacket, while the girl sits passively on fluffy pillows, wearing a gray-and-pink cardigan, gray trousers, and pink Mary Janes. The only difference between the painting and the fashion advertisement is that the boy in the painting proudly wears pink, which was considered a suitable color for boys at the time. Another example of contemporary innocence is found in Figure 3.10, an ad from Dior in 2010, in which a girl sits on a Louis XVI-style sofa. In this advertisement we see how pink has become the major determining factor of gendered innocence. The visual intertextuality here comes from the aforementioned historical visualizations of romantic childhood. As in *The Age of Innocence* (1788) by Sir Joshua Reynolds, so also in the Dior ad the girl is placed in the foreground of the image. She looks small and innocent but not lost in thought, because she gazes seriously out of the frame and at the viewer. She is aware of the audience and the camera. The ad constructs the girl's innocence and youth with many different techniques. She sits with her feet on the sofa, dressed in a pink bell-shaped princess dress, golden ballet flats, and a large silk hair flower. The color palette is pastel-based, with tones of dusky pink, pearly gray, and light blue that make the child's skin look translucent and the girl herself almost incorporeal.

Figure 3.10 A sophisticated version of contemporary pink innocence. © Dior Kids 2010.

Colorful children's clothes were common up until the 1770s, as we can also see from Hoppner's painting. However, the girls' white dresses are also evidence of how, at the time, bleaching and inexpensive cotton were revolutionizing children's clothing. White became the dominant color for children's wear and other colors were made visible in ribbons and sashes, which were easy to remove for laundry,[40] as demonstrated by the girls' pink sashes in the image.

In contrast to the late nineteenth century, white no longer plays as important a role as a symbol of innocence. The role has been transferred to two other colors: pink and light blue, particularly their pastel versions. Both pink and blue are interesting in terms of the history of color representations. While pink was still valued in the late Middle Ages, its popularity and appreciation decreased to a new low in the 1800s. Pink was defined as the most artificial of the colors, as a simple blend achieved by mixing white into the noblest of colors (red). Pink was thought to stand for everything that was vulgar, artificial, and off-putting.[41]

Despite this downright loathing of the color, pink and light blue were seen as children's colors, but contrary to how they are today. Pink as a girls' color has a relatively short history, as Jo Paoletti describes in *Pink and Blue* (2012).

Up until the First World War, boys were dressed in pink, while the color for girls was blue.[42] This was because pink, like red, was connected to strength and decisiveness, while blue had been linked to girls since the Middle Ages because it referenced the Virgin Mary.[43] Traditionally, red has been associated with fiery passion, love, eroticism, pornography, and active sexuality. However, blending it with white literally "dilutes" it: at the same time as white lightens the red color, it also fades out the interpretations related to sex, passion, sensuality, and the body.

This was turned on its head after the Second World War, when the connotations of pink changed to the complete opposite—girlish sensitivity and grace. Pink also became the symbol of homosexuality due to the Nazis branding homosexuals with a pink triangle in concentration camps.[44] Blue became the masculine boyish color, partly because it was a popular choice for military uniforms.

In both the Moschino Bambino and Dior advertisements, the innocence of the girls is emphasized by what are ultimately weakened versions of the colors black, blue, and red.[45] In terms of color history, pastel tones relate not only to children but also to the upper classes in the eighteenth century, among whom they became popular. Even today, pastel pink and pastel blue are considered more refined than bright fuchsia or electric blue. In the Dior ad, the pastel tones accentuate not only the girl's innocence but also the understated bourgeois charm of the upper-class brand. In sharp contrast, the cheap pink and blue products included in supermarket selections are linked in people's minds to the lower classes.

Colors thus play a specific role in constructing gender-specific social codes.[46] But they not only indicate gender but also make claims about sexuality. When pink started to be seen as the "weak color" in the 1800s, it became disconnected from the masculine and strong color red. However, due to its signals of weakness, blendedness, and artifice, it gradually also became a symbol for homosexuality, which was considered vulgar and perverted.[47] There is still a clear link between pink clothes and gender and sexuality. Due to the meanings of femininity and homosexuality associated with pink, it is no wonder that the color is seldom seen in boys' clothing, whereas for girls it dominates the shelves.

Blue for a Bouncing Boy?

The cooler palette of boys' clothing is usually chiefly blue. It is interesting that before the 1700s, blue was generally considered to belong to women, while light blue was a shade for peasants and other lower-class people.[48]

In today's clothing world, blue distinguishes boys from girls. An almost polar opposite of the representation of femininity in the Dior ad is provided by an ad for casual boys' clothing by the Italian brand Gianfranco Ferrè, depicted in Figure 3.11, featuring three boys playing on scooters in a similar manner to

Figure 3.11 Sprightly boys on their scooters. © Gianfranco Ferré 2007.

the little boy on the Harley Davidson in the Moschino advertisement. Unlike the classical beauty of the Dior ad, this image draws us to the present day. The short-haired models are dressed like grown men in casual, brightly colored clothes: T-shirt, sleeveless vest, and short-sleeved shirt. These are not pastel tones but pure and bright shades of blue, red, and white. In terms of color history, they can be linked to the purity and simplicity of the modernist palette. Unlike pastel tones, they signify brisk masculinity.[49]

The dominating tone in the image is the blue of the scooters and the seaside. These days the color is self-evidently linked with boyhood, but this was not always the case: as an imported product, blue was once the most expensive pigment in Europe, and yet together with green it was linked to vegetation and death, and was so seen as inferior to red.[50] In his history of the color blue, the art historian Michel Pastoureau describes how blue had little or no significance. It wasn't even the color of the sky, which authors and artists described as being white, red, or golden.[51] Gradually the connotations of the color changed, however, and by the late Middle Ages, it began to take over from red the highest status in the Western color hierarchy.[52]

The new appreciation for the color blue derived from many issues related to the new social order of the Modern Age, and from changes in the ways that society and the world as a whole were viewed. As European societies increased in complexity, their color scales were transformed. The six main colors—white, red, black, blue, green, and yellow—were joined by countless other shades. They were combined into diverse codes and symbols. Blue first became fashionable in the 1700s among both women and men. Its popularity was furthered by Goethe's novel *The Sorrows of Young Werther* ([1774] 2013), whose eponymous character wore a blue coat. Goethe's description gave rise to "Werther mania," through which readers started to associate blue with romantic, unrequited love.[53] Goethe describes the blue coat as follows:

> It cost me much to part with the blue coat which I wore the first time I danced with Charlotte. But I could not possibly wear it any longer. But I have ordered a new one, precisely similar, even to the collar and sleeves, as well as a new waistcoat and pantaloons. But it does not produce the same effect upon me. I know not how it is, but I hope in time I shall like it better.[54]

The popularity of the color was also seen in eighteenth-century painting, an example of which is Figure 3.12, *The Blue Boy* (c. 1770) by the English artist Thomas Gainsborough. For the contemporary viewer the boy dressed in blue may seem an iconic example of blue as a boys' color. However, up until the mid-nineteenth century, blue did not necessarily refer to boys.[55] In the painting, the color blue is associated with youth and boyhood, to the boy's innocence and separation from adulthood. Interestingly, the most important feature is not the color but his costume-like outfit, which was also considered a sign of innocence and childhood—a history that still lives on in children's fantasy outfits and fancy dress. The painting popularized this androgynous costume look for boys.[56] Another important feature of the painting is class: the boy portrayed in the painting was not a member of the aristocracy; nor was the painting done on order.[57] Despite this, *The Blue Boy* became the most famous painting of boyhood through countless imitations.

Only at the beginning of the twentieth century did blue become a favorite color in European society. Besides youth and suffering, the color was associated with the French Revolution and the American Civil War, and thereby with development, Enlightenment, dreams, and freedom. Thanks to these positive connotations, the color blue was first linked with masculinity, becoming a favorite for clothes for boys, as well as men. Blue took over from black in uniforms, business suits, shirts, jackets, and sporting clothes. It also became the symbol for freedom, thanks to blue jeans.

The blue tones of the Ferrè ad carry with them all of these centuries-old layers of meaning. For the contemporary viewer, the primary color palette tells us that these are undoubtedly male children, engrossed in masculine activity in a setting (seaside and scooters) that hints at freedom, leisure, and carefree play. The models' childhood is underscored: they are small in proportion to the blue grown-up scooters, and they seem unaware of the camera and photographer. Instead of posing, they are immersed in their toys.

Figure 3.12 Portrait of a prepubescent boy. Thomas Gainsborough, *The Blue Boy* (c. 1770). © Getty Images. Photograph by The Print Collector.

Gendered Innocence

Placed in contrast to their visual counterparts from the eighteenth and nineteenth centuries, the ads for Silvia, Dior, and Ferrè (Figures 3.2, 3.10, and 3.11) fall into place on a historical continuum. Since the end of the 1800s and, particularly, during the 1900s, ideas concerning the distinctions between girls and boys and the gender-specificity of clothes have only been reinforced. Today, innocence is not a gender-free state but a thoroughly gendered, commercialized, buyable, and wearable commodity. In fact, the idea of gendered innocence is already present in the iconic paintings by Reynolds and Gainsborough. Both imprinted the idea of a passive girl and an active boy through the children's poses: while *The Blue Boy* stands commandingly on a hill and stares right at the viewer, the girl in Reynolds's painting sits passively and looks away from the viewer.

The paintings illustrate the contemporary gender theorist Judith Butler's idea that gender is performative.[58] According to the theory, gender is a culturally, historically, and socially constructed category. Although the world—at least according to most advertisements—seems to be split into two types, girls and boys, there is no reason to assume that "girl" and "boy" reflect any prevalent natural order. A child's gender is not just something that is observed at birth or by ultrasound prior to it. Instead, it is a category within which the child becomes rooted at the latest when the obstetrician announces the sex at the birth. After this proclamation, the child's future will be carefully gendered, with everything from the name and the personal identification number (which in Finland, for example, includes a numerical code indicating gender) to clothes and toys specifying the child's gender. All this may seem natural, but it isn't. Every year intersex children are born bearing physical properties from both sexes. There are also many girls who don't want to dress and behave like girls, and ditto boys. Adults and children alike are required to conform to one gender or the other, and if a child should defy this requirement, he or she (or his or her parent or guardian) is likely to be branded as weird. Under pressure from gender-normative practices, it is difficult for children to act in contravention of common practices.

Advertising does not just reflect the gender symmetry of our social reality. As representations, fashion advertisements are inevitably also abstractions of what we understand of reality or, in this case, of gender.[59] Therefore advertising must be seen as a form of communication. One of the main "messages" of clothing and advertising is gender: they both stylize or stress certain aspects of gender at the expense of others. Advertising for high-end fashion is just one part of the cultural context within which we try to work out what gender is and what it means, and it reduces these questions to their essentials.

It should be noted that although human existence comprises countless ambits (political, professional, educational, creative, artistic, religious, spiritual, and so on), it is the one related to gender that seems to be emphasized in fashion and its advertising, also for children. It seems that everything is viewed through gender-tinted glasses, and consumers are addressed primarily according to their sex. In a way this is no wonder: gender is an important part of our definition of who we are as people in contemporary societies. For many, seeing themselves as a woman or man is very important, and those who cannot or do not want to place themselves in either category can easily feel left out.

The way in which advertising brings in gender roles from infancy can be examined, for example, through an ad for the Italian brand Baby Graziella, as demonstrated in Figure 3.13. It features two toddlers in a leather-clad car interior reminiscent of a 1950s' Cadillac. The children are placed in the front seat, one at the wheel and the other in the passenger seat. The one who is dressed in a light-blue knitted vest, white polo shirt, and blue trousers appears to be driving the car, while the one attired in a white knitted dress and jacket watches from the side, with a hand on the driver's shoulder. At first sight it depicts two young children playing at driving a car.

The image advertises baby clothes that fit in with a middle-class, leisurely lifestyle. Presumably, the children are not expected to play in the mud wearing these light-colored clothes, but to sit gracefully in a pushchair. The ad does more than market knitwear that hearkens back to a nostalgic past. It adopts a stance on the children's genders and imagines specific roles for them. Suddenly the initially innocent playfulness of the image takes on a more serious tone. Although their sexes are not self-evident to a viewer, the babies are coded through specific clothes to appear as a girl and a boy. The boy's clothes are pale blue and he is placed at the wheel of a car, which is another common gender stereotype: although the child can hardly walk or talk, he is already a car enthusiast. The passenger, on the other hand, is clearly depicted as a girl. The light-colored dress does this without question. Unlike the boy, she does not drive. From infancy, she assumes the role of the passenger. This conventional setting is accentuated by the 1950s-like styling of the advertisement, recalling a time whose gender system is stereotypically regarded as stricter than our own.

Although masked in the guise of innocent play, this image not only repeats culturally dominant stereotypes of girls and boys; it also sells them. The consumers who are attracted to the image's visual arrangement may end up buying the brand's baby clothes. Those who are displeased by the advertisement's gender-normativeness do not form a part of the brand's target audience. The ad makes use of the history of childhood, while also recycling these gender stereotypes. It reinforces traditional gender values, giving the impression that these are the values represented by the brand in question. Therefore it not only constructs the models' gender roles but also builds the brand's identity.

Figure 3.13 Driving a car is child's play—if you are a boy. Girls sit obediently in the passenger seat. © Baby Graziella 2001.

The visual world built into this ad tells us that the categories of "girl" and "boy" are conceptual generalizations. At the same time they have material consequences, most evidently in the types and colors of the children's clothes. The concept of gender performativity helps us to see the porousness of the conventional categories: it would not be impossible to read the child in the driver's seat to be a girl, even though it would certainly not be the primary interpretation of the image. From the perspective of social constructionism, what we see as natural boyhood or girlhood is actually closely linked to the concept of gender and its normative ideas on femininity and masculinity.[60] Our reading of the children as girl and boy is based on the usual meanings associated with children's clothes and gender. For us to see the children as two girls, we have to activate a process of information production that challenges stereotypes and actively works to prove that alternative readings are possible.

The Attraction of the Fashion Image

The reading of the aforementioned Baby Graziella ad shows that our understanding of childhood, girlhood, and boyhood is formed on a much more abstract level than by looking at a child's anatomy. In that ad, the interpretation was primarily

4

EROTICIZED INNOCENCE

Innocence has become a powerful code. This derives not only from the styling of modern advertisements but also—and especially—from the ancient trend of trying to determine people's characters from their clothing.

The American sociologist Richard Sennett has made interesting interpretations of the relationship between clothes and character.[1] He has researched the changing correlations between private and public life, all the way from the Roman Empire to today, and proposes that the boundaries between the public and the private have faded and been blurred. An essential driving force of the changes was the new concept of the personality and its place in public, which became popular in the 1800s. The triumph of personality was linked to Enlightenment philosophy, which supplanted religion and upheld science and reason as the ways of explaining the world. In such a world, the person became a new kind of source for finding the truth. Three central properties of the personality were defined. First, it was thought that different people had different personalities. Second, it was believed that each persona had its own look. Thirdly, and perhaps most importantly in terms of clothes, it was said that a person is exactly what he or she looks like, and therefore people who look odd are also odd. When people's looks change, so does their personality. This type of thinking—detecting a causal relationship between personality and clothes—is still quite common, especially so in relation to children. However, we should perhaps not think so much about a child's personality, but instead of what clothes *do* to children, and the responsibility of the parents in sending messages about their child through its clothing.

Clothes as a Revelation of Personality

In the nineteenth century, people started to construct their personalities by consciously manipulating their appearance. Sennett refers to that society as a

---

Figure 4.1 From the series *Twins*, Helsinki, 2010. © Heidi Lunabba.

"collection of personalities." The gist of it is that material objects such as clothes became symbols through which the personality was highlighted.[2]

At that time, clothes were seen as guides to a person's authentic ego. It was believed that one could get to know an individual by focusing on his or her most concrete elements—clothing details, ways of speaking, and behavior. The appearance was not divided from the self but was considered to hint at the private person beneath it. Neither did the self go beyond the person's appearance.[3] This belief in clothes as revealers of the personality mystified the appearance. The secularized understanding of looks also led to a new kind of logic: in order to learn the truth about someone, one must stand back and let the "ocular gastronomy" do its work. In other words, intensive observation could disclose the truth.

The details of the body and their observation became a method for constructing and understanding the personality. Premodernist nineteenth-century French authors such as Gustave Flaubert and Honoré de Balzac described reality painstakingly; as Sennett says, they were great reporters of the nineteenth century. By paying attention to details in an anonymous city, the writers sought to reveal things about individuals, on the one hand, and about the society at large, on the other. In other words, details did not just shed light on personality; they could also unveil the state of society.[4]

Even if today we don't believe that clothes reveal our identities or that by changing clothes one can change one's whole personality, the way we dress has become a very important method for adjusting our image. Adapting Michel Foucault, clothes could be called one of the essential "technologies of the self" of today's culture.[5] Foucault described how people can affect their own selves, their thinking, and their being by various methods, and how we can change to achieve our ideal selves. The idea of a link between clothes and personality construction is particularly strong when it comes to children. Buying fashionable clothes for children tells of the parents' desire to reflect an image of success. At the same time, clothes also contain a powerful message of what constitutes the right or wrong kind of childhood. There are strong opinions concerning these norms that regulate the style and cut of the garments. In fact, children's clothing shows that modern subjectivity is constructed around a concept of normality that centers on values and properties that could be called middle class: it should be neat and tidy, understated and concealing.[6]

The theories connecting clothing to personality construction date back to the nineteenth century. That was also the time that established the links between childhood innocence, clothes, and visuality. The period is characterized by the trend of the personality—including clothing as an element of it—becoming a part of the public sphere in Europe's new urban centers. People started taking their own and others' appearance seriously and believed that clothes held the key to deducing what kind of person a random passerby was. As the interpretation of clothing details became more common, people became particularly aware of the relationship between their appearance and the self. Perhaps they didn't want to reveal who they were to others.[7] Another consequence of the trend was the increasing homogenization of clothes aided by the technical developments in clothing production. By dressing in the same way as everyone else and blending into the masses, one could make it impossible for others to judge one's character. Then you were no longer an individual who stood out but a face in the crowd.

The change didn't by any means eliminate observation; if anything, it made it even more careful and detailed. This tradition is still present in fashion, almost unchanged. High fashion and people who know fashion are usually recognizable from details: the fabric, the cut, the sewing. Of course, the brand logos that are visible on clothes today are expected to reveal the wearer's fashion sense at first sight. For example, if a child wears a shirt with a polo player or a crocodile on the chest, others can interpret from it that the child is fashionably dressed. Additionally, the logo denotes the wearer's wealth and shows that the child supposedly wears quality clothes, with a higher level of design than their cheaper counterparts—which is not necessarily true, of course.

Although these days we understand that appearances can be deceiving and don't necessarily tell the truth about a person's real self, we still look for outward signs on the basis of which we can draw conclusions about inner characteristics. Dress codes have loosened, particularly among adults, but for children they are still quite strict, and clothes are believed to affect the child's developing self and personality. Paradoxically, the strictness of the codes in children's wear is visible in the fact that fashion catalogues continuously toy with breaking the rules. That is probably one reason why children's fashion is advertised using images in which the boundaries between childhood and adulthood, and innocence and sexiness, are ambiguous.

Snow-White Innocence

Most of the children's advertising that can be classed as ambivalent plays with the tension between innocence and experience. An example of this tension is seen in Figure 4.2, which is an advertisement by Dior from 2007. In it we see a young girl in a bright, white room, dressed in white clothes and shoes. Sitting on a white neoclassical Louis XVI chair looking bored or tired, she dangles a white teddy bear between her legs.[8] The white teddy is a reference to a romantic bourgeois childhood: playing with stuffed animals is children's work.[9] The advertisement resembles a situation where the girl has grown tired of playing and has sat down for a break. The arrangement is very natural: this is how we understand a tired child to look. It is common to portray tired children publicly, and it is considered a sign of their innocence. A grown-up sleeping in a public place causes confusion because it breaks a social norm related to adulthood, but for children it is allowed because they are young. The ad in question recycles

Figure 4.2 A drowsy child or a languid seductress? Sexuality is constructed ambivalently in children's fashion advertising. © Dior Kids 2007.

the idea of the romantic and pure, white bourgeois childhood, which appeared in the nineteenth century at around the same time that the first laws restricting the use of child labor were passed. As the use of children for labor reduced, their emotional value and irreplaceability as sentimentality-awakening creatures grew. People's concept of work changed, and play, although financially unprofitable, became children's work.[10] From this perspective, the child resting on a chair is a typical example of an ideal childhood.

There is another element in the image that is more important than gestures or the pose as a representation of innocence: the color white. The room is white, the teddy is white, and the girl is dressed in white. White has always been a children's color, symbolizing purity, joy, virginity, and innocence. Especially in the nineteenth century, white clothing marked the boundary between children and adults: children wore simple, loose, white dresses.[11] In Ancient Greece, white related to smoothness, transparency, lightness, and dryness: white was the color of light. In medieval theological discourse, white became imbued with Christian meaning. It became a symbol for divine light, and referred to the dazzling purity of Christ resurrected and to a light that can only come from God.[12] In Christian discourse, white was linked to the Resurrection and to the resulting joy and happiness, which is why early Christian art always dressed Jesus and the angels in white. In the hierarchy of colors, white became the most noble color at the highest level, related to faith, lightness, and immateriality.[13] This is why the color was linked almost exclusively to children in medieval Britain, for example.[14] White clothes referred to the purity and morality of the body. Deceased children were dressed in white and placed in white coffins, and those attending the funeral were expected to wear white. Besides its Christian symbolism, the color white had meanings related to the untaintedness and incorporeality of a small child's body.

In the increasingly secularized culture of the nineteenth and early twentieth centuries, white clothes became a sign of the bourgeoisie. Mothers dressed their children in simple white clothing to denote the children's innocence and the family's cleanliness and wealth: it demonstrated that the family had several outfits for their children, so that dirtied ones could be changed.[15] The idealization of the color white derived from the Christian tradition, in which women were represented as white angels. When the Christian connotations became secularized, women became "domestic angels" instead. Their sublime glow became a sign of inner and outer beauty. Whiteness was also a question of race: white women were defined as a particular caste characterized by spirituality, incorporeality, and etherealness.[16] In other words, whiteness guaranteed moral and racial superiority to women. The Dior advertisement draws from the tradition of the white glow. The tired child on the chair exudes the same upper-class purity and goodness as her mother.

Ambivalence of Innocence and Sensuality

Paradoxically, the white color—or non-color—of the Dior ad is so strong that the invisibility, lightness, and transparency become very visible and palpable. The trick in the advertisement is that while the whiteness constructs an image of innocence, it is so excessive that it paradoxically emphasizes the color of the Caucasian girl. The girl's skin color, the redness of the hair, the parted lips, and the direct gaze open up an interpretation of the girl being older than she really is. Red hair has since Ancient Rome been a symbol of fire, passion, love, blood, and violence.

Unlike the innocent little girl painted by Reynolds, the Dior girl is not lost in her childishness but looks directly out at the viewer. A possible reading is that this is not just an innocent child tired of playing with her teddy. The arrangement repeats the cultural archetype known from women's fashion advertising. The details of the Dior ad break down the traditional views on girlhood, according to which girls should be respectable and asexual.

Ironically, this ad and others like it make financial profits from using a childish figure that has purposefully been stripped of all financial benefit and utilitarian thinking. The affective and emotional value that became the core of childhood innocence has turned into a very effective tool by marketing machinery. The image of an innocent, pretty, and cute girl attracts the adult gaze and tries to awaken feelings of sympathy that will benefit the brand.

The technique used here is very common in fashion images. The adult's eyes are drawn to the fashionable clothes through the interplay of sensuality and innocence. Some researchers believe that the sexualization of childhood is not a culturally marginal phenomenon, or a new thing caused by capitalist consumer culture; they say sexiness has always gone hand in hand with innocence.[17] Others, conversely, believe that the fashion industry specifically generates and promotes childhood sexualization and has irretrievably changed the concept of childhood.[18] The problem is that defining childhood as innocent fails to take children's sexual rights into account while ultimately reinforcing the eroticism of innocence. The idea that innocence is sexy is built into the modern discourse of innocence, and that is exactly what the fashion industry makes use of.

Lower-Class Symbols

Naturally, the clearest signs of sexuality can be found where the self-evident norms of innocence are broken. A suitable example is Figure 4.3, which is an advertisement by Fornarina, an Italian streetwear brand for children and young people, photographed by Francesco Musati and Valentina Aimone, who are responsible for developing the brand's sassy and streetwise identity. It features a girl wearing typical little-girl clothes: a sleeveless white top with a pink heart and angel-wing pattern, and blue jeans. The clothes in themselves are in no way sexy; rather, they reinforce the idea of the innocent little girl. It is everything else in the image that provides a flagrant contrast to the innocence of the clothes. The girl has been placed on a leopard-skin stool in a bright red room. Her face is heavily made up, her lips and nails are red, and her hair is curled in waves reminiscent of 1970s' disco (or twenty-first-century Madonna). A tasseled brooch has been pinned to the breast of her heart-patterned top.

For centuries, the colors, patterns, and materials of clothes were subject to strict rules that attempted to set the boundaries for decency—for instance, in terms of what attire was suitable for each social class. In that system, certain colors, patterns, and fabrics could signify, for example, a respectable woman versus a prostitute. Prostitutes wore striped hoods in Britain and striped capes in France, all the way up to the eighteenth century, and in the mid-nineteenth

Figure 4.3 The little girl's innocence is challenged by visual connotations of lower-class sexuality. Fornarina. Photograph by Francesco Musati and Valentina Aimone. © Fornarina 2001.

century this became a fashion trend.[19] Over time, the stripes turned into a ribbon that the representatives of the profession were supposed to attach to their arm or shoulder. Later the ribbon became a tassel that was first worn on the shoulder, but later was used to cover the nipples of women in striptease and burlesque shows.[20] When these kinds of dress codes were abolished, it became significantly more difficult to determine a stranger's sexual status. This led to a certain miniaturization, that is, an emphasis on the details of garments.[21] Because women were supposed to cover up their bodies in public, details such as seams, the way buttons were attached, and the quality, color, and tone of the fabric became signs for a woman's social and sexual status. Too low a cut in the front or too high a hem at the ankle were read as signs of sexual promiscuity. The body was also observed. Nails and cuticles, the color of the teeth, the condition of the skin, and the amount of makeup could offer enough information to determine the respectability of a lady. A woman's only option to avoid being branded disreputable was to conceal her body.

The same principle still applies: if a woman's skirt is too short, her heels are too high, or she shows too much cleavage, her credibility will suffer, for example, in the workplace.

The dualism between innocence and sexuality reached a peak in Victorian times.[22] Innocence was idealized and children's sexuality was defined as something both forbidden and tempting. This dichotomy produced the image of the pure, white, virginal middle-class child that was sentimentalized in art, literature, and popular culture.[23] At the same time it generated the opposite: the idea of a sexual child specific to a certain class, which was used as the basis for controlling working-class and poor children. This figure was also immortalized in the visual and literary culture of the time.[24]

The Fornarina ad can be seen as a comment on the history of miniaturization, achieved by using certain details as conflicting signifiers of the body. The heavy makeup, the tassel, the intense crimson of the background, and the leopard pattern are all things we have learnt to read as signs of a grown woman's active sexuality, of a lower class, and of an animalistic, possibly prostituted body. In connection to a child they create an intentional conflict between chaste innocence and low-society, grown-up sexuality, which the brand wants to present. Simultaneously, the girl's clothing—a top, jeans, and sneakers—is not sexual but innocent. The ambivalence between innocence and sexuality is constructed by highlighting the cuteness of the girl through her innocent clothing and juxtaposing it with the other signs in the image that communicate sexuality.

The Fornarina advertisement suggests that by dressing in that brand's clothes, little girls can consciously play with this history and build themselves a streetwise image. The message in the ad is that chasteness and sexiness have become properties that can be constructed through clothes, speech, gestures, and styling. The visual opposite of the sexualized girl is the girl we might see in an educational image, an incorporeal being focusing on her studies.[25] The sexualized girl and the brainy girl need each other. The imagery of the fashion industry tends to favor the former, although some "nerdy" schoolgirls in glasses are also featured.

The concept of respectability comprises values that are closely related to class, gender, sexuality, and race. As we found previously, class is an essential part of the categorization of a woman.[26] As the analysis of the Dior and Fornarina advertisements demonstrates, class is also an important factor in the formation of meanings related to girlhood. The ads prove that respectability and morals are not just applied to women; judgment is equally passed on girls and their clothing, and more broadly speaking on children in general. By observing children we can determine whether they come from a moral or immoral family. If a child is dressed in revealing or flashy clothes, we tend to conclude that he or she has been exposed to premature sexualization. Class-specific symbols of sexuality have taught us to think that.

Serious Play

The Dior and Fornarina ads contain ambivalent blends of innocence and experience, and a play with signs of adult maturity, which can be found in many *Vogue Bambini* fashion editorials.

One example from 1995 is constructed around children playing at a swimming pool. Figure 4.4 comes from a fashion editorial: a red-haired girl poses in a bikini with the bust part filled with two orange balloons, accentuating the girl's innocence. She is laughing while she plays with something that isn't yet a part of her life: breasts. The strong green and orange colors of the image emphasize childishness here; besides pastel pink and blue, bright colors are deemed suitable for children.

A somewhat more serious game is going on in Figure 4.5, another editorial from the same year, in which a boy and two girls illustrate the story of "a very secret mission" by the Italian brand Young Versace. The start page of the editorial features two long-limbed, red-lipped, red-bikini-clad prepubescent "Bond girls." They lean against the shoulders of a "James Bond" figure clad in black suit and sunglasses. The second image of the editorial has only the boy, now without his suit jacket, with red lipstick stains all over his face and chest, which the editorial's narrative connects to the girls' red lips. While drawing from children's detective games and the world of grown-up movies, this article assigns highly stereotypical roles to the models. The girls are almost like Playboy models, automatically displaying their bodies for all to see, while the boy is a crime-solving, womanizing agent. Hidden in the innocent role-playing scenario is the assumption that girls and boys adopt different action parts simply due to their gender, already when playing games.

Yet another fashion editorial, also from 1995, this time entitled "Simple, Somewhat Royal Lines," features a girl that appears to have been playing princesses. In the opening photograph, a large-eyed blond girl stares straight out at the viewer. She wears a white dress and peeks out from beneath a veil-like curtain. The image draws from a long cultural history of representing virginity and inevitably brings to mind icons depicting virgins. Virginity is considered by some a cultural symbol that upholds the patriarchy, with the assumption that girls in particular should reach adulthood without losing their maidenhood. A virgin is an adult with no sexual history, who is presumably still asexual. Although "virginity" technically refers to the hymen remaining intact, the word is also extensively used when speaking of inexperience.[27] The difference between experience and inexperience is conceptually the distinction between a grown-up and a child, and this is imitated by a diverse range of cultural representations. The second image of the same article (Figure 4.6) has the same girl sitting in a white dress, with a crown of flowers, in a tiled space. Although this arrangement also repeats some of the traditions of virginal representation, both images are

Figure 4.4 A little girl plays an adult woman in a swimsuit fashion editorial. *Vogue Bambini*, May–June 1995. © Vogue Bambini/Condé Nast.

also toying with the tension between chastity and sexuality. In the first image, the girl's serious gaze challenges the impression of a virgin lost in her childhood innocence; in the second, the girl's unkempt bleached hair and trainers that hang open indicate modernity and that something has happened. The former image's veil of innocence has fallen from her eyes. The little girl's status as an untouched virgin is also shattered by styling the girl in the fashion of the Italian porn star and former member of Parliament Ilona Staller, aka Cicciolina, whose trademark pose used to involve virginal, white clothes, and a flower wreath on her bleached hair.

The fourth example, Figure 4.7, also from 1995, features two androgynous children. They pose in a white studio for an article entitled "Back to the Future." They are both clad futuristically in silver-colored garments and Dr. Martens, and their hair is sprayed with a silvery shimmer. Their brows and eyes are made up. The figures are highly reminiscent of boy band singers of the mid-1990s, with their self-assured poses and contemptuous downward looks at the viewer. What is interesting about the editorial is that despite the boy band association, neither

YOUNG VERSACE

UNA MISSIONE MOLTO SEGRETA

ma è solo un gioco tra fiction e ironia

Figure 4.5 Gender difference in a Versace Junior fashion editorial. The long-legged "Bond girls" in their bikinis lean against the "Bond boy" in his black suit and sunglasses. *Vogue Bambini*, January–February 1995. © Young Versace 1995.

child's gender is entirely unambiguous here. They combine both boyish and girlish characteristics. The first child's shaven hair would generally be considered a sign of masculinity, but the same child's midriff-baring top is a clearly feminine garment. Their facial makeup is very feminine, whereas the fact that the second child wears nothing under the silver jacket is a particularly masculine trait. The children's surrendering way of posing to the camera and the direct eye contact with the viewer are typically feminine. While the editorial appears to support the idea of an androgynous, gender-norm-transcending future, it does also claim that a child is not innocent or helpless but a self-aware actor who can express his or her girlhood or boyhood in contravention of prevailing norms with the help of fashion and makeup. The editorial seems to suggest that clothes and makeup are important ingredients in gender construction.

Figure 4.6 The girls in the Aquachiara fashion editorial are simultaneously portrayed as innocent children and sexy vamps, with connotations of images of the pop star Courtney Love and porn star Ilona Staller. *Vogue Bambini*, May–June 1995. © Aquachiara 1995.

An analysis of fashion advertisements and editorials demonstrates that fashion culture needs the concepts of both the virginal and the sexual child. In particular, it seems to need a hybrid of both of these. Sigmund Freud stated that virginity is needed in a patriarchal social order because it guarantees men the right of ownership of women.[28] This is reflected most clearly in the Versace "secret mission" feature, but the swimming costume editorial and the one based on virginity and its loss also fall into this category. The last example's futuristic punk attitude, on the other hand, reads as a critique of innocence and intactness.

The images make us consider the fact that childhood innocence is above all a sign of adults' rights to own children. While each of the examples describes the unequal distribution of power between adults and children, they also demonstrate how culture fetishizes the innocent child and lifts her or his supposed pre-sexual identity into the spotlight. Paradoxically enough, an innocent child is actually a

Figure 4.7 A fashion editorial "Back to Future" suggests that the future is androgynous: boys can also wear make-up. *Vogue Bambini*, November–December 1995. Photograph by Nick Ferrand. © Vogue Bambini/Condé Nast.

symbol of availability and ownership. The fashion industry recycles this conflicting image of the innocent/sexual child, but it is also able to challenge this view.

An analysis of fashion images demonstrates that childhood innocence isn't— and never has been—unchanging. In fact, the boundary between innocence and sexuality has always been uncertain—as it is in this book's examples. Innocence has always been considered to be easy to spoil, which is why we want to protect and control our children. At the same time, the ambivalence also articulates an interpretation that has been overshadowed by the innocent child: not even a century ago, when innocence first became established as the main characteristic of childhood, did people believe that complete innocence of a child would be possible or even desirable. Therefore the authorities recommended that instead of keeping children in sexual ignorance, they should be taught what was chastely named "enlightened innocence."[29] In reality, the schooling of children to be chaste in body and spirit was done using techniques that would today be considered barbaric. For example, parents were recommended to pour hot water or candle wax onto the hands of masturbating children. The objective was to extinguish sexual impulses and to plant morals in children's minds. The brutal instructions show us at least that innocence was not considered an inner property of a child but a virtue that could be acquired.

Race and Innocence

When the childhood ideal is a white, middle-class, and incorporeal figure, the ideal shouldn't be too difficult to challenge, as the advertisements described in the preceding sections have shown. The ideal figure of the innocent child has been divested of all class, sex, and racial differences, which offers high-fashion advertisers opportunities for interpreting childhood differently. Innocence is no longer necessarily white. In fact, some of the fashion images from the twenty-first century offer examples of the opposite happening: signs of sexuality being adjusted to be more innocent.

For example, Figure 4.8 is an advertisement for the American fashion brand Ralph Lauren from the spring of 2010. It features two children, a girl and a boy, who bring a new perspective into a familiar arrangement. Having started in 1967 as a necktie business, the company has in recent decades become an icon of American sportswear and casual clothing, whose advertising has followed its time, with all the political twists that has implied. Therefore it is no wonder that this ad reflects American multiculturalism of the twenty-first century, with black children posing in a setting reminiscent of the White House gardens in the style of a miniature Barack and Michelle Obama.

They wear classic clothes. The curly haired girl wears an empire-waisted, pink-and-white-striped, lace-edged lightweight dress, while the boy has a blue-and-white-striped jacket, collared shirt, tie, and loose-fitting checkered trousers. Through their innocence-referencing colorways, these clothes construct a gender gap between the children. The clothes exude neatness, cleanliness, and a strong middle- or upper-class identity. Although the details turn the children into miniature adults (with both looking directly into the camera, the girl wearing pearls and the boy, a tie), their animal companions also emphasize their cute innocence and youth. The girl, who sits on a chair by a low table set with tea, has with her a white rabbit, which symbolizes virginity. The boy, in turn, holds a yellow Labrador puppy.

The main difference between this Ralph Lauren ad and other similar representations of innocent and middle-class childhood lies in the fact that the children are not Caucasian. This is still very rare in fashion advertising: in the materials I analyzed, comprising thousands of fashion images, there were almost no other arrangements like these, with the exception of the multicultural images produced by Benetton. The observation reflects two things. First, it tells

Figure 4.8 Michelle and Barack? Children's fashion advertising has been very white but this is slowly changing. © Ralph Lauren 2010.

us that the world of Western fashion images has long been very white, ethnically speaking. Second, it reveals that the visual history of the innocent child is the history of the Caucasian child. Ralph Lauren's ad indicates that times have changed: the buyers of expensive fashion products are no longer necessarily white and middle class, and the innocent child is no longer exclusively white.

The advertisement is a clear exception in the Western tradition, in which white skin color has symbolized innocence and purity, whereas non-whiteness has signified sexuality and dirtiness.[30] The ad also opens new viewpoints onto the US colonial history, in which the white man encountered exotic otherness, subjected it to his colonializing gaze, and redefined it from his own point of view. In the global—and immediately after President Obama's election, somewhat more multicultural—world of fashion, the eyes cast over black children do not necessarily, at least at the representational level, follow the gaze of the white Western man described by Edward Said, which exoticized black and Asian people (children) and reduced them to feminine, weak, and passive viewing objects.[31] In this sense the Ralph Lauren advertisement can be seen as part of a post-colonial critique of fashion and its advertising. "Post-colonialism" refers to the period of time following colonialism, when colonized countries became independent nations from the mid-twentieth century onward. As a form of cultural critique, post-colonialism records how racism, slavery, and other forms of xenophobia still exist in art, literature, and fashion. The aim of this stand is to analyze "optical colonialism" and to decolonize: to change the ways in which the dominant Western culture represents other cultures and peoples.[32]

The Ralph Lauren ad is also a telling example of how malleable and flexible the concept of innocence is, and how it is continuously adjusted by taking influences from diverse historical and cultural sources. The children in the ad are located in a setting that until the twenty-first century was available exclusively to white middle- and upper-class children. The children in the Ralph Lauren advertisement make visible the bond between innocence and race, offering a platform for discussing racism, which reared its head at the same time as the discourse on innocence became established in the 1800s. At the time, racialism aimed to establish a racial hierarchy between the peoples of the earth.[33] It stated that it was possible to determine from the shape and physiology of the body—especially that of a child—what different races were like in terms of character, intelligence, and sophistication.[34] Races with their diverse gendered and sexualized properties were thought to develop through a gradual progression.[35]

It was claimed that non-white children developed sexually more quickly than their white peers and thereby also reached the peak of their mental development during puberty. Eugene S. Talbot, a researcher of degenerative evolution and heredity, proposed that after puberty, "because of mental atrophy," black people "remained through life seemingly enslaved to the sexual impulse." Additionally, he claimed that the conflict between the growth of the brain and the genitals during puberty resulted "in the triumph of the reproductive" over the intellectual.[36] In both Europe and the United States there has been a long tradition of seeing black people as hypersexual, unintelligent, and dirty, compared to whites, who are considered chaste, intelligent, and clean. Racialism is closely linked to people's understanding of reason, which is represented by white Westerners. In this context it is set against carnality and sexuality, which through history have been symbolized in non-white, non-Western peoples.[37] Even in the late nineteenth century, the sexual customs of non-Western people were commonly considered the opposite of the civilized.[38]

Sigmund Freud, the father of psychoanalysis, was one of the most prominent debaters of child sexuality in the late nineteenth and early twentieth centuries. He turned attention away from racialism to the study of neuroses and proposed that the origin of sexual neuroses could be traced to sexuality-smothering civilization. In his view, non-Western countries could not have neuroses, because they had no sexual inhibitions. In the early days of the 1900s, Freud turned his eyes to Ancient Greek mythology and developed a theory on the sexuality of children drawn from the myth of Oedipus Rex. It became a central theory through which the sexuality and development of children started to be seen. It has actually been suggested that Freud turned attention from race to sexuality because Europe was characterized by increasing anti-Semitism at the end of the nineteenth and beginning of the twentieth century. The politically jagged atmosphere was evident in the growing intensity of categorizing people according to race. Being Jewish, Freud perhaps wanted to avoid being racially branded himself and therefore linked racial discourse with primitivism and women.[39]

Although the terminology has changed, today's theories probably owe more to Freud than to anyone else. Thanks to him, racialist thinking was also superseded in psychiatry, even if it is still alive and well in popular culture. The Ralph Lauren ad, for example, carries with it the complex history related to innocence, race, and sexuality. Ultimately, it reveals that whiteness is still the norm in our innocence-visualizing children's fashion advertising, and that it is easy to stand out from it with images such as the Ralph Lauren advert. The ad is unique in its stand against historic and stereotypical racial discourse. It also suggests that things have changed since the late nineteenth century, even though the early twenty-first is still branded by racism and nationalism.

The Ralph Lauren advertisement shows how small the elements are with which the image of innocence can be constructed or challenged. Usually, skin color is associated with sexuality, but here it is placed in the context of upper-class innocence. It is noteworthy, however, that the children in the advertisement are not very dark-skinned. Studies have shown that in commercial fashion advertising, African Americans are shown with lighter skin color and more European facial features than in supposedly more artistic fashion editorials, for example.[40] In the Ralph Lauren ad, the connection between skin color and sexuality is "lightened" and the children become more innocent as a consequence.

Feminized Asia and Hot Latina Girls

The Ralph Lauren advertisement depicting the black "presidential couple" is an exception in the visual history of innocence. In most images with non-white children, the children's bodies are presented in a thoroughly sexual light. *Vogue Bambini* ran a fashion editorial on children's swimwear in 1996. Its title was "Orient. Two Friends for a Long Hot Exotic Summer" (Figure 4.9).

The two-spread report is photographed in a lush green environment reminiscent of an Oriental temple garden, with two children—an Asian girl and boy—almost blending into the vegetation. This associates them with nature more closely than a parkland setting. The children pose for the camera looking submissive, quite the opposite of the "lightened" children in the Ralph Lauren advertisement. They are dressed just in swimming costumes: she wears a bikini while the androgynous boy has on swimming shorts. The report seems to suggest that fashion and sex tourism are both industries that exploit children. This is evident from the title of the swimsuit report, bringing the commercial exploitation of children into the interpretive frame of reference for the image series by hinting at the sex tourism that heads to the Orient.

Figure 4.9 "Optical colonialism" is a recurring theme in children's fashion advertising. Asian children are often depicted as weak and passive objects of a Western (male) gaze. *Vogue Bambini*, 1996. Photograph by Aldo Fallai. © Vogue Bambini/Condé Nast.

Interestingly, as far as I have been able to find out, this report did not stir any controversy. The reason may lie in the presentation context, but it may also be that Western people are used to seeing dark-skinned children as exotic "others"—even as sexual partners. For a long time, non-Western countries and their peoples were considered a *tabula rasa*: untouched and innocent virgins until Western man conquered them and their lands. In colonialist thinking, the Orient, that is, the Far East, was considered a feminine continent. This is evident, for instance, in the fact that in Western representations, Asian men are feminized and stereotypically shown as delicate, passive creatures—in contrast with Africans, for example, whose dominant characteristic was oversexualization.[41]

The Orientalist tradition is also visible in the visual and textual rhetoric of the *Vogue Bambini* fashion editorial. While it turns the children into passive objects of the white fashion magazine reader's gaze with its evident racial consciousness, it also constructs an idea of them as objects eroticized by the fashion industry and by Western culture. The report follows a formulaic way of representing the Asiatic. The concept of the stereotype is highly applicable here: it refers to a simplistic, eye-catching, and easy-to-understand representation that encapsulates a large amount of complex information and connotations.[42] The problem with stereotypes is that they create a hierarchy of values between "us" and "them." Even though they only tell one part of the truth, from a single perspective, these fragments are utilized in ranking and valuing the phenomenon in question. This means that stereotypes are always linked to the distribution of power in society: the dominant culture reinforces its own identity by marginalizing and stereotyping other groups.

In the report, "Asianness" is forced into the mold of certain fetishized and generalized properties: feminine, passive, and delicate. Although a dainty build is common to almost all child models, in Asian children—especially the boy here—it is indelibly linked to passivity. He looks at the camera very submissively. The delicate features and passive attitudes conform to the emblematic characteristics assigned to the entire continent.[43] The fashion editorial, presented in journalistic style, also reminds us of the way in which non-Western children's bodies have become surfaces onto which Western sexual fantasies and taboos are projected. At the same time it manifests the colonialist "white gaze": the Western person's way of controlling non-Western bodies with their gaze and their camera.[44] In this sense, the *Vogue Bambini* editorial forms a part of the so-called optical colonialism, that is, the tradition of the objectifying gaze. It derives equally from nineteenth-century racialist theory and its imagery of "primitive peoples" and from the Western way of productizing racially specific oddities.[45]

Another example of the use of race and ethnicity is visible in Figure 4.10, a Dior advertisement from 2001, in which a little girl poses in sunglasses and glossy lips in the fashion of the pop star Jennifer Lopez. The long-haired girl is at the forefront of the image, wearing tight-fitting, brightly colored clothes that bring out her golden skin hue. The chestnut hair that runs down to her shoulders is long and full-bodied, framing a delicate face featuring the large sunglasses. She has her hands on her hips and looks at the camera over her glasses. The background is blue and the image is lit so that she appears to be in the heat of the sun or under spotlights, which creates a hot and lively atmosphere.

The girl figure in this ad is attention-provoking for two reasons. First, it presents the young girl as a small adult who poses to the camera with self-assurance: hand on hip, she looks over her sunglasses directly at the viewer. Second, through the visual resemblance to Jennifer Lopez, she is coded as Latin American, which is also a rather rare find in Western fashion imagery in general, and in Dior advertising in particular.

The advertisement makes effective use of stereotypes connected with Latin Americans: romance, sensuality, sexuality combined with simultaneous

Figure 4.10 This advertisement for sunglasses utilizes the theme of the "spicy" Latina. © Dior Kids 2001.

childishness, exoticism, bright colors, rhythmic music, and olive skin.[46] When further stereotyped physical properties are added to this—red lips, large backside, big hips, generous breasts, small waist, and skin-tight clothes—you end up with a figure constructed on the basis of sexuality, fertility, carnality, and race.

Although the girl in the Dior ad does not have all of the properties belonging to the Latina stereotype, everything from her pose and her look to the styling and the color palette in this image contains the beginnings of the trope, which is presented as a natural and authentic quality that she possesses. The stereotype is familiar from popular culture imagery, for example, from the television series *Desperate Housewives*, where the actress Eva Longoria plays the fierce character of Gabrielle Solis, or from *Modern Family*, with Sofía Vergara as the typically passionate Latina. This makes a huge contrast to the languid white girl on the chair in the other Dior ad in Figure 4.2.

The two Dior images (Figures 4.2 and 4.10), the Fornarina and Ralph Lauren ads (Figures 4.3 and 4.8), and the representations of virginity and Asianness in the fashion editorials all suggest in different ways that innocence is not a self-evident attribute of children regardless of skin color. The girl in the white room is simultaneously the Madonna and the whore; the Fornarina advert suggests active sexuality through details linked to the working classes; black children are "innocentized" by lightening their skin color; Asian children are passivized and objectified under the viewer's gaze; and the Latina girl is given the hallmarks of a future hot vamp. Despite the differences, each example contains recognizable class-specific and racist discourse. While the Dior and Fornarina ads play with social status, the swimming costume editorial with the red-haired girl with balloons in her bikini turns body parts signifying a woman's sexuality into a little girl's fun game. The editorial that toys with the idea of the loss of virginity through the Cicciolina-type girl, the Versace agent mission, the swimsuit report with the Asian children, and the ad with the hot Latin American girl in turn draw attention to the interplay of innocence, open sexuality, and the objectifying, racializing gaze in children's fashion advertising. The Ralph Lauren ad is the only one to break down racial stereotypes.

Consumption of Otherness

The images and editorials I have analyzed in this chapter commodify the interaction between childhood innocence, sexuality, class, and race. They turn children into consumable and enjoyable spectacles. Looking at it from a traditionally feminist point of view, one can well say that fashion advertising and fashion editorials subject children to a typically fetishizing and racializing adult gaze. As such, advertisements representing children are just another link in the chain of representations that objectify both women and non-whites.[47]

In the stereotypes related to children, black children are considered oversexualized; Asians, feminine; and whites, asexual. This kind of racist discourse is still evident in fashion advertising. It appears that advertising does not just recycle the ideology of white childhood using stereotypes; it also constructs "othernesses" that are of lesser value than the supposedly ideal childhood. But fashion advertisements can also be used to criticize the idea of the universality of childhood, and to draw attention to the differences between children and childhood. How childhood is defined in each case depends on how the meanings related to culture, race, ethnicity, nationality, gender, and class are woven together.[48]

Fashion houses offer consumers identity and lifestyle projects tied into their advertising images.[49] These images aim to speak to many consumer groups. Fashion brands make use of racialized representations of childhood to create an impression of the brand as a multicultural resource. Stereotypes play their role in this: the use of cultural attributes reduced to certain limited characteristics is the way for brands to accentuate and essentialize differences.[50] It means some properties have to be highlighted and other marginalized. For this reason fashion advertising relies so often on a familiar formula that depicts whiteness as innocent, blackness as sexual, Asianness as passive, and Latinness as passionate.

This kind of "othering" and consumption of otherness is characteristic of brands.[51] They will assume strong cultural meanings and link them to themselves and their products. By making use of otherness in their representations, advertisements and fashion editorials suggest to viewers and readers that they can also be a part of some of the symbolic meanings related to childhood by buying these fashionable clothes. They also show that today's fashion consumer does not live in a parochial monoculture but in a multicultural, global world. Paradoxically, multiculturalism in the fashion world is achieved by recycling tired stereotypes used many times over by Western popular culture. Therefore it is no wonder that fashion imagery that toys with multiculturalism always contains a glimpse of stale racist discourse.

5

FASHION AS THE SEXUALIZER OF CHILDREN?

In the spring of 2010, *The Sun* announced that Primark was selling "paedo bikinis." It was referring to padded pink swimwear tops with gold stars, which the clothing chain was selling to seven- and eight-year-old girls, as shown in Figure 5.2. It was not long before indignant British parents and child welfare authorities were calling on consumers to boycott the company. Primark was accused of promoting pedophilia by making little girls attractive to male perverts. Finally David Cameron, the Conservative leader, stepped in, saying he thought Primark was "encouraging the premature sexualization and commercialization of childhood." After Cameron's intervention, Primark's representatives admitted their mistake, withdrew the bikinis, and donated the profits to children's charities.[1]

Throughout the start of the twenty-first century there has been a lot of debate on whether commercial businesses exploit children and prematurely sexualize them. For example, in 2006 the Australian think tank The Australia Institute published a report entitled *Corporate Paedophilia*, according to which photographs of sexualized children are increasingly common in advertising and marketing.[2] According to the report, children under the age of twelve, girls in particular, are dressed the same way as adult models in advertising, which sexualizes their innocence. The report suggests that while early sexualization used to take place mostly by showing children sexual materials, things have now changed and children are pressured to adopt a "sexualized appearance" and behavior models.

One year after the "paedo bikini" scandal, the UK saw the publication of the so-called Bailey Review, which examined the supposed sexualization of children in the country.[3] The report was commissioned by the government and its main message was in line with that of its Australian counterpart. According to the review, today's culture has become more commercial and sexual, and sexualized representations

Figure 5.1 From the series *Twins*, Helsinki, 2010. © Heidi Lunabba.

Figure 5.2 Primark stores in Britain withdrew padded bikini tops after the company was accused of promoting pedophilia. *The Sun*, December 1, 2011. © The Sun 2011.

have become an everyday occurrence. In such a cultural environment, which is defined in the review as typical of late capitalist, media-oriented societies, children are said to grow up too fast and lose their right to be children. Both reports also say that children are pressurized to have sex before they are ready, and that parents are powerless before increasingly obtrusive imagery.[4]

The Bailey Review suggests as solutions placing magazines with sexual imagery out of children's reach in shops, censorship of TV programs, age restrictions on music videos, and easier installation of parental control software.[5] The Australian report proposed that the country's government set up a specific authority for the protection of child innocence, with the mandate of controlling media content.[6] In it, a team of experts comprising psychologists, pediatricians, primary school teachers, and criminologists would keep an eye on the media with the aim of guaranteeing the opportunity for all children to develop and grow up out of reach of sexualizing content.[7]

This kind of control of media content, with undertones of an Orwellian totalitarian state, is based on two assumptions. Firstly, that society used to be more innocent. And secondly, that the progression away from innocence has a self-evidently negative impact on the psyches and "normal" development of children.

The argumentation used in the official reports is very much along the same lines as the debates found in the media. The press loves to report on cases such as the Primark scandal, and comes up with sensationalist terminology such as "paedo bikini," "crop top," and "child porn" to define the phenomenon at hand as succinctly and eye-catchingly as possible. While the media purport just to describe a phenomenon, they are in fact judging it, for example, by branding bikini tops pedophiliac and the companies that sell them, immoral.

The thought of children being corrupted has not just come up due to recent developments, however; discussion has been ongoing for some time in the world of the fashion and fashion advertising. Related debates in the Anglo-American media over the last few decades could well be described as having gone from one scandal to the next. One high-fashion brand exceeds all others in this respect: the American company Calvin Klein. Its advertising has roused stormy controversies and impassioned arguments since at least the late 1970s. Usually the debate has centered on the use of child and teenaged models, whose innocence the advertisements have been said to corrupt, regardless of the fact that the models have mainly been young adults.[8] One scandal in particular did focus on children—on boys in particular—as both models and victims. This was a children's underwear campaign which we can see in Figures 5.3 and 5.4. The company was going to launch the campaign on February 17, 1999, on New York's Times Square, during New York Fashion Week.

The campaign was designed by the agency CRK Advertising, and photographed by the famous Mario Testino, who is renowned among other things as the creator of the "heroin chic" trend.[9] The black-and-white images feature three children. Dressed in white underwear belonging to the collection, they are jumping on a sofa, as children are wont to do. According to the ad agency, the campaign was "intended to show children smiling, laughing and just being themselves" and to "capture the same warmth and spontaneity that you find in a family snapshot."[10]

The campaign never made it as far as the billboards, however. The images were published in advance in newspapers such as the New York Post and magazines such as Martha Stewart Living. This raised an uproar and led to the cancellation of the outdoor advertising campaign. Some readers, including psychologists, members of the conservative American Family Association (which purports to maintain "American family values"), and the then mayor or New York, the Republican Rudolph Giuliani, demanded it. They said the campaign was "immoral" and reminded them of "kiddie porn" and "pedophile-friendly porn."[11] Even some advertising industry employees said Calvin Klein was "treading in a very dangerous place," and that "kiddie-porn is a very real problem and to even play in the area is not appropriate."[12]

The opponents of the campaign saw something in the ads other than innocent children jumping on a sofa. They were especially concerned about Testino's way of photographing one particular child—the little boy wearing white Y-fronts (Figure 5.3). The claim concerning the detrimental and pedophilia-friendly effect of the image was essentially caused by the fact that the viewer's eyes were drawn to the "clearly outlined genitals of the little boy" through the underpants.[13] In contrast, no one expressed concern for the little girls in another photograph of the same campaign, even though one was wearing a sports bra. If the same logic had been followed, and on the basis of general worries related to girls, one

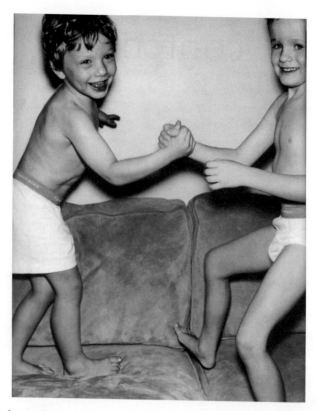

Figure 5.3 Accusations of child pornography were made against Calvin Klein in relation to children's underwear advertisements. Calvin Klein children's underwear. Photograph by Mario Testino. © Calvin Klein 1999.

might well have expected comments on how the bra brought out her breasts and thereby contravened the ideal of girlish virginity and innocence.[14]

Eventually the controversy surrounding the campaign that had aimed for the warmth and spontaneity of a family photo led to Calvin Klein pulling the images from public view just one day before the intended launch.[15] The company cited as the reason that "the comments and reaction that [they had] received today raised issues that [they] had not fully considered."[16] Although the campaign was never seen on Times Square, Calvin Klein did achieve something: the company's sales skyrocketed.

Sexualized Culture?

Examples such as the "paedo bikini," the government-commissioned reports, and the Calvin Klein underwear campaign show that scandals related to children's clothes and how they are visually represented are not rare in today's culture.

Figure 5.4 The concerned voices argued that the advertisements drew attention to the little boy's "clearly outlined genitals". © Calvin Klein 1999. Photograph by Mario Testino.

Similar examples pop up in the media almost every week. Many adults are concerned that the way children are dressed or photographed can prematurely sexualize their bodies. Girls' swimsuits, crop tops, and thongs and boys' y-fronts are seen as symbols of grown-up sexuality, which does not yet belong in the innocent and asexual period of childhood. The discussion usually involves the demand that children should be allowed to be children for as long as possible— as if clothes could deprive someone of this opportunity.

The discourse that claims our culture to be particularly sexual and childhood innocence to be in danger of corruption is affected by a lack of historical perspective.[17] Another problem is that it takes the idea of sexualization as a given and implies that this phenomenon—which is not explained any further— corrupts the authentic innocence of childhood. "Sexualization" is like a force that arises from "commercial culture," attacks children, and harms them. This undefined force is something negative and has obviously disadvantageous consequences, such as sexual abuse, early maturity, pedophilia, and child pornography.

What the proponents of the point of view forget is that "sexualization," "child pornography," and "pedophile-friendly porn" are not absolute terms that provide a definite description of a phenomenon. They are, as Austin says, performative—that is, they constitute active reality construction on the speaker's part. Sexualization takes place at the instant when an advertising image (for example) is declared to be "sexualizing."[18] There is a huge gap between the exploitation rhetoric and any factual proof of it. The fact that someone claims it to be so is regarded as sufficient proof. In contrast, the proof provided by many researchers showing that children and adolescents are not in any particular danger and that they are able to consciously navigate the world of media representations, especially with the guidance of adults, is disregarded by the sexualization rhetoricians.[19] As the previous chapter indicated, the image of detrimental sexuality is built through non-middle-class and non-white symbolism. We have learnt to link these to the lower social classes, to prostitution, pornography, and dark skin. What is displayed underneath revealing clothes is not skin but the sexism of the culture, which instructs girls—and increasingly boys, as the Calvin Klein controversy suggests—to see themselves narcissistically already in prepubescence. Revealing clothes are claimed to offer girls and boys a commodified sexuality that restricts their freedom and their choices, which is why they must be protected from sexualizing culture.[20]

"Proper" and "healthy" sexuality is implicitly perceived as a white, middle-class, heterosexual, and monogamous phenomenon that is ultimately intended for reproduction of the species. These are the objectives of maintaining childhood innocence for as long as possible, and they are considered to be jeopardized by the aforementioned sexualizing forces. While signs of innocence are considered safe, sexual symbols that fall outside of the ideal are presented as negative and detrimental to a child's psyche and body. The boundary between innocent and dangerous is not universal, however, but culturally specific and historically fluctuating.[21] For example, the clothes and images that are considered to be examples of sexualization do not just reflect the fact that children's bodies and attire might be increasingly influenced by forms of presentation absorbed into the mainstream from pornography. It is a question of middle-class values being undermined.[22]

The idea of the links between clothing and sexuality was not invented by our contemporary culture. Generalizing somewhat, one could claim that in Western culture clothes have always been used to draw attention to body parts that are considered sexy, and that we have learnt to read the public display of certain body parts as a suggestion of the wearer's desire or readiness to have sex. The problem is that the suggestion has become the whole message, reducing the whole wearer to a sexual object and erasing any form of agency from her (or, occasionally, him). This is considered particularly problematic in relation to children because the prevailing understanding of childhood does not encompass the idea of a child as an active agent or a sexual being.

Alternatives can be found to the child-victimizing discourse from within academia in particular. Several studies have shown that the problem is not so much with the fact that girls may be sexual or that they reveal it with their clothing, but with the cultural imperative that wants to keep them innocent, virginal, and ignorant. In this interpretation, the clothes branded as detrimental by the sexualization discourse are actually shown as symbols of girls' independence, sexual power, and strength. The problem then becomes "perverse men" and the dirty gaze they direct onto children, even though women are at least equally active participants in the public worry debates and the attempts to dictate what kinds of clothes girls are allowed to wear.[23]

The controversy arising from the Calvin Klein campaign is particularly interesting in that it was based around a little boy, whereas most of the debates in media and in research focus on girls. Demonstrations of this include the ban on shorts described in Introduction and the "paedo bikini" case discussed in this chapter. Unlike boys' clothes, girls' clothes are thought to carry with them valuable symbolic information of what girls are like and how they are seen.[24]

Generally speaking, there has been much less talk about the links between boys and their clothes, even though this is changing, now that men are increasingly interested in fashion and grooming, and with the appearance of peer-reviewed journals such as *Critical Studies in Men's Fashion*. Whereas girls are placed in the danger zone as victims of possible manipulation and sexualization, many consider the clothing choices of boys to rather be expressions of their freedom of choice. It is noteworthy that the concerns related to girls and their loss of innocence have sexual overtones, whereas for boys the concerns are mainly related to crime, drug and alcohol abuse, or violence.[25] The unrest and indignation raised by the Calvin Klein campaign seem to indicate a change: the corporality of little boys has become more visible in a new way. The fact that the ads' critics' eyes were drawn to the boy's flapping underpants and that they immediately interpreted it as bulging genitals reveals that little boys' bodies have for many people also become an object that is susceptible to sexual exploitation.[26]

The claims of the sexualizing gaze may feel odd particularly to those who have grown up in a culture where naked or half-naked children running around and jumping on furniture are still a common sight. Although the "paedo bikini" scandal and the Bailey Review are specific to Great Britain, the Rush and La Nauze report to Australia, and the Calvin Klein scandal to the United States, the forms of reaction that can be found in them have become very common around the (Western) world when it comes to visual representations of children and to kids' clothes. The typically American distaste for nakedness or half-dress in little children has led to repudiation of the work of artists such as Sally Mann and Robert Mapplethorpe, among others.[27] Therefore I believe that the reception of the campaign describes not only the American context but also how fashion images featuring children are seen and endowed with meaning more generally.

Children's Clothes as Moral Guardians

The links between clothes and sexuality are one of the enduring subjects of fashion studies. The language of fashion is intertwined with the language of sexuality. Sexuality is one of the fundamental ways of understanding the function of dress. Clothes evoke interpretations of sexual allure through cut, material, color, and style. The intimate relationship between the body and clothing makes any item of dress or adornment potentially sexually charged.[28] Even though the debate around children seems to suggest otherwise, the question is not of a distinction between sexual and non-sexual, but between acceptable and unacceptable sexuality. Certain forms of sexuality demand negotiation.

The roots of the subject lead back to debates in the Judeo-Christian world of the morality of garments from the point of view of religion. Well before today's secular considerations of sexuality, clothes with cuts, materials, colors, or styles that could be interpreted as sexually attractive were considered problematic.[29] Back then the wrong clothes did not act against the codes of middle-class ideals but against God's will. Wearing the wrong kinds of clothes was sinful. God's will defined some garments as more susceptible to sexual associations, and thereby less moral, than others. Also all kinds of beautification and vanity were sinful. Simple dress and makeup-free skin spoke of a sinless spirit. As we discussed earlier, the rules set by Christian culture changed through secularization and were absorbed into the norms of middle-class life. The morals of dress in Western societies no longer spring from religion, but from social class.[30]

Another method for controlling sexuality in premodern Europe were sumptuary laws,[31] which were designed particularly for regulating consumption of clothes, food, and furniture but also played a central role as moral guardians.[32] On the one hand they regulated and reinforced the social hierarchy and moral rules and regulations, that is, prevented ordinary people from imitating the appearance and clothing of rulers and aristocrats; on the other, they stigmatized certain groups of people as immoral or otherwise unpleasant. Those who were branded were forced to dress in ways that revealed their social status.[33]

In a secularized culture, the construction of decency has an affinity with the habitus of the upper classes. Proper femininity, for example, is produced as a sign of distinction from the lower-class sexual woman. By the end of the nineteenth century, ideal femininity was established as middle-class womanhood: "[It] was seen to be the property of middle-class women who could prove themselves to be respectable through their appearance and conduct."[34] The same applies to girls. Having sexualized parts of their bodies highlighted is considered especially detrimental to white middle-class girls.

They have to prove themselves to be innocent through their appearance and conduct. The need to prove one's innocence is revealing: it is not considered a natural given.

It is actually no wonder that revealing or form-fitting clothes should still cause a primitive counter-reaction in some people. The phenomenon that is today referred to in terms of sexualization stems from at least as far back as the 1950s and the period's general disapproval of teen fashions, and, on the other hand, from centuries-old discussions on sin, morality, and class. What these discourses have in common is that the figures of the fallen woman and the sexily clad youth act as symbols into which the moral dilemmas related to clothing are condensed. In Judeo-Christian culture, a prostitute represents sin; in secularized culture, a child or teenager wearing sexy clothes represents either a lower-class problem child or the victim of cultural sexualization. Their clothes carry meanings associated with the stigma of the whore at the bottom of the social hierarchy. It makes the clothes look questionable on someone who is not a prostitute—or, to be exact, it makes them look like a prostitute.

Fetishized Innocence and Concealed Corporality

A somewhat more advanced theory on the relationship between sexuality, clothes, and the body can be found in the 1930s. It has been attributed to the British psychologist John Carl Flügel, who is said to have called it the theory of the "Shifting Erogenous Zones." However, Flügel did not actually use this concept in his book, *The Psychology of Clothes.* Rather, it was a term coined in the 1960s by the costume historian James Laver, who, in his turn, does not claim ownership of the concept but attributes it distantly to "some psychologists."[35] Be that as it may, the theory of the Shifting Erogenous Zones claims that there are no specific sexual clothes, but that rather our interpretation of sexiness changes along with fashions. The interesting thing about the theory is that it tells us about the importance of baring and covering as definers of seductiveness. While clothes cover us, they also reveal parts and attract attention to our bodies. They accentuate certain body parts and draw the eyes to them.

Although Flügel's fashion theory is mostly seen as a curiosity in modern fashion studies, it does contain an important idea of ambivalence from the point of view of this book.[36] Flügel believed that fashion changes as our concept of what is sexy changes. In other words, fashion develops through the clash between modesty and showiness. The clash generates a conflict, which is visible wherever a war is waged between social status and sexuality. Therefore the idea of class plays a crucial role even in this theory, as a determinant of both fashion and sexuality.

Flügel's thoughts have later been expanded on, and some have proposed that the ambivalence is not so much related to clothes but to identity. Fashion changes alongside our concept of ourselves and our identities.[37] This view is derived from the theory of postmodernism that defines the self and identity as fragmentary and dispersed.[38] Besides clothes, ambivalence characterizes human identity: neither has one single, immutable meaning. Paradoxically, this is considered a problem when it comes to children. While children are still changing into the adults that they will become, in essence they are supposed to stay the same (innocent).

In some researchers' opinions, the emphasis on innocence has turned it and the clothes that signal it into fetishes in our neoliberal and fragmented world.[39] Fetishized innocence symbolizes what is lost. The fetishistic nature of clothes is related to the proximity of a garment to the body. Clothes aren't a part of the body but they are not wholly separate from it, either. They form a kind of boundary between the body and the outer world. In classical Freudian theory, fetishes are linked to suppressing a pleasure obtained through vision. In Freud's example, a clothing fetishist suppresses the vision of his mother's "castration" and instead idealizes her clothes in order to prevent himself from seeing the "awful" truth.[40] The way fetishism works in the case of children is that adults refuse to see the child's body as sexual and instead idealize his or her innocence-signifying clothes. This prevents the adult from seeing the truth—that is, the fact that the child is not necessarily innocent in the first place.

Today's sexualization debate related to clothes and visual representations has traces of Christian discourse, class consciousness, and theories on erotic body parts and fetishes. All of these are based on the idea that clothes symbolize a secret and concealed corporality. Clothes are understood to reveal or fetishize a sexual or erotic body part of an adult. In the case of children, the train of thought is the opposite: the clothes fetishize the innocence of childhood. When a child is dressed in a garment that signifies innocence, then also the child is seen as innocent. But when he or she is dressed in a sexually loaded garment, he or she becomes sexual. This understanding of children still has echoes of John Locke's ideas of the child as a *tabula rasa*.[41]

This is not the whole truth, however, and that is what is often forgotten by those who speak of sexualization. Clothes have no fundamental meaning in themselves, either innocent or sexual. What actually happens is that clothes are used to actively construct the meaning of the child as innocent or sexual.[42] We don't necessarily have to believe that skintight clothes, for example, signify sexuality; it is just that we have learnt to do so over a long period of time. In our visualized and media-oriented Western culture, the question is not just about clothes. It is also about how clothes are communicated to us through advertising and what additional meanings the visual representation adds to the clothes and the child's figure.

No Underwear! Obsession for Men!

Calvin Klein has consciously built an image as a taboo-breaking advertiser. Often it has overstepped the mark for the American audience, and the company's campaigns have aroused a lot of debate.

In 1980, the American model and actress Brooke Shields posed in a Calvin Klein jeans ad. Shields, who had already played a child prostitute in Louis Malle's film *Pretty Baby* (1978) and a nature child shipwrecked on a tropical island in Randal Kleiser's depiction of prepubescent love, *The Blue Lagoon* (1980), caused indignation with the following remark: "Do you wanna know what comes between me and my Calvins? Nothing." The comment was interpreted as meaning both that Shields wore no underwear beneath her jeans and that she (underage at the time) had had an affair with the designer. Another scandal arose in 1992 when the young actor Mark Wahlberg, aka Marky Mark, posed in an underwear campaign immortalized by Herb Ritts. In the TV ad, Wahlberg appeared in boxer shorts, blatantly groping his crotch and claiming to have lost his virginity even though his mother thought otherwise. It was a continuation of other, similar campaigns by Calvin Klein, in which athletic and handsome men appeared in underpants that highlighted their buttocks and bulging genitals. Many were disgruntled by the campaign, claiming it was too openly homosexual.[43]

In the 1990s, Klein's campaigns were almost without fail turned into huge media spectacles that ended up making headlines. For example, the *Obsession for Men* campaign from 1994 caused concern because it launched a new kind of fashion icon: Kate Moss. Moss, nineteen at the time, was photographed lying naked on a sofa. Pictured sometimes biting her nails, the vulnerable, childlike Moss, who looked underage, was said to resemble an undernourished child. Her appearance was the initial impulse for what was later known as "heroin chic"[44] and the "kinderwhore look."[45] Heroin chic referred to tired, apathetic, and gaunt-looking models, whereas kinderwhore was constructed using Lolitaesque baby doll dresses, tousled hair, hair pins, and bows. Another essential aspect was poses that imitated childhood innocence: grown women biting their fingers and staring at the viewer wide-eyed and head cocked. The provocativeness of the style came from the blend of childishness and grown-up sexuality.[46] It was disturbing because the kinderwhore look openly suggested that innocence is sexy. In Moss's figure these characteristics were combined in a way that made consumers accuse Calvin Klein of child exploitation and objectification of teenaged models, even though Moss was of age at the time.[47] The way she looked was enough. This proves how delicate the distinction is between inexperience and adult sexuality.

Calvin Klein's reputation as a daring advertiser peaked in 1995, when the company published a jeans campaign photographed by the fashion photographer and the maker of Madonna's *Sex* book Steven Meisel. The campaign was inspired by a 1970s' retro look meant to recreate the back pages of adult magazines of that era, and featured models in racy poses and situations.[48] The campaign included both videos and photographs. In the TV ads, young models stand before a cheap-looking imitation-wood wall, while an older male voice (belonging to Steven Meisel) asks them provocative questions and makes intrusive insinuations about their looks. Once again, critics claimed that the campaign was tasteless and suggestive. In contrast with the aforementioned campaigns, but like the 1999 case, this one was pulled from the market quite soon after being first shown on television.[49]

The interpretations of the 1999 Calvin Klein children's underwear campaign drew from the company's previous scandals, and the debates that were conducted in relation to it have also affected the interpretive framework for the crop top and child bikini debates of this millennium. Klein's campaigns have taught people to react in a certain way whenever the brand name is even mentioned. One could say that they have worked as a kind of test lab for developing the formula for purposefully creating controversy. At the same time, they have formed the interpretation of the detrimental effect of advertising on children. This is a card that can be played every time shocking images are shown.

The paradox seems to lie in the fact that while we want to see children as active participants alongside adults in consuming fashion and formulating meanings, we also see them as vulnerable.[50] The thought of possible threats to children is nothing new; in fact, various corruption theories have been proposed ever since children were defined as innocent. It has been suggested that interpretations related to child exploitation are signs of uncertain times, and that the child-abusing monster has reared its head whenever society is undergoing change.[51] When people feel that they are losing their grip on life, on their work, or on their future, they fixate on the idea of saving the children and their innocence.

Worried discourse on children is not just a modern phenomenon. During the golden age of industrialization in the mid-nineteenth century, there was discussion on how child-abusing monsters would lurk in the dark alleyways of industrial towns, through which working-class children had to walk to work.[52] Protecting children from threatening adults can be considered one of the main reasons for the passing of child labor legislation. At the same time people wondered whether children were innocent at all, or already marked by sexuality. The question was: Where do children acquire sexuality?

The Child Freed from Innocence

The French philosopher Michel Foucault is perhaps the best-known analyst of sexuality. He represented a new kind of tradition of sexual research in claiming that sexuality cannot be biologically defined.[53] He suggested that sexuality should be viewed as a cultural and historical construct, therefore offering an alternative to sexual essentialism. For him, a fundamental aspect of defining sexuality was the division between respectable and depraved sexuality and between permissible and criminal sexuality. What was defined as permissible and desirable was marital, monogamous, heterosexual sex aimed at conception. Homosexuality, prostitution, and child sexuality were instead excluded from the ambit of propriety. Due to this definition, a sexual hierarchy had formed in Western society, in which certain forms of sexuality were unfairly repressed. The American cultural anthropologist Gayle Rubin considered such forms to be fetishism, sadism, masochism, transsexuality, transvestism, exhibitionism, voyeurism, promiscuous homosexuality, commercial sex, and pedophilia.[54] The researchers said that sexuality had become a weapon with which to repress, dominate, and punish those who did not fit within the category of respectability.[55] One problem with this sexual hierarchy was that, despite attempts, it was impossible to punish criminal acts. Mostly individuals whose sexuality was deemed a threat to children and their innocence in particular were punished.[56] The attempt to protect children against sex crimes had generated a discourse of vulnerability, in which adults were seen as enemies of children. Paradoxically, then, society had come to a point where emphasizing the differences between adults and children had produced the concept of the perverse monster whose only aspiration in life was to have sexual relations with minors.[57]

Between the 1960s and the 1980s, attempts were made to dismantle some of the repressive systems built around sexuality and to bridge the categorical differences between adults and children. The sexual revolution challenged the norms and modes of behavior related to sexuality.[58] The liberation movement wanted, among other things, to make extramarital sex acceptable, to normalize homosexuality, and to give children the right to express themselves sexually. Gayle Rubin, for example, called for "pluralistic sexual ethics" and "democratic morality," and proposed that sexual acts should be evaluated based on the parties' treatment of each other—whether the relationship involved reciprocal consideration or forcing, and how much pleasure the different parties obtained from the relations.[59] Another solution that was offered was the removal of sexual boundaries between adults and children.[60] The proponents of the sexual revolution defined childhood as a symbol filled with political desires and freedom, and turned the child into a figure onto which they projected the idea of an unoppressed, free future sexuality.[61]

Sensual Children in Advertising

The May/June 1982 issue of *Vogue Bambini* contains a fashion editorial entitled "Femininity and Sensuality." It begins as follows:

A few years ago Irina Ionesco published images of her daughter in *Playboy*, portraying her naked and in a sexy pose. Then, *Pretty Baby* came out: a movie pretending to be serious but which ended up creating paedophilic fantasies. Nowadays no newspaper can not discuss this phenomenon where a six-year-old girl looks like a twenty-six-year-old woman.[62]

The start of this multipaged editorial is intentionally provocative. The images accompanying the text feature a girl, clearly under the age of ten, dressed in white clothes that reference innocence in similar fashion to the Dior girl posing in the white room in Figure 4.2. In some of the photographs, the girl wears a traditionally Kate Greenaway-esque little-girl dress, whereas in others she has on more modern white trousers, a T-shirt, and braces—or just the trousers and braces, posing bare-chested. She is made up like a grown woman, with lip gloss on her full-bodied lips, visible eye makeup, and a cloud of curls on her head or under her hat. The famous fashion photographer Herb Ritts took the photographs, and the girl poses like an adult, looking the viewer in the eye with a serious gaze. As in the Dior ad, this girl is presented as a Lolita or prepubescent temptress.

The text goes on:

> It would be indecent to hide behind sentences that condemn commercialization of girls only because of the discomfort of admitting that sensuality and childhood eroticism exist. It is possible that a fourteen-year-old girl is taking the pill and a three to four-year-old child has sexual instincts which she or he may satisfy without being threatened to go to hell if they are "caught" doing so.... An eight-year-old girl is not a child anymore, and while she is not an adult either, her sexuality cannot be neutralized with some excuse.[63]

The frame of reference for the editorial is clearly the upper-class fantasy of an innocent child, but it is also undeniably anchored in the freedom speech discourse of the sexual revolution. The text seems to be speaking the language of the theorists of its time, almost demanding that the reader understand that a small child cannot be seen as an asexual being. While on the one hand it admits that consumer culture involves the potential threat of little girls being exploited, it also stresses that even very young children are already sexual. Herb Ritts's way of photographing the girl accentuates this dualism. The white clothes and the girl's shirtlessness in one image emphasize her childishness, while her direct gaze and adult makeup bring out her sexuality.

In addition to this editorial, several 1970s' issues of *Vogue Bambini* feature advertisements with children posing in the nude. In one ad, two naked boys and three naked girls pose for a jeans advertisement, while in another five naked boys surround a naked grown man with hairy chest and a moustache. Even though in today's cultural environment it would be unheard-of to publish something like this, it is not that long since nudity of children and adults was considered a perfectly normal and possible form of representation in fashion advertising.

From Liberation to Seduction

Advertising images featuring naked children and fashion editorials that openly discuss little girls' sexuality may today seem extreme. Even in their own time they did not receive unreserved support, although I have found no evidence that these particular examples were publicly debated. The rhetoric of sexual freedom had its opponents. Criticism arose primarily from two American sources. One was the feminist movement: researchers speak of the so-called feminist sex wars.[64] Another source was the former psychoanalyst and later best-selling writer Jeffrey Masson. Like the radical feminists, Masson opposed the removal of sexual boundaries between adults and children.

The feminists claimed that pornographic representations not only *represented* exploitation of women and girls but actually *constituted* exploitation, for which reason pornography should be banned.[65] Masson, for his part, turned attention to Sigmund Freud's "seduction theory."[66] The United States had already been under the influence of Freudian thought for decades, and his psychoanalytical theory had become the cornerstone of the American culture of therapy. Freud's adaptation of seduction theory was "discovered" at the time and brought up as counterforce to the sexual revolution's discourse.

At the end of the nineteenth century, the theory of seduction was not generated as the result of purposeful deliberation but as a kind of by-product when Freud was trying to determine the origin of neuroses by using the technique he developed that we now know as psychoanalysis. The starting point of the theory was that sexuality is received by children from the outside. Freud had reached this conclusion after listening to the hysterical symptoms of his patients.[67] Based on what his patients told him, Freud deduced that psychic disorders that appeared in adulthood were due to traumatic seduction experiences that had taken place in early childhood.[68]

Masson freely adapted Freud's theory and found proof in it of extensive sexual abuse of children in the patriarchal social order. Masson's speculations turned seduction theory into a theory on child exploitation, in a form that had nothing much to do with Freud's ideas. Masson's interpretation became popular in the cultural atmosphere of the United States in the 1980s, despite being criticized for being purposefully engineered to achieve certain ends, and for politicizing Freud's seduction theory.[69] It was used in arguing against violence toward children. Masson's ideas were supported by new information on the history of childhood. One particularly prominent idea was that of the psychohistorian

Lloyd DeMause, who said that the history of childhood was entirely a history of abuse, and that children had never been cared for properly until modern times.[70] DeMause was not alone in his beliefs. Some pediatricians pointed out that child abuse had not stopped, even though children were better cared for than in any preceding century.[71]

Debates raged around child abuse and allegations of mistreatment of children flourished. The child abuse argument became a tool for political battle and influence.[72] The perpetuators of the abuse debate have modified public opinion and affected the way in which children are treated. As the cancellation of the Calvin Klein campaign and the withdrawal of the "paedo bikinis" prove, they have been and continue to be very influential. In contrast, the fashion editorial pondering the sexuality of little girls and the advertisements featuring nude children, with their sex-positive attitudes, seem to have been irremediably left behind.

Feminism has proved that in a patriarchy, women and children are in a submissive position compared to men. Child abuse and violence against women are only seen as possible in societies where there is gender inequality. The seduction of girls, in particular, is considered a part of the patriarchal family structure: the more power men have, the more likely fathers are to commit incest with their daughters.[73] The proposed answer is not removing the sexual boundaries between adults and children, but destroying the patriarchal system as a whole, as it is this system that is seen as the basis for exploitation of both women and children. Today's commercial culture is seen as a continuation of the patriarchy and therefore repressive.

Protection or Control?

The negative interpretations of the Calvin Klein ad campaigns and the "paedo bikinis" were founded on a growing worry over the status of children in adult culture, and of grown-ups' understanding of the differences between themselves and children. The debate was particularly rooted in the need to free children from adult repression and sexuality. As we have discussed before, the "battle" had two opposing sides with the same aim but different methods.

The first camp was pushing for emphasizing child sexuality instead of suppressing it, whereas the second believed that an emphasis on child sexuality cannot form the future of a civilized culture, as it already forms its past and present. Permitting sexual relations between children and adults would make it impossible to intervene in child sex abuse, and would mean subjecting children to the sexual demands of adults.[74] The first camp argued that controlling representations does not give children freedom, but rather subjects them to new forms of control. The second camp saw a continuum between representations and child exploitation. As we have seen from the reception of the Calvin Klein campaign and the subsequent crop top and "paedo bikini" debates, the latter camp has received more support.

The interpretation of Freud's seduction theory has over time formed the established view, which can be brought up whenever there is a question related to child representations and clothes. According to this notion, the images of the Calvin Klein campaign and the pink padded bikini bras, for example, are authentic proof of the fact that exploitation has taken or will take place. The logical conclusion is that because children must be protected from exploiting adults, offensive representations and prematurely grown-up clothes must be censored. At this point it is worthwhile to recall the fashion studies that have mapped the links between clothes and sexuality, as well as constructionist representation theory—the idea that neither clothes nor images are in any mimetic relationship to reality. Instead, the meanings of both the bikinis and the visual representations are constructed through an interpretive community that generates the view that an image is offensive or a garment sexualizing. Realistic representation theory interprets the images and garments in a single way, by positioning the child as the potential—and likely—victim of adults and the fashion industry.

Children's Fashion: Fantasy or Reality?

The Calvin Klein campaigns and the "paedo bikinis" are also possible to interpret in an alternative way: from the perspective of fantasy. The clearest expression of this idea came from the Italian film analyst Teresa de Lauretis in the same year that Masson published his views.[75] De Lauretis's interpretation of Freud is completely different from Masson's. She draws attention to the significance that Freud assigns to fantasy as a part of human identity-formation.

De Lauretis points out that the ability to fantasize is a heavily visual skill: it is like a stage, or a stream of consecutive images, in the middle of which the subject is positioned.[76] Fantasy is also linked to the metaphor of the mirror. The idea of the link between fantasy, subjectivity, and the mirror was first proposed by the French psychoanalyst Jacques Lacan. He connected this trifecta with the development of a child at the age of around six to eighteen months. At that age, children do not yet understand the world symbolically (through language) but observe it through their eyes and other senses. Lacan defines the so-called mirror stage as an important milestone in a child's development: in it, the child sees and recognizes herself in a mirror and forms an understanding of herself as an image external to the self. This recognition is characterized by a fantasy of the self. Lacan's claim is that the human self is constructed from the very start through alienating reflection and fantasizing.[77]

Fashion and its images are a special form of fantasizing the human; in many ways we become gendered and sexualized individuals through fashioning ourselves.[78] De Lauretis divides fantasy into two separate acts: "imagining" and "imaging," of which the latter is achieved with the help of various technical aids.[79] The creation of public images such as Calvin Klein's advertising is a creative activity made possible by our ability to imagine, while the advertisements are materialized fantasies, the result of imaging.[80] Children's clothing and their advertising are materializations of the imagined child's life. Still, this idea, clothing and advertising as fantasy, gets easily lost when it is connected to children — as we have seen in this chapter. It seems that apart from specifically designed costumes such as those of Superman or Little Red Riding Hood, which underline their fantastical nature, regular clothing, including underwear for children, is a very serious game with boundaries that should not be crossed.

The Calvin Klein campaign is an example of how childhood is turned into a public fantasy whose meaning is formed depending on how the viewers of the images imagine childhood to be. The campaign and the bikinis are seen as concrete examples of exploitation if we believe the radical feminists' or Masson's theory. However, if we think of the images as public fantasies without a direct connection to children, the campaign can be seen to draw from the history of innocence, where play (in this case, jumping on the sofa) is children's work. A few examples of children jumping on sofas can be found in fashion advertising, and they don't usually awaken any kind of debate.

Looking at Children: The Problem of the Adult Gaze

Of course child abuse is not just a fantasy but pitiless reality. In the case of fantasies such as images and clothes, however, especially in fashion and advertising, it is misleading to assert that an image or a garment mirrors reality. They are attractive fantasies that give us snapshots of a lost childhood that we are never to regain, and invite us to take a look into the intimate world with which children are traditionally associated. Children's fashion advertising permits us to look at children — in fact, they pretty much *demand* that we look at and admire them.

Part of the problem is that even though children have become active consumers of fashion, they are still most often regarded as passive recipients of the adult gaze, in the same way as women were long seen as objects of the male gaze — as discussed by the British film director and feminist scholar Laura Mulvey in the 1970s.[81] She argued that the pleasure in looking (*scopophilia*) comes from voyeurism — a one-way viewing situation in which the viewer has power over the object.[82] She also claimed that the viewer's pleasure is nearly always sexual in nature and that the viewer experiencing this pleasure is a man, while a woman is the passive object of the "male gaze." [83]

Analyzing the responses to the Calvin Klein campaign and the bikini top scandal from Mulvey's perspective, it is evident that fashion photographs and clothing represent children as the scopophilic target of the adult gaze, which also makes the boundaries of proper gazing and proper clothing of a child rather restrictive. Fashion images featuring children represent voyeurism, due to the unidirectional nature of the viewing and the inequality in status of adults and children.

This inequality in the viewing relationship and the idea of the objectification of children under the adult gaze have drawn some researchers to problematize the way that fashion images visualize the fantasy of childhood innocence. For example, Richard D. Mohr claims that adults who look at advertisements featuring children are inevitably taking part in "everyday paedophilia."[84] By this he is not referring to actual pedophiles, that is, people who fantasize about or carry out sexual acts with minors, but to the imaginary figure of the child that is needed for maintaining the normal social order. Sexually titillating images of children, which Mohr calls "paedophiliac representations," are ones in which "youthfulness sexualizes the image and in turn the image enhances the sexiness of youth."[85] According to this logic, almost all fashion advertisements and reports with representations of children are sexualizing in nature, solely because they feature under-aged children. Mohr claims that without the culturally constructed figure of the pedophile it would not be possible to look at children innocently.

Mohr's interpretation is extreme, but it expresses a paradox of our time. While all parents want their fashionably styled children to be looked at, the limitations for looking are very strict because there are only a few acceptable ways of looking (such as admiration). Mohr thus expands on Mulvey's thoughts on inequality of the gaze. In his view, a grown-up always appears as the active viewer who defines how a child is looked at, while the child's task is to fulfill the grown-up's gaze, that is, be its passive target.

Of course it is quite a generalization to claim that our culture needs the figure of the evil pedophile to take on inadmissible ways of looking, in order that "the rest of us"—adults who are sane and healthy—may look at children innocently. It is important to recall that a gaze and an interpretation that focus on details of the body—*in casu* a boy's "bulging genitals" or a girl's bikini top—do not just describe a phenomenon, that is, "genitals" or "bikini top." They interpret and evaluate the image and the garment in a specific way. This way of looking, which could be called indiscriminate assumption, relies on representational realism. It confuses pieces of clothing and images representing children with actual children.

The Calvin Klein and "paedo bikini" cases are paradigmatic. They represent a process by which certain kinds of interpretations, when repeated over and over, are turned into unquestionable truths. They are also paradigmatic in another way: they prove how easily images or clothes related to children can be confused with flesh-and-blood children.

The reactions to the Calvin Klein campaign also bring out the differences in attitudes toward the bodies of little boys and girls. For the most part girls, like grown women, are assumed to be carnal, sexual creatures, but the same does not apply to boys or men.[86] Young boys and men are not traditionally seen as sexual.

The main criticism concerns the middle-class ideal of masculinity, in which a man is determined through factors other than sexuality: his mind and reason. An openly sexual man falls outside of the category of this gentlemanly figure. He is either the predatory pedophile or a homosexual. When analyzing the reception of the campaign, we may wonder whether it was ultimately about rejecting homosexual fantasies.

The boy's white underpants, which were a miniature version of Calvin Klein's standard men's underpants, are key here. Worn by grown men, they have been associated with an eroticized male body and gay aesthetics at least since Mark Wahlberg's time. Calvin Klein has also become known as a brand favored by gay men.[87] The biggest crime of the campaign may have been to associate the white underwear with its non-straight connotations to the body of an innocent boy.

6

HETEROSEXUAL INNOCENCE

The spring 2010 issue of *Vogue Bambini* has two fashion advertisements that typify the current conceptions of the associations of the colors pink and blue with childhood innocence, children's gender differences, and the heterosexuality masked as innocence within these. The first (Figure 6.2) is a full-spread advertisement featuring four long-haired girls in what looks like a shop interior. They pose with sweet smiles and are dressed in summery clothes: dress or skirt, sleeveless top, three-quarter-length leggings, frilly espadrille wedges with silk ankle ties, summer hats, and sunglasses worn on top of the head. The second image highlights just one of the girls. She is spreading out her skirts and looking at the viewer with childishly cocked head. The bottom of the image bears the brand name: Laura Biagiotti DOLLS. The name and the mannequins in the background that are dressed in similar clothes as the girl's emphasize the girls' dollishness.

A few pages on, in the same issue, there is an advertisement for another high-end children's clothes brand, Trussardi Junior, featuring four short-haired boys (Figure 6.3). They are photographed in a studio, against a white background. Arranged close together in a group, the boys are laughing, leaning against each other, and seemingly doing some brotherly jostling. They are identically dressed in blue jeans, white shirts, blue knitted vests, and blue trainers. The brand name, Tru Trussardi Junior, is again printed in large letters.

Both ads sell products, the former for girls and the latter for boys. In this way, the advertisements try to build fashion-conscious consumers out of children.[1] At the same time, they are selling something else: a dichotomous gender system and the related sexuality. Unlike the examples discussed in the previous chapter, neither of these images has caused any counterreactions to my knowledge. They are most likely considered ordinary and safe, even though they sell gender and sexuality just as much as the prior examples. Because these advertisements do not question the norms related to upper-middle-class childhood, and because they conceal sexuality beneath supposedly

Figure 6.1 From the series *Twins*, Paris, 2012. © Heidi Lunabba.

Figure 6.2 Girls pose like dolls in pink summer dresses. © Laura Biagiotti DOLLS 2010.

neutral clothes and innocent poses, they are easy to read as more authentic representations of childhood.

Nevertheless, the Biagiotti and Trussardi ads demonstrate how childhood is thoroughly gendered. Neither of the advertisements represent childhood per se, but both of them make it known that these children are girls and boys. They state that childhood is dichotomous and that girlhood and boyhood are constructed through differing clothes, poses, and behavior patterns.[2] Even though pink was previously associated with boys and it is not that long since little boys wore skirts, it wouldn't occur to anyone to think that the children dressed in pink are boys. One would also find it difficult—although not impossible—to see the jeans-clad gamboling figures as tomboy girls. In any case, the stereotypical gender codes in the examples are based on and generate an unquestioned interpretation of girlhood and boyhood in most people's minds. The dress codes and visual representation methods are so well established that anything else would probably feel strange. Like the fashion historian Elizabeth Wilson wrote in 1985, fashion is obsessed with gender.[3] Contemporary (children's) clothes draw attention to gender so that one can understand, usually at a first glance, whether the person is a woman or a man, a girl or a boy. We expect people to look like one of these genders and if they do not, we are easily confused. The gendering of a child starts very early—in utero, in fact, as many parents these days make use of advanced medical ultrasound technology. Once a baby is born, it is dressed in clothing that follows the prevailing gendered color scheme, assigning the newborn

Figure 6.3 Masculine boys do not mind the camera when they wrestle in a brotherly fashion with their friends. © Tru Trussardi Junior 2010.

with a specific gender. When we see a child, we tend to think that the child's clothing reflects his or her biological sex. But what we actually see is a *gendered appearance* that we assume to be an accurate depiction of the "true sex" underneath the clothes. Dressing a child according to predetermined gender codes is an articulation of gendered power on a bodily level, reproducing the body as already gendered and sexualized.

The aforementioned advertisements are a textbook example of how clothing carries gendered meanings and assigns them onto bodies. The way children are dressed generates continuous gender interpretation, as clothing draws attention to the body and to the physical differences between girls and boys. Clothes are so gender-coded that a child's sex could be discerned even without the child being present. Contemporary Westerners understand skirts to stand for girls and a jeans/shirt/vest combination to signify boys, even without looking at the child. In this sense, clothing does not refer to the biological body but to culturally constructed ideas about femininity and masculinity. Still, clothing tends to naturalize this thoroughly cultural order, to make it appear as fact rather than construction.[4]

The child models in the advertisements are secondary: they merely reaffirm the reading we have already made from the clothes. But if we do observe the models, we see that they also have a purpose, which goes beyond what can be discerned from their clothes. Through their poses, the child models reveal things about the gendered relationships between girls and boys. This makes the advertisements a textbook example of the division noticed by Erving Goffman: boys are pictured as active doers, playing rather than posing for the camera, while girls are shown as childish, doll-like figures whose job is to smile and obediently pose for the camera.[5] In this sense the images follow the tradition of hyperritualization of the inequality between genders, in which girls and women are represented in a subordinate position to boys and men.

The Laura Biagiotti and Trussardi ads are not interesting just because of their old-fashioned gender ideas, however. They are particularly fascinating because they fail to awaken any passionate response, even though they clearly communicate that girls and boys are not innocent (androgynous and asexual) beings, but gendered and sexualized, and subject to a specific hierarchy. Although cases such as those described in the previous chapter attract the most attention and debate in the media, the majority of fashion ads are exactly like this: they reiterate views on how dichotomous gender differences should be constructed between girls and boys from when they are babies. The images form a part of the process that ritualizes the staging of girls as pink-clad, cute, and infantile dolls posing to the camera, while boys are active players that are focused on each other and care little about the photographer. Girls are turned into little children through the use of pink clothes and stuffed toys; similar infantilizing elements are missing from ads featuring boys. These boys are dressed in miniature men's clothes, and shown as a jostling band that has ended up in front of the camera by accident. They seem to possess a grown-up masculinity that takes control of both their attire and the photography session. Girls are left in the role of onlookers and models displaying clothing and their own bodies.

Fashioning a Heteronormative Childhood

Conventional gender differences also reinforce and normalize the idea of children's heterosexuality. Following the thoughts of the American gender theorist Judith Butler, the cute girl and boy representations in *Vogue Bambini*, and in the Laura Biogiotti and Trussardi Junior advertisements in particular, are typical examples of how sexual desire is fantasized to appear between genders that are considered opposites.[6] To use the terms applied in gender theory, the "feminine girls" and "masculine boys" of the fashion advertisements embody the heteronormative gender system.

The American literary critic Michael Warner is usually credited with the development of the term "heteronormative."[7] It describes how heterosexuality is so highly institutionalized in social practices that it starts to look like asexuality and as the only acceptable model of behavior. The term underscores the fact that heterosexuality is not actually any more natural than other forms of sexuality—only more common, if that.[8]

In other words, the concept of heteronormativity draws attention to the ways in which sexual hierarchies are created, established, and maintained. While heterosexuality is given priority, people with other forms of gender identity and sexual orientation—gays, lesbians, and transgender people among them—are marginalized. Usually this prioritization is not done consciously; in fact it is mostly tacit and subconscious. In this sense, heteronormativity can be likened to Louis Althusser's ideology.[9]

The Laura Biagiotti DOLLS and Tru Trussardi Junior advertisements are models of how we subliminally teach normality. Both settings are so ordinary that they are seldom questioned. Of course, at the same time they are public fantasies, interpretations of "girls," "boys," and "heterosexuality" by the dominant gender system. The ads popularize the thought that feminine girls and masculine boys grow into heterosexual subjects. In our media-oriented culture, the advertising world relies on the power and influential nature of images and clothing. Some say that the impact of advertising is based on quick recognition and the fact that an advert repeats a stereotyped understanding of gender through the ways in which models pose and are dressed.[10] This is probably true. The reactions to unsettling photographs reflect the fact that the frame of reference for these photographs is imagery that awakens no passions.

We must not think that gender-normative advertisements only reflect the values and attitudes of the dominant system; they also actively generate definitions of reality through exclusion.[11] To use the terminology of Teresa de Lauretis, advertising is a "technology of gender," meaning that it produces popularized information on what and how a gender and its related sexuality are and should be.[12]

Even tiny babies are paired up in girl-and-boy settings in fashion advertising. With slightly older children this kind of pairing is a rule rather than an exception. A good example of this is Figure 6.4, an advertisement for the brand Braez, dating from 2001. In it, tones of blue and red are used to signify both gender and the fact that the children belong together. The children are holding hands. On the one hand the gesture symbolizes innocence and friendship, but on the other, in the adult world it refers to sexual attraction between the two parties. This is why gay couples, for example, still find it hard to walk hand in

Figure 6.4 Innocent heterosexuality? © Braez Junior 2001.

hand in public: the gesture implies that they have sex. This kind of intimacy is not read into the gesture of holding hands when it comes to children, but at the same time children of opposite genders in particular are encouraged to show this kind of affection. In reality, then, holding hands is not innocent but implies some degree of a hope of future intimacy. The underlying gender ideology of hand-holding becomes most tangible when thinking about two boys. Unlike girl/boy or even girl/girl pairs, two boys are seldom encouraged to hold hands.

The Braez ad also indicates gender differences through the children's styling, poses, and clothes. The girl's code includes long blond curls, light skin, a body-hugging red jersey dress that has been lightened to pink through batik dyeing, embroidered flowers on her denim jacket, and her serious, even withdrawn (i.e., passive) expression. The boy is coded with short, dark hair, slightly darker skin, the bright-red color of his figure-concealing, loose shirt, and his loose, patched jeans. His expression is slightly more active, looking at the camera open-mouthed, as if about to say something. He is also standing a little further forward than the girl, almost as if to protect his shy friend. Both children are barefoot and seem natural, despite the studio environment.

The photograph has the air of a hasty snapshot, which makes its subject—the girl–boy pairing—seem even more natural. The image was staged and constructed, though. The girl is more feminine than the boy, which is accentuated, besides the aforementioned elements, by the fact that she is slightly shorter and is standing a bit further back. This setting reinforces some of the most persistent cultural conventions, which state that boys must be taller, more masculine, and more active than girls. In this way, the advertisement already imagines these children within the structures of heterosexual gender, affection, and romance. These kinds of ordinary-looking images featuring seemingly conventional children carefully shore up the idea of the naturalness of this setting, while also training children and adults alike to adopt and learn the rules of what girls are like, how boys should look, and what kinds of couples they should form.

Kissing Children

Some of the models in advertisements that reiterate the stereotype of heterosexual romance are babies and toddlers. For example, Figure 6.5, which is a 1993 advertisement for the brand Baby's, is obviously connected to the gender ideology that defines heterosexuality as natural. It features two very young children in a lush Alpine-style environment. They are identically dressed in corduroy trousers, autumn jackets, and stiff ankle boots that don't directly indicate gender. Our gender assumptions are based on the styling of their hair. One of the children has plaits and so is coded as a girl, while the other's short hair signifies boyhood, in accordance with stereotypes.

Many of those who are involved with children know from everyday experience that the gender codes of children's clothes and styling are incredibly strict. Excessively feminine clothes or long hair will subject a boy to comments from the outer world, especially once he goes to school. For a little girl, on the other hand, growing long hair is usually the first step in the process of becoming a heterosexual girl. Even if her hair has been bobbed for the first few years of her life, the hair-growing project will usually start by the time she goes to school, at the latest. It is surprising how much discussion among adults a girl's hair will invite, and what kind of anxiety ensues if a girl aspires to cut her long hair short. If her hair is long and voluminous, it is admired and styled, whereas short hair either is ignored or generates questions of whether she intends to

Figure 6.5 An innocent romance. © Baby's 1993.

grow it out. The same applies inversely to boys. Even if a boy's locks have been allowed to flow freely for the first few years, once he goes to day care or, at the very latest, school, his parents will be pressured in different ways to cut them.

The children in the advertisement are pictured kissing each other with eyes closed—a familiar gesture from romantic love stories. Kissing is one of the strongest cultural expressions of emotion, and it signifies the fulfillment of a relationship: the ideal of romantic love. This is one of the reasons that so many couples are pictured kissing in their wedding photos. Although love has been spoken and written about since the times of Plato and Sappho, it was not until the modern age and, particularly, the nineteenth century that romantic love became the essence of heterosexual relationships.[13] Like childhood innocence, romantic love is presented as a natural phenomenon, even though in reality it is the product of an urbanized, capitalist society.[14]

The pertinent thing about the romantic love ideal in terms of childhood is related to sexuality: the nineteenth-century nuclear family ideology linked love to romance and to sex between people of opposite gender.[15] Romantic love became the symbolic basis for marriage. It did not befit children or youths. In contrast, children became material symbols of the fulfillment of romantic love between a man and a woman.

In the Baby's advertisement, there is a suggestion of romantic love between two presumably innocent toddlers. Of course these kinds of situations do happen in everyday life; children are encouraged to express their feelings in certain ways, to certain people, with certain kinds of gestures between boys and girls.[16] The ad turns this ideologically highly loaded theme into innocent play. This kind of play will only attract attention when a tacit, unquestioned norm is violated, for example, by encouraging two boys to kiss each other on the lips. The natural setting of the Baby's ad supports the notion of the innocence and naturalness of this kiss: this is the way it's meant to be; this is innocent. The naturalness of the kiss is also underlined by the somewhat androgynous appearance of the children. The children are like the two halves in Plato's myth of the original human being, the Androgyne. According to this myth on the origins of man and woman, Zeus cut the Androgyne into two, causing the two halves eternally to desire one another. When they came together, the two halves threw their arms around one another and entwined in a mutual embrace.[17]

Heteronormative Messages of Clothes

As we have seen, clothes have never been neutral in meaning or used just for covering the body. Instead, they have always had the task of adapting a person to his or her social environment. Seen in this way, it was never a question of just clothes. Children's clothes and accessories are also material objects that tell us how we should approach, speak to, and speak of a child, and how children should interact with each other. The ideas of passiveness and activeness displayed in children's fashion advertising often also apply in our everyday encounters with children. We will speak more softly to a child recognized as a girl based on clothing, whereas boys are expected to exhibit masculine behavior and emotional control from when they are very young. In these ways we teach sensitivity to girls and assertiveness to boys. Ultimately the dichotomy constructs the idea that women and men are opposites and therefore complement each other. In the Baby's kissing image (Figure 6.5), for example, the antagonism is naturalized. When the ad is mirrored to the history of childhood innocence and romantic love, we see that it makes use of the traditional meanings of innocence associated with roundness and nature, in order to make the image and the situation believable. In other words, the image makes use of certain accepted stereotypes to ensure its message is not disturbing. With this gesture, the brand takes part in recycling and reinforcing the naturalness of the idea that heterosexuality is the default.

At the very least, the gender ideology of this advertisement is evident in the fact that, although similar advertisements can be found in every issue of *Vogue Bambini*, only one example was found among all the thousands of images of two children who are clearly interpreted as boys kissing each other (Figure 6.6). This is a one-spread advertisement from 1999 by Moschino Junior for waterproof clothing, featuring two boys. In the first image, we see one of the boys dressed in a gray sweatshirt with a nimbus and lightning drawn on it, staring at the viewer with a wide grin. The other boy, dressed in a red waterproof jacket, is depicted pecking the other boy's cheek, not his lips, with his eyes shut, in a friendly manner.

In contrast, there were some examples of two girls nearly kissing on the mouth (see Figure 6.7), and more of two boys or two girls hugging. Evidently the heterosexualization of childhood takes place in fashion imagery in much the same way as it does for adults—same-sex intimacy is there, but in the margins. It most often requires opposite genders, that is, children coded as a feminine girl and a masculine boy, between whom an assumed relationship (i.e., sexual desire) can be fantasized. Even if the children are placed in a natural setting or pictured in the form of a snapshot, the sexuality displayed in the image is no more natural than its genders are.

The standardized innocence of childhood and its obvious assumptions of gender dichotomy and heterosexuality are some of the manifestations of heteronormativeness. The gendering power is particularly strong and unquestioned in representations of children. The status of gender dichotomy and heterosexuality is interesting in relation to children, because as the Braez and Baby's adverts attest, it is considered just as natural, artless, and inborn as the children's innocence. In fact it is innocence.[18]

Innocence works as an invisibility cloak, covering heterosexuality either in lightweight figure-concealing, childish clothes or specifying it in colors such as pink and blue. The concept of heteronormativity is helpful in understanding the norms that define childhood and the ways in which innocence masquerading as asexuality is used to sweep gendering and sexualizing meanings under the carpet.

Learning Heterosexuality

The examples given here also demonstrate how fashion advertising fetishizes gender differences. This kind of thinking has a long history, going as far back as late nineteenth-century theories on psychoanalysis, sexology, and psychiatry, early twentieth-century educational ideology, and the popularization and commercialization of all of these.[19]

Figure 6.6 A rare sight: a friendly kiss between boys. © Moschino Junior 1999.

The bridge-builder was once again Sigmund Freud. Firstly, Freud's ideas form a part of the history that ingrained the thoughts on girls, boys, and heterosexuality that today's commercial culture so skillfully recycles. A second reason that Freud is so important is that his theory is by far the best-known and most widely used basis for theories on children. The impact of Freud's "new theory of sexuality" has even been compared to the degree of influence of Charles Darwin and Karl Marx,[20] while Freud's renown in twentieth-century Western culture has been likened to that of Albert Einstein.[21] Thirdly, today's child psychology still clearly draws from Freud's theories, even if his name is no longer really mentioned. Child developmental psychology is based on the idea that a child will undergo certain stages of development to end up at the heterosexual awakening that awaits at puberty.

According to Freud, we become heterosexual and normal—that is, dichotomously gendered—adults through what is known as the Oedipus complex. This is named after the myth of Oedipus Rex, according to which Oedipus ended up murdering his father and marrying his mother in trying to avoid the fulfillment of a prophecy.[22] Freud claims that the story is a cultural metaphor, in which "patricide" and "maternal incest" symbolize the parental love that is an essential part of a child's sexual development. The love displayed by a little boy for his primary care-giver, that is, his mother, represents the initial stage of a grown man's object of desire. For girls the setting is more complicated, as

Figure 6.7 Almost kissing. Advertisements depicting girls kissing are more common than similar ones of boys. *Vogue Bambini*, September–October 1993. © Vogue Bambini/ Condé Nast.

they must transfer their initial maternal love to their fathers.[23] Unlike boys, girls must relinquish their maternal love and turn it into a feeling of identification. They then compete with their mothers for their fathers' love. In the female Oedipus complex, the love for her father becomes the model that a girl is assumed to later transfer to other men.[24] Freud's complicated system is based on a love triangle involving the mother, father, and child.[25] Its frame of reference is heterosexuality, toward which he assumes every child's normal development leads.

Heterosexuality and the radical gap between genders are still an unquestioned norm in literature on child sexual development, even if Freud and the Oedipus complex are not directly named.[26] For example, the way that literature describes the understanding of gender by girls and boys is that a child will recognize at the age of three or four that he or she is a girl or boy, and that this understanding remains unchanged and ever-present from then on. Additionally, it is said that at around the same age, children develop a clear concept of gender roles, that is, what girls versus boys look like and how they act. Although Freud's ideas regarding penis envy can be seen as symptomatic of the gender system and repression of women typical of the time, people are still quite likely to state that girls will wonder whether they are missing something because they lack a penis.[27] In other words, the benchmark for childhood is still a boy, and girls are measured against it. The worst of it is that esteemed current experts still repeat the Freudian theory that sexuality awakens at puberty and is stronger in boys than in girls. In fact, from the point of view of gender theory, sexual desire is not a force of nature that will simply take over a subject. It is just that certain kinds of sexual gestures and evidences of desire are considered more acceptable and beneficial in boys, whereas in girls they are often branded alarming. Girls are supposed to be well-behaved and obedient, while boys are permitted significantly greater freedom of expression in the area of sexuality.[28] That is to say that expressions of sexual desire are primarily controlled by socially defined rules of behavior, not by the fact that boys experience essentially stronger desires than girls.

This is even more striking when considering transgender or gender-variant children. Although there is a growing body of literature on intersex and trans children,[29] there were no examples to be found in the research material, despite the fact that in recent years some transgender children have even become celebrities. One of them is Jazz Jennings, a transgender girl who first appeared in the media at age six and became the celebrity "transgender tween" at the age of fourteen. She has authored the memoir *I Am Jazz*, and has her own reality-television show (*All that Jazz*), a YouTube channel and the Web-based video campaign #SeeTheRealMe for a cosmetics brand, and was named one of *Time* Magazine's "25 Most Influential Teens" in 2014.[30] Even though Jennings is clearly a fashion icon—alongside grown-up transgender women and men such as Laverne Cox, Andreja Pejić, and Carmen Carrera—transgender and gender-variant child models are not present in children's fashion advertising.

Grown-Up Babies

Fashion advertising from the end of the last century and the beginning of this one indisputably demonstrates that gender-specificity in children and the related sexuality are not something that only affects children in adolescence. On the contrary, childhood is coded according to gender and sexuality from infancy. Advertisements do not always even need babies: it is enough of a hint to have color-coded clothes.

In the last decade, babies have become increasingly visible figures in children's fashion advertising. On the one hand, this can be seen as a logical development in the ambition of consumer culture to penetrate always new areas of life. On the other hand, it is an effort to commercialize infancy by placing babies in easy-to-distinguish, stereotypical gender pigeonholes by using clothes, body styling, and poses. Even newborns are shown in fashion advertising as already heterosexual little women and men. Babies are displayed in ever more imaginative settings doing

Figure 6.8 Siblings, friends, or a miniature couple? © Ferré 2003.

things that are completely unfamiliar to their age group, which indicates that a child's progression toward grown-up gender, sexuality, and consumerism really starts at birth. It is no exaggeration to say that if we are to believe the world of fashion advertising, our society is full of prematurely aged adults in the guise of infants. There, babies don't play or really even cry; instead they sit, look at the camera, and smile, and sometimes hold hands with another baby in a way that once again evokes meanings related to heteronormative relationships in the viewer's mind.

Most of those who have observed babies know that their genders are very difficult to tell apart based on their appearance, so advertisements emphasize gender using clothes. In advertising, two babies are often clearly coded as a girl and a boy through their attire. Feminine girls wear dresses and masculine boys wear trousers. Quite often the baby girl is shown just looking, whereas the boys always seem to have some kind of a task to perform—like fiddling with a shoe, as we can see in Figure 6.8, which is an advertisement by the Italian fashion brand Ferrè from 2003.

7

QUEER CHILDREN IN FASHION ADVERTISING

If a child is sexual from the start, one could ask whether some other kind of sexuality than heterosexuality could not be linked to childhood. After all, our society contains plenty of adults who define themselves as non-straight. Despite what the ideology of childhood innocence would have us believe, innocence as we know it is not asexual but heterosexual. As we have seen in the preceding chapters, innocence is a category that excludes non-white, non-middle-class, and non-heterosexual children.

In order for innocence to maintain its place and status as the primary definer of childhood, it needs as its opposites not only adulthood but also non-innocence, that is, sexuality. As we saw in Chapter 6, research literature and media debates usually define child sexuality as a problem that must be solved. Several books have been published in recent years on the conflicts of interest between consumer culture and childhood.[1] These works do take a stand on child sexuality, but their perspective is limited to the assumption that consumer culture and excessively revealing clothes subject girls, in particular, to "predatory pedophiles" and "steal" their innocence. None of the books in question starts with the assumption that sexuality may not be a problem. For the writers it is a problem and therefore they are unable to see anything but the innocent victim-child who is exploited in various ways.

The possibility of a child being homosexual is considered an even bigger problem than sexuality in general; it is nearly completely taboo. Even Freud defined homosexuality as a sign of a disorder in a child's normal development. These days people still don't want to discuss the possibility of children being homosexual, but would rather pretend that there is no problem as long as it is not talked about. Many non-heterosexual children grow up without meeting any children like themselves. Fortunately, recent popular culture representations have started to include more gays and lesbians. There is a growing body of LGBT-inclusive children's books, which can be seen at least as some sign of the beginnings of sexual equality.

Figure 7.1 From the series *Twins*, Helsinki, 2010. © Heidi Lunabba.

The Tombstone of Heterosexuality and Gender Nonconformity

The idea of the gender-variant or non-heterosexual child brings up the striving to trivialize and pathologize all non-normative forms of childhood. It shows us that the innocent child is like a protective shield for adults; if we can convince ourselves that a child is innocent, we don't have to trouble our minds with whether the child is heterosexual or not. And whereas innocent, gender-conforming — or *cisgender*[2] — heterosexual children just appear in the world, gender-variant and non-heterosexual children only come about through deliberate action. Giving birth to a transgender or homosexual child requires political will, conscious choices, and theoretical midwifery. Non-straightness and gender nonconformity are still viewed by our culture as something that never appear in childhood, but only afterward — not until the person comes out of the closet by telling others about his or her sexual orientation or nonconformity. The logic behind the coming-out theory is the idea that while helping the individual in question, it also helps the surrounding community to become more accepting of homosexuality and gender variance.[3] In other words, the supposition is that non-heterosexuality or gender variance are not just a private matter that remains behind closed doors and only concerns the person's nearest and dearest but a life-changing and possibly emancipatory identity for the whole community.[4]

By the time someone comes out and announces his or her non-heterosexuality, for example, he or she is usually so far from childhood that the "(parental) plans for one's straight destination" have been extinguished a long time ago, as the American gender theorist Kathryn Bond Stockton puts it when writing about queer childhoods.[5] She finds it ironic that whereas a heterosexual child is a gift of life, a non-heterosexual one is a "tombstone of heterosexuality." By this Bond Stockton means that the arrival of a gay child means the metaphorical death of the heterosexual child, because the coming-out process traditionally also involves the *a posteriori* construction of a homosexual childhood. By narrating a retrospective life-story, the person can find a logical — that is, natural — explanation for the feelings of being the odd one out and the outsider in childhood. The coming-out process incorporates the construction of a narrative that demonstrates that the person never had a heterosexual childhood at all. The same applies to gender-nonconforming children. Their arrival indicates the metaphorical death of the gender-conforming child and explains that the person in question never was a girl or a boy to begin with.

In other words, non-heterosexual and gender-variant children do exist, but mostly as retrospective and imaginary constructs. They can be considered as cultural constructs — very similar to fashion images. This is noteworthy: after all, we tend to assume that we live in a society where different expressions of gender and sexuality are real and permitted and non-heterosexuals and gender-variant women and men are guaranteed the same rights as straight gender-conforming people.[6] This openness is limited to adulthood, however, and does not apply to children. Children are under particular sexual control and protection. One of the forms of this protection is that grown-ups try to write off any characteristics that may indicate homosexuality or gender nonconformity appearing in childhood—femininity in a boy or masculinity in a girl—as passing stages.

Girls and boys who break the gender norms of femininity for females and masculinity for males are accepted as long as it looks like a temporary experimentation phase. However, a feisty tomboy is much more acceptable than a girlish boy.[7] The answer is found in gender hierarchy: whereas a girl's boyishness is seen as an attempt to rise through the hierarchy, a boy's girlishness is the opposite. Nevertheless, it is worth noting that a boyish girl will come up against opposition if she goes "too far" in her tomboyishness, for example, wanting to dress in boys' clothes. Not many descriptions of girlish boys exist in literature. One such work is *My Princess Boy*,[8] which is about a little boy who loves pink princess clothes. The book has been well received, but it has also sparked a debate where some have suggested that feminine boys are "perverted" and that children shouldn't be "burdened" by offering them understanding of different gender arrangements because the bipolar arrangement is the norm. While there are plenty of examples in literature of girls being boyishly sprightly and assertive in a perfectly acceptable way, boys won't go unpunished for being feminine. There isn't even an established term for the male counterpart of "tomboy," or conventional cultural representations.

The Polymorphously Perverse Child

Freud's theory of the "polymorphously perverse" child offers some tools for breaking down the heteronormativity hidden in the concept of innocence. When giving up his seduction theory in the early twentieth century, Freud discovered that "children are naturally polymorphously perverse."[9] By perverse he means that a baby has no specific object of desire and no particular erogenous zone on the body: an infant's whole body is erogenous. The concept of the polymorphously perverse child refers to the fact that a child is sexual from birth, and open to various possibilities. A baby's sexuality is not yet affected by upbringing or culture.

For Freud, one of the main proofs of total sexuality—or the queer origins of gender and sexuality—was a baby's "pleasure-sucking." By this he meant the "rhythmic repetition of sucking contact with the mouth (the lips), wherein the purpose of taking nourishment is excluded."[10] Pleasure-sucking originates in breastfeeding, which links it to the pleasure obtained from a vital bodily function.

However, according to Freud's observations, pleasure-sucking was usually followed by tugging on another body part, such as an earlobe or the genitals. It wasn't far from this to masturbation, that is, the purposeful search for sexual pleasure. Freud's contemporaries disapproved of masturbation, but for Freud the main discovery in this observation was that pleasure-sucking was not directed outward, but was a sign of autoeroticism. Freud defined pleasure-sucking as the foundation of all eroticism.

Even though Freud was concerned with sexuality, his idea of polymorphous perversity can also be applied to gender. The constructionist theory argues that gender is not a given but performative, in the sense that that the body becomes gendered "through a series of acts which are renewed, revised, and consolidated through time," as Judith Butler writes.[11] While Butler sees gender as the material effect of power and discourse, more recent accounts have shifted focus to analyzing how "matter itself comes to matter," as Karen Barad puts it.[12] This viewpoint focuses on the active agency of matter itself, outside of the representational frame. It argues that, for example, a child's bodily matter does not merely passively wait to be assigned a gender through practices such as christening. Instead, the child's material body is, like desire, polymorphously perverse; by "touching itself" it opens up an infinite set of possibilities for becoming a gendered adult.[13]

Even though we may be accustomed to thinking that the child's gendered body is just a concrete fact, both Butler and Barad agree that this is not the case. The gendered body is no less phantasmic than desire. This is clearly demonstrated by children's fashion advertising. The adverts are materialized fantasies about a child's gendered and sexualized embodiment. Like sexuality, embodied gender is also a *relation* between corporeality and the imagined body.[14] The phantasmic body and its sexuality exist separately from the material body that moves through the world.

Queering Childhood

Polymorphous perversity is very close to the concept of "queer" as it is used in contemporary research. Queerness has gained increasing visibility during the past decade or so, and not least in fashion studies. Historically, the term "queer" has been used in many ways: to signify strange, abnormal, or atypical, or as a colloquial and abusive word for homosexuality. In its theoretical form, as *queer theory*, it was first defined by Teresa de Lauretis in 1991, and queerness was established as a method that has been successfully used to criticize identity-based gay and lesbian studies and to challenge heterosexist assumptions about what passes for theory and knowledge.[15] De Lauretis's ideas were swiftly adopted in cultural studies, where it has become an analytical concept, a way of reading cultural texts and visual representations (such as fashion advertising) against heteronormative assumptions. Queer theory points out how heterosexism has shaped knowledge by marginalizing non-heterosexual experiences, and aims to offer alternative ways of understanding and seeing.[16] In this context, it means acknowledging the paradox that while a child can be seen as sexual, it cannot be seen as non-heterosexual, and that while a child is gendered, it cannot be gender-nonconforming. In other words, we imagine a child has a determined sexual orientation and gender at birth, while in reality both develop over time.

Contemporary critical gender research and queer theory are widely in favor of the idea that gender and sexuality are formed as a result of various cultural, technological, and medical practices. Fashion advertising and children's clothing indicate how society guides children toward normative gender and heterosexuality in innumerable ways, without ever mentioning other possibilities. Despite the fact that Freud considered a gender-conforming, heterosexual adult the only "proper" outcome of a child's development, he was very progressive in paving the way for studies that recognize gender variance and bringing his new understanding of childhood to light. Freud's theory has opened up opportunities for modern researchers to imagine new kinds of childhood narratives—ones that are not predetermined according to the ideology of heteronormativity.

Today's developmental psychology has adopted Freud's idea of the linear development curve, but still largely rejects the notion of a child's preordained sexuality and gender. Quite often it will define non-normative forms of sexual expression and gender as important and valuable, but ultimately as phases of "experimentation." Adolescence is connected with sexual awakening and the beginnings of sexual interaction—by default with the opposite sex.[17] Childhood is seen as a changing state, at least to some extent, but adulthood is characterized by the permanence of the identity that is achieved after the upheavals of childhood and adolescence. While gender is assumed as an objective fact that can be observed even before birth through advanced medical ultrasound technology, the grown-up's sexual identity is considered to be the outcome of the changes undergone during childhood and puberty.

Queer theory criticizes developmental psychology for these views, because a child is not just guided by defined development stages but also by a multitude of factors and life-changing events. The development stages might not define the ultimate end result in terms of the person's gender and sexuality. In other words, you aren't just born a heterosexual, gender-conforming girl or boy. It is more likely that one grows into a specific gender and heterosexuality through highly complex psychological processes and in the cross-fire of the culture's prevalent expectations. Furthermore, gender and sexuality are not separate but entangled, affecting and materializing each other.

As in constructionist studies overall, the starting point for this book is that things don't necessarily have to be as they are. They are possible to change. One launching pad for change comes from Freud's concept of the polymorphously perverse child, as long as it is used separately from Oedipal development curve theories. Polymorphous perversion refers to the potential that every human being has for different genders and sexualities from birth. From this point of view, being gay, lesbian, or transgender should not appear as any kind of mystery, let alone a problem requiring solving, but as just one option in a wide scope of sexualities and genders.

A perversion is not a deviation from nature, but from a socially construed norm.[18] The idea that a person develops through a set number of phases to reach gender-conforming heterosexual adulthood should be seen in the light of the heterosexual norm that defines what is "normal."[19]

The concept of the polymorphously perverse child is very useful when combined with the concept of the "queer child." It refers to the cultural figure of the child with whom there is "something wrong" from the normative perspective. Probably everyone has come across some child who will object to being quiet, run amok when it is time to sit down nicely, and fail to observe commands or behavior rules. This everyday occurrence could be thought to reflect something more theoretical; the queer child is a concept that criticizes the in-built heteronormativity of childhood innocence. It describes all of the children who do not or would not like to fit in with the norms of the innocent heterosexual gender-conforming child. It questions the prevailing understanding of innocence and draws attention to the fact that all of the children who are branded as sexual by our culture are also branded as in some way damaged or defective. This not only opens opportunities for many different forms of gender and sexuality for children; it also becomes a metaphor for a kind of gender and sexuality that adapts and changes throughout life. In other words, it suggests a lifelong polymorphous perversity and a contradiction of stifling norms.

Androgynous Cross-Dressers and Feminine Girl Couples

With heterosexuality being defined through innocence, how does children's fashion advertising imagine other forms of sexuality? To answer this question we must once again look into the past: at the women's liberation movement of the early twentieth century and the late nineteenth century's sexology debates, when it was still thought that there was some correspondence between sexual orientation and appearance. Material manifestations in clothing and makeup, for example, produced interpretations of sexuality; while proper middle-class feminine clothing was salient proof of a girl or woman's place as a procreator of the species, excessively visible makeup or variations in garments (too revealing a neckline or too high a hemline) were interpreted as signs of loose morals. Meanwhile, a man's feminine gestures were indications of homosexuality. Another aspect of the links between clothing, sexuality, and meaning is found in cases of conflict between garments and the anatomical body. Cross-dressing was considered strong evidence of non-heterosexuality.[20]

These views still live on. We look for hints on a person's gender and sexual orientation from his or her clothes and personal styling.[21] Women and men whose dress practices and gender concur with culture's expectations are automatically assumed to be heterosexual, whereas material signs such as a woman's shaved head or manly clothes are interpreted as stereotypically lesbian, and similarly a man in feminine clothes must be gay. Children are not excluded from this dichotomy, hence pink meaning girl and blue meaning boy, even though less than a century ago the opposite was true.[22] If a contemporary boy wears pink—not to mention a skirt or a dress—grown-ups will worry and start to ask whether there is "something wrong"—implying that the boy might be homosexual. Gender-nonconforming and non-heterosexual children have no established or accepted visual and material history of their own. It has to be constructed from the material and visual history of dress practices coming from adult homosexuals. Children's fashion advertising offers examples of this, especially in the form of depictions of androgynous girls.

As we can see in Figure 7.2, the Italian clothing brand I Pinco Pallino does not rely on traditional feminine/masculine representations in its advertising. In the brand's Christmas advertisement from 2007, we see a typical I Pinco Pallino child model: a red-haired young girl standing with her hands in her pockets, looking straight into the camera. She is cross-dressed in shades of brown, in an outfit consisting of a pinstriped suit and sequined vest worn over a collared shirt.

The girl's appearance with her red hair, brown pinstriped suit, white shirt, and sequined vest and her serious demeanor looking straight at the viewer turn her into an androgynous miniature grown-up. A contemporary viewer might associate the look the girl embodies with Tilda Swinton's androgynous character Orlando in the eponymous movie by Sally Potter (1992). The iconography of this girl figure dates back much further than the 1990s, however, to before the invention of the concept of innocence on the one hand, and to the late 1800s and early 1900s, on the other, with their sexological debates and the idea of the New Woman. She is a ghostly materialization of the premodern child, in that she is not an innocent child but a miniature adult, whose primary attribute is social status, which takes shape through her clothes and the cameo brooch pinned to her collar. At the same time she shares a lot of the visual/material coding of butch lesbians and the New Woman as they

Figure 7.2 A girl dandy does not draw from the conventional visual-sartorial codes of innocence. © Pinco Pallino 2002.

were represented around the beginning of the twentieth century.[23] Up until the 1920s, in Western societies, being a woman was largely associated with wearing skirts and dresses. Unlike boys, girls never ceased wearing a dress, and therefore remained more like infants throughout their lives. A skirt was thus also an important marker and material proof of a woman's social inferiority. The figure of a woman in masculine clothing made manifest the changes taking place in the social status of women.

The fashion advertisement taps into the paradoxical nature of the devastating First World War. While it killed more people than any war before it, it also radically and irrevocably changed the social status and employment patterns of women. It gave them opportunities to adopt masculine tailoring and comfortable clothes, releasing them from the corset of femininity. The atrocity of the war gave birth to the independent young modern woman—the *flapper*, or *garçonne* in French—who was able to move about, ride a bicycle, or even play golf. Her style carries with it the metaphorical death of the prewar gender system and became the emblem of modernity, novelty, change, youth, glamor, and sexual subjectivity. She abandoned the Edwardian model of fashion—the frilly petticoats, S-shaped corsets, and large hats—in favor of loose-fitting tunics and trousers.[24] The flapper's societal freedom and the new gender order changed her into an androgynous, flat and geometrical, boyish figure. Upper-class and bourgeois women in particular adopted the look of the nineteenth-century male dandy and used it to symbolize their independent status, in which they had no need for men.

This was a radical change at a time when most bourgeois women still wore movement-restricting hoop dresses and corsets. Women were prisoners of their clothes, which was seen as a reflection of their socially subordinate position. Gradually, loose clothing and low heels that permitted free movement became a symbol for the women's liberation movement, and this material history is still reflected in women's business suits.

The I Pinco Pallino advertisement also makes references to late-nineteenth-century sexological discourse, in which it was thought that homosexuality could be discerned from a person's clothes. Besides Sigmund Freud, these ideas were popularized in the beginning of the century by Richard von Krafft-Ebing and Havelock Ellis. They thought that a man who embodied femininity and desired other men was actually a woman trapped in a man's body, and vice versa.[25] Sexologists considered masculine dress in women as a definite sign of lesbianism. Simultaneously, the I Pinco Pallino advertisement can also be linked to the concept of the "third sex," which has historically defined sex and gender variations beyond the dimorphic model common in the Western world before the Enlightenment, and still common in non-Western cultures.[26] Combining the cultural, medical, and sexological histories with fashion history, the I Pinco Pallino advertisement produces several interpretations. What we see can be understood as a self-assertive modern girl, a lesbian, or perhaps even a budding trans boy.

The material details in the I Pinco Pallino advertisement link the dandy girl to the history of the modern sexual child, which has been differentiated from the grand narrative of the innocent childhood. This view was actually supported by Freud, who thought masculinity was natural in a girl.[27] Freud based his perhaps surprising view on the idea of a single original androgynous gender, already defined in the Greek myth of Androgyne. Freud believed that girls and boys gradually derived from this original state of being. He saw a girl's development toward feminine womanhood as a process of shedding her original masculinity and adopting a new feminine and receptive role. If this didn't happen and the girl didn't accept that she was different from boys, the result was a "masculinity complex" and a masculine lesbian who was left at a childish level. This violent fantasy still lives on: although tomboyishness may be encouraged, girls are expected to become interested in boys in adolescence at the latest. On the other hand, feminine girls are automatically considered heterosexual, even though they might well be feminine lesbians, that is, femmes.[28]

The representations of androgynous girls in children's fashion advertising are also linked to trends in women's fashion, particularly the so-called lesbian chic, in which the conventional visual codes of masculine lesbianism are softened and androgynized into seasonally repeated styles.[29] The girlish androgyny in the I Pinco Pallino ad is wholly commercialized. It has turned nineteenth-century dandyism into part of a girl's wardrobe selection through the use of sellable consumables. At the same time the dandy girl is a continuation of the girl culture and "girl power" debates of the late twentieth and early twenty-first centuries, which have included a lot of discussion regarding what makes a "strong girl," how she behaves, and what she looks like.[30] A dandy girl differs significantly from her more girly sister: whereas a feminine girl will wear a (pink) dress and pose nicely for the camera, a masculine one wears loose, comfortable clothes that permit physical movement and are in low-key colors, and responds to the viewer's gaze self-assuredly.

The world of fashion advertising also features a lot of girl couples. Whereas male couples and groups suggest asexual social fellowship, with girls the idea of an erotic charge is permitted—as long as the girls are feminine. Fashion photographs have plenty of pairs of girls, staged intimately close together. A Fisichino swimming costume advertisement (Figure 7.3) provides a typical example. The girls in the advert are like mirror images: they wear the same swimsuit and both have long blonde hair. They are looking in each other's eyes with their arms around each other's shoulders, smiling.

The advertisement can be read as a stereotypical representation of either friendship or desire between girls. It toys with the assumption of the subjects' innocence, while also eroticizing them by directing the viewer's gaze toward the hourglass waists suggested by the swimming costumes. Meanwhile, the belts at the girls' hips direct the eyes toward their crotches. The belts delimit the groin area and make it the center of focus. The triangular areas demarcated by the belts are unlikely to refer to the sexual maturity of these little women, but rather emphasize their inexperience.

The interpretation of the swimsuit advertisement accentuates the girls' innocence and the eroticization of it, but there is also a third possible reading. In it, the girls exist only for each other, which is evinced in their likeness to one another. Their similar appearance draws from the technique of "twinning," common in fashion photography.[31] In lesbian history, twinning is linked especially to the tradition of romantic friendship, meaning the love between "two equals"—that is, two people of the same sex.[32] The way twinning works in advertising is that representations of same-sex pairs are purposely open to simultaneous interpretations of friendship and unconventional sexuality.[33] Therefore the girlhood depicted in the ad does not restrict the reading of the image to sisterhood or friendship, but leaves it open to the thought of the two being lovers.

Figure 7.3 Twins, friends, or lovers? Twinning is a recurring theme in adult fashion advertising, suggesting same-sex desire. © Fisichino 2007.

Not for Sissies! Hegemonic Masculinity

There is no official term for the opposite of "tomboy." Masculine girls are accepted, even admired, but the figure of a feminine boy is a cultural taboo.[34] My research material did not contain a single girlish boy. Whereas tomboyishness has positive connotations, such as confidence and independence, femininity in boys is shunned and considered pathological.

This is rooted far back in history, among other places in the model of humanity presented by Freud, where it is the duty of a girl to envy her superior in the sexual hierarchy (i.e., the boy).[35] Conversely, a boy who identifies with feminine girls is somehow seen as relinquishing his power, and is therefore dismissed as weak.

Modern studies of masculinity generally consider Freud the first theorist of masculinity.[36] He questioned the supposed naturalness of masculinity and did not take heterosexuality that is usually linked to it as a given.[37] Later psychiatric theories have rejected Freud. A normal boy's development includes masculinity as if by nature. This was particularly influenced by the increasing conservatism of psychiatric discourse between the 1930s and 1960s. At that time, mental health was connected to a carefully outlined conception of gender, heterosexuality, and marriage. Later conservative psychiatry defined heterosexuality as the unproblematic and natural climax for a boy's development. Any other rendition of gender and sexuality was pathologized and defined as the result of a dysfunctional adult/child relationship. Psychoanalytical treatment gradually became a tool for normalization, used to try to mold patients into a carefully delimited heteronormative gender arrangement.[38]

Several critical masculinity studies have drawn attention to the ideological nature of conservative psychiatry, where masculinity and heterosexuality are factors that are desirable for a boy to possess. In today's critical gender theory, masculinity is usually understood to be a cultural construct, and the prevailing concept of masculinity is known as hegemonic masculinity.

Hegemonic masculinity is based on the superiority of boys and men over girls and women.[39] The ideal boy is aggressive, assertive, self-confident, and, most essentially, heterosexual. The most prominent element of hegemonic masculinity is power, which can be political, economic, social, or physical. With this power, a man can control either the society or his own surroundings.[40]

Boys and men are tempted, sometimes forced, to take on the ideals of hegemonic masculinity. A man must *prove* his manhood; in other words, masculinity is an ideal that is pursued in different ways.[41] Cultural masculinity is first and foremost a representation, materialized in a warrior-like, manly appearance. It dictates what a man should be like: how he should behave and feel. In critical gender studies, hegemonic masculinity refers to the generally accepted and in many ways bolstered view of the masculine gender and sexuality, which does not care whether real boys or men actually meet the ideal or not.[42]

Additionally, hegemonic masculinity is only open to heterosexual men; others are branded as deviant, sick, or feminine, that is, non-masculine.[43] This strict model of manhood also probably explains the lack of girlish boys in advertising for boys' fashion, as the imagery usually shows boys as energetic children who are clearly coded as boys by their gender-conforming clothes.

Homosocial Little Boys

Advertising with boys often features groups of boys. This is because boyhood is not constructed just in contrast to girls and femininity but also in relation to other boys. The journey toward masculine adulthood demands friendship, camaraderie, and fellowship between boys. Close friendships and social ties between boys are described in critical masculinity studies with the term "homosocial." It refers to relations between boys or men in which masculinity, heterosexuality, and a mutual hierarchy are built and reinforced through competition and the kind of jostling seen in the Tru Trussardi Junior ad in Figure 6.3. The concept also refers to groups of friends, masculine exercise of power, and heterosexuality, which are seen as the foundations for the social order controlled by men and for the subjugation of women.[44]

For many researchers of masculinity, homosociality denotes both misogyny and homophobia, whereas others use it as a positive descriptor. The Finnish youth researcher Tommi Hoikkala, for example, describes homosociality as a kind of fellowship, referring to his observation that boys like to do things in groups surrounding a certain interest, such as football.[45] Although Hoikkala attempts to emphasize the fact that relationships between boys are not just based on negative things, such as fighting and violence, his asexual redefinition paradoxically ends up reinforcing the fear of homosexuality often latent in masculinity and represented through hypermasculine representations such as the men of Tom of Finland. In other words, sexuality is at the heart of masculinity and therefore also in relationships between boys or men.

The most interesting interpretation of homosociality so far has been given by the American literary critic Eve Kosofsky Sedgwick.[46] In her view, the patriarchal social order was not always built around repression of women, compulsory heterosexuality, or homophobia. To support her argument, Sedgwick refers particularly to the Ancient Greek society, which, while patriarchal, did not condone homosexuality but viewed it as an essential part of the culture. It was permitted between men belonging to the higher social classes and adolescent boys. These relationships were described using concepts that today are applied to heterosexual love. The essential aspect of these erotic relations was mentoring: the young boys were apprentices to whom the older men taught citizenship skills, among others. Sedgwick concludes that although heterosexuality is an important aspect of patriarchal society, homophobia is not.[47]

Another crucial determinant factor of homosociality is competition between men. It is seen in literature and films, for example, as love triangles in which two men compete for the same woman's favor. Homosociality is a tie that binds the two suitors to the object of their affection, but also to each other.[48] The choice of object, in fact, is affected less by who she is than by the identity of the sparring partner. In this way, the relationship between the competing suitors can be stronger than that between the suitor and the object of desire.[49]

The boundary between homosociality and homosexuality is fluid, and the concepts are closely interwoven. Homosociality is also a concept of sexual politics, defining the ways in which sexuality and sociality are related. Analyzing advertising for boys' fashion from this perspective, one can find many examples that simultaneously represent friendship between the boys and contain the possibility of homosexuality.

The possibility for the Sedgwickian perspective on a homosocial relationship appears, for example, in a full-spread advertisement for Moschino Bambino e Junior, as demonstrated in Figure 7.4. It features three children: two boys and a girl. The boys stand side by side and appear to be looking at the girl, who sits further away and is turned toward the viewer. The boys seem to be seeking the girl with their eyes, but she is out of their reach. The photograph links the boys to each other through their intimate posture and their similar yet inversely color-coded clothes: one's outfit consists of a white shirt and blue trousers, and the other's is the opposite. There is also a very subtle hierarchy between the boys: the dark-haired boy is somewhat more masculine, standing with his hands in his pockets and slightly in front of the more feminine blond boy.

Gentlemanly Looks

Homosociality is also a determining factor in Figure 7.5, a 2001 advertisement for the Spanish brand Peter John, which makes suits for young boys. It features two male children. The boys conform to traditional gender roles, with their short hair and their traditional mark of modern masculinity: a man's suit. The history of men's suits is of particular interest. It is rooted in the army and in uniforms. Initially, uniforms represented military and political power within an army, but gradually they were turned also into civilian wear—especially during and after the French Revolution, when they started by representing the rebelliousness of ordinary people and slowly turned into various new kinds of outfits. Similar developments took place in the United Kingdom, where the models for military uniforms turned into men's suits. Military symbols transformed piecemeal into symbols of authority and social status.[50]

The staging of this image taps into the military and masculine history of suits, which is accentuated by a small drawing above the brand name, featuring London's hallmarks: Big Ben and a Royal Guard. At first sight, the image seems to represent asexual friendship. An alternative reading is possible, however; whereas the friendship style of homosociality highlights competition and banter, the boys in the Peter John advert are looking each other in the eye, smiling sweetly. The military authority linked to men's suits and the competitiveness and jostling related to social friendship are completely absent. Instead, the image has the kind of warmth one is used to seeing in representations of girls' friendship. The masculine dress code, the styling, and the intimacy of the boys' gaze and pose bring some sexual tension into the photograph, which does not sit easily with the idea of asexual fellowship.

Even though everyday speech stereotypically links femininity to homosexuality and defines masculinity as heterosexual, every subject's original state of being is polymorphous perversity.[51] The individual identity depends on

Figure 7.4 Two boys and a girl. An erotic love triangle? © Moschino Bambino e Junior 2001.

how strongly masculinity and femininity eventually become manifest. The Peter John advertisement makes use of both masculine and feminine signs and ties the boys together through their gaze and similar dress, which opens up possibilities to interpret the advertisement with a suggestion of romantic love.

Secret Friendship

In a third example (Figure 7.6), we see an expression of friendship between boys. This advertisement moves clearly toward the gay end of the homosociality continuum. It is an advertisement for I Pinco Pallino from 2001 and it comprises two images in the fashion of Polaroid snapshots. The ad makes use of a photo album-like layout: the images are arranged vertically on a white background, with the brand name at the bottom. It features two children who could be assumed to be boys based on their light-colored shirts and shorts, and the styling of their hair. In the upper image, the boys are photographed from behind, with their arms around each other in a natural setting. In the lower image, the same boys are pictured from the side, with one standing behind the other, leaning his head against the other boy's neck and holding his hand. Both images are imbued with intimacy.

Figure 7.5 Two boys in suits exchange gentlemanly looks. Friends or lovers? © Peter John 2001.

The cropping, angles, and immediacy of the pictures give the whole image narrative a feeling of secrecy. Although the loose clothing, the boys' unawareness of the camera, and the nature in the background mean that the image draws from the visual repertoire of childhood innocence, the boys are placed in poses that contain suggestions of romantic relationships between adults. This pair of boys is pictured with an air of voyeurism, which accentuates the interpretation of it containing something that should not be said out loud.

Fair Sailors

The final example comes from a sailor-themed campaign by the jeans manufacturer Diesel and dates from 2007 (Figure 7.7). It adds further new perspectives on homosociality. The advertisement depicts four children from a bird's-eye view playing cards on the deck of a sailing ship on a sunny day. One of the children (a girl) is asleep; another (a boy) is squinting up at the camera.

Figure 7.6 Boys in an intimate embrace—love or friendship? © I Pinco Pallino 2001. Photograph by Mauro Balletti.

A third (boy) lies relaxed with his head resting on his hands and his eyes closed, while the fourth (girl) is fiddling with her cards. With its gender symmetry, the ad initially appears to allude to heterosexuality, in the form of future couples practicing typical social interaction patterns on the sunny sea. Despite this, the symmetry is broken in several ways. Firstly, the children are dressed in unisex style, in pale-colored sailor-type outfits. Anti-normatively, the clothing does not clearly indicate either sex.

The sailor outfit is one of the most classic and global icons in children's wear. It has been used as work clothing, uniforms, fashionable attire, and fancy dress costumes. The outfit took its recognizable form, with the white or blue loose-fitting shirt, neckerchief, wide-leg trousers, and white hat, during the nineteenth century. Apparently, the wide trouser legs were necessary for sailors to roll them up for deck work. The neckerchief could be used as a sweatband.[52]

No one knows exactly why the outfit became fashionable, but there were probably at least a few factors at play. The outfit was officially adopted as the uniform of the US Navy in 1813, and the British Navy in 1857. At around that

Figure 7.7 Fair sailors. This advertisement by Diesel plays with the multiple meanings of the sailor outfit. © Diesel 2007.

time, in 1846, Queen Victoria had a sailor outfit made for her son, the future King Edward VII. When an image of the boy in his suit was published, the outfit quickly became a popular form of dress for boys and girls, and the colors blue and white began to symbolize the sea, the beach, leisure, and freedom. By the end of the nineteenth century, it had become the most common outfit for well-dressed children, and it remained so until the 1940s. From then on it became popular as a fancy dress costume, and as such it was taken over by popular culture: sailors became an icon in musicals, variety shows, Hollywood movies, animated images, and drag shows. Gay culture in particular influenced the fetishization and sexualization of the sailor outfit. In the late 1990s, the French fashion designer Jean-Paul Gaultier's brand adopted sailor stripes as part of its core image.[53]

The Diesel advertisement references the history of the sailor outfit becoming a part of the middle-class child's wardrobe. At the same time it has connotations of the outfit's more ambivalent history, which is stylized especially in the boy who is lying down with his hands behind his head on the right-hand edge of the image. He is positioned as the center of attention. The figure is familiar from classic gay fantasies, for example, Thomas Mann's novella *Death in Venice* and the movie of the same name, directed by Luchino Visconti.[54] In the story, the main character, Gustav von Aschenbach, is passionately in love with the fourteen-year-old Tadzio, a gorgeous, precocious boy in a sailor suit. The boy's exoticized southern Italian figure also creates associations with the boys in Wilhelm von Gloeden's photographs and the French sailors in Jean Genet's novel *Querelle of Brest* (1947), which Rainer Werner Fassbinder turned into a movie that feasted on gay clichés (1982). Additionally the photographed boy reflects a touch of the sailor aesthetic familiar from Jean-Paul Gaultier's ads and the visual style of the French artist couple Pierre et Gilles (although without their trademark lavish glitter and glitz).

While the image has something very innocent and heteronormative about it, the boy's figure opens up a new level of interpretation that chafes against these norms. The boy illustrates the idea of the queer child, which is associated with homosexuality. The boy on the right-hand side is the most clearly eroticized of the children. He is lying down unaware of the camera, as an object surrendering to the viewer's gaze. The boy's gendered signs also take the viewer's thoughts back to the androgyny that was popularized in advertising in the 1990s as a way of breaking some of the strict confines of hegemonic masculinity, and making way for homoerotic views and desires.[55]

Fabulous Gays in Fashion Advertising

It is evident that advertisements reveal a world that is still sharply divided into two gender categories. At the same time, it is this normativity that offers the opportunity for questioning classifications and testing boundaries. These are things that advertisements typically do, as some of the aforementioned examples prove.

The queer connotations of advertisements are not just figments of a researcher's imagination, but correlate closely with the increasing cultural and social prominence of homosexuality in the 1980s and 1990s. It became visible especially in consumption and advertising, where representing sexuality was no longer tied to making an individual sexualized body evident in the sense of coming out of the closet. Instead, marketers and advertisers helped to turn gayness into a desirable lifestyle.[56]

It has become increasingly common since the late 1980s to speak of non-heterosexual consumers. Some researchers call this the "pink economy,"[57] and especially in the United States and the UK it has led to a new consumer category,[58] the "gay market."[59] In the 1990s, despite—or perhaps because of—the global recession, more and more companies started trying to attract homosexual consumers to their products. At the same time there was a rise of prime-time TV shows and films featuring gay and lesbian main characters.[60] Talking of sexuality, and particularly representing it visually, became commonplace and definitively shifted from the margins to the center of popular culture. While gays and lesbians had previously faced the problems of invisibility, living a double life, conforming to heterosexual clothing norms,[61] and possibly having to come out, during the 1990s gays and lesbians turned into a public and fetishistic spectacle intended for all and sundry to enjoy.[62]

For advertising, the crucial question is how to address both heterosexual and non-heterosexual consumers at the same time. In the early 1990s, studies were made, for example, on how to hide various codes in advertisements that attract diverse consumer groups.[63] One such example is seen in Figure 7.8, a Ralph Lauren fashion editorial from 1996 featuring a boy dandy. The title of the editorial is simply "Dandy." The cultural history of the dandy is particularly interesting. On the one hand, the dandy is defined as a "clothes-wearing man": a man who is particularly interested in his physical appearance, in refined speech, and in leisurely hobbies, and who takes the refinement of his appearance to the extreme. In fashion history, the dandy has become a symbol for a distinct clothing style and a pattern of behavior, summarizing the masculine idea of the modern fashionable individual: the modern stylish man. The dandy marks a shift toward modern society where the structure of the ruling elite loosened and the middle classes gained more space, also in terms of defining fashion.[64]

But this is not all the dandy stands for. His particular style was distinguished from the suit-and-tie style of the gentleman we saw in the Peter John advertisement in Figure 7.5. The gentleman and the dandy may seem almost synonymous but this is not the case. The gentleman was associated with a good family and seen as a cultured, courteous, and well-educated man with qualities of refinement. Sophisticated dress was part of the gentleman's appearance, but it was not all he was. The dandy, on the other hand, was regarded as a man with a particular interest in fashionable dress; unlike the gentleman, the dandy did not necessarily come from a good or upper-class family. The dandy's appearance differed from that of the gentleman: while they both dressed well, the dandy was a more flamboyant dresser. The dandy is thus the prototype of a male consumer of fashion. He is an entrepreneur of style who is enmeshed in the life of idle worldliness and luxurious consumption. The dandy is devoted to the management of impressions and attention, as Thomas Carlyle writes in *Sartor Resartus*.[65]

But the dandy as a figure also questions the rigid boundaries of sexuality through the details in his clothing. Roland Barthes turned his analytical eye on those revealing details in his theory of the dandy.[66] Unlike many fashion scholars, Barthes not only understands the dandy as a historical figure and a symbol of modern identity; for him, the dandy symbolizes a special kind of dressing technique. In other words, for Barthes, the dandy is first and foremost a theoretical and analytical tool. His essay "Dandyism and Fashion" is often read as a critique of mass-produced fashion, due to his statement "fashion killed dandyism." However, less attention has been paid to his ideas about detail. Why does Barthes stress the near-invisible details, the *je-ne-sais-quoi* quality of appearance? Because that little next-to-nothing is the crucial signifier of the dandy's difference. And this is not different from unfashionableness but from heterosexuality. For Barthes, the details form a discreet sign that only communicates to the person's peers: other homosexuals.

Figure 7.8 A boy dandy. An interest in flashy fashions is often interpreted as a sign of homosexuality. © Polo Ralph Lauren 1996. Photograph by Nick Ferrand.

Of course, the dandyish boy in the Ralph Lauren ad is far from discreet. On the contrary, he is extremely flamboyant, sporting thick, blow-dried blonde hair, and in the second image of the editorial, an orange silk blouse, a fox stole, big golden rings, red socks and shoes, and a black velvet suit. These material details hark back to the mid-eighteenth century and the flamboyantly dressed macaronis, whom fashion historian Peter McNeil has described as the first homosexual subculture.[67]

This kind of strategy is known as the double marketing strategy, meaning that some of the signals built into advertisements speak to straight consumers, while others speak to gays. The assumption is that at least some consumers are aware of how homosexuality has been represented through history. For a long time, however, advertisers did not admit that they were designing advertisements also for gay consumers, because they feared it would scare away their clients. Instead of politics, advertisers claimed to be doing "just business."[68] This is not the case today: certain non-heterosexual groups—in particular well-educated, urban gay men without children—have more money to spend than the average family. As the stigma of homosexuality has worn off, advertisements for products such as fashion, travel, and alcohol especially have started including openly gay and lesbian depictions.[69] Homosexuals have become good consumers, which has raised their social status in a money-loving world that believes in consumerism.

8
SEXUALIZATION IS THE NAME OF THE GAME

I will end the book by looking at children's advertising from one further viewpoint: that of child models and how they have become a part of the fashion world and its imagining machine. Even though children have always had a spot in fashion advertising, like the previous chapters so eminently prove, they have usually remained as anonymous children, and the concerned debate has focused on the images and clothes and their assumed effects on children. But since the first decade of the new millennium, the child model has become a phenomenon, and the focus and the debate have somewhat shifted from images to the models. There is even a new strand of guidebooks. They give adults advice on how to transform their offspring into super models and paint (a rather rosy) image of the occupation while they also market modeling as a desired way of life for children. The rise of the child model is also very visible in *Vogue Bambini*. In the 2000s, the magazine frequently published thick catwalk issues in which the child models were photographed on a runway, modeling the latest children's fashions. This has transformed child modeling into a desirable occupation and an interpretative frame through which eligible childhood is understood and negotiated in contemporary culture. In this process celebrity child models play an especially central role. They mediate fashion for their peers but they also articulate the fashionable lifestyle. This is at least partly due to the fact that the models are also child celebrities. They may be child stars from films or television series, or the children of adult celebrities.

This has also brought about a new discourse on the loaded relationship between children, fashion, and visuality. On the one hand, celebrity child models are admired and seen as ideal children who represent an ideal life. On the other hand, the child model phenomenon has also intensified the debate on children's sexualization. This proves that children have become an integral part of the global image-making machine. Their presence as admired idols or as pitiable

Figure 8.1 From the series *Twins*, Helsinki, 2010. © Heidi Lunabba.

victims in fashion advertising has a purpose: to create publicity and to increase sales and the value of the brand, for example.

The concerned debates center especially on little girls even though there are some celebrity boys, such as Romeo Beckham, who also work as models. However, while boy models are admired and treated as active agents whom modeling cannot harm, girls are not granted similar agency. They are often seen as victims. The girl models create concerned debate and have also created real-life actions, as will become evident in this chapter. This kind of gender dichotomy regarding modeling and the worry about children's sexualization is telling. While the girl may be seen as the ideal fashion consumer and in some cases an admirable fashion icon, she is also seen as the weak and easily abused victim and their parents as thoughtless dupes. Boy models, on the other hand, seem to be able to maintain their agency even if they enter the world of fashion modeling. This dichotomy constructs the ideal child as a boy.

Child models thus occupy an interesting place in the affect-driven consumer culture. They are cultural barometers of sentiments and attitudes toward girls, boys, images, fashion, and consumerism. Their work also opens doors to further discussion about the extent to which child modeling relates to the demand for constant "self-editing" and "self-branding," and to what measure celebrity models encourage ordinary children to internalize ideas about the self as a "marketable product" and to see themselves as "entrepreneurs of self."[1]

Child Modeling — A Rising Trend

Although very little research has been conducted on child models, the subject is clearly popular in the mass media. In 2011, for example, several newspaper articles were published on the topic of celebrity child models who set trends and fashions. A report in the largest Swedish daily newspaper *Dagens Nyheter* pondered why well-known fashion houses use "super-young celebrities" as their faces.[2] According to the report, "girls are the new fashion icon."

The article reported that the then eleven-year-old Kiernan Shipka, who became widely known from the American television show *Mad Men* (produced by Matt Weiner), has worked as a model for major fashion houses since then. Another fashion celebrity featured in the article is one of the world's best-known fashion bloggers, the then fifteen-year-old Tavi Gevinson. Gevinson is by no means the only one to blog about children's fashion. On the contrary, recent years have seen an upsurge of adult bloggers who style their children and represent them as fashion models in their blogs.

The fashion reporter proposes that the key to understanding the popularity of child models is the unspoiled nature—that is, innocence—of childhood.

She argues that fashion brands are increasingly conscious of the fact that the negative publicity received by grown-up stars (such as, say, Kate Moss with her cocaine abuse) may be detrimental to the brand's image.[3] Here freshness and innocence are not external properties but refer to something completely different: the child's as yet unlived life, which gives the brand the power to adapt the child as much as it likes.

The newspaper article reported on a real rising trend. In the autumn of 2010, for example, the fashion house Miu Miu made a campaign featuring the child actress Hailee Steinfeld, who played a quick-witted tomboy in the Coen brothers' film *True Grit* (2010).

Marc by Marc Jacobs, on the other hand, used Elle Fanning, who had completed an impressive role as the daughter of a washed-up Hollywood star in Sofia Coppola's *Somewhere* (2010). Her sister, Dakota Fanning, is also a face of Marc Jacobs. The link between fashion and film has grown ever stronger.[4] Any clothes worn by a Hollywood star will increase the renown and desirability of a brand. Based on the newspaper articles written on child stars as fashion icons, one may conclude that the same phenomenon has arisen in the world of children.

In both the Miu Miu advertisements featuring Hailee Steinfeld and the Marc by Marc Jacobs campaigns featuring Elle Fanning, grown women's clothes were modeled by adolescent girls. While both fashion houses clearly draw from the premodern history of childhood, highlighting the miniature adult within the child, their editorials also construct and circulate the age-old understanding that the difference between grown women and little girls is but a question of nuance. A grown woman is more or less a little girl in adult clothing.

Both of these editorials also elicited some degree of debate. The fourteen-year-old Hailee Steinfeld, who was the face of Miu Miu, was immortalized by the well-known fashion photographer Bruce Weber. In the photographs, the young actress is styled in the fashion of a 1940s Hollywood movie star and is placed in diverse settings to show off dresses, bags, and shoes. In one image, she is lying down on the grass holding a shoe, as if she had fallen over. In another, she poses like a grown woman in a mink stole, and in a third she is standing by a railway track and leaning on a concrete post that bears a sign saying "Private property. No trespassing." One of the campaign's images in particular led to discussions on the limits of propriety: in it, Steinfeld was sitting on the railway track. This time the discussions were not related to sexuality; instead, the ad was found to be irresponsible for "showing a child in a hazardous or dangerous situation."[5] The advertisement was withdrawn from public view because the staging was thought to encourage young girls to commit suicide.[6] The ad campaign for Marc by Marc Jacobs was photographed by another well-known fashion photographer, Jürgen Teller. It features the then thirteen-year-old Elle Fanning, who is styled to look very innocent and childish while modeling women's fall clothes that are too big for her. Although the fashion images were seen as "sophisticated" compared to her sister Dakota Fanning's debut with the same designer in 2006, some also wondered whether it was appropriate for the fashion world and fashion consumers to "love" a thirteen-year-old girl.

In contrast, an advertising campaign for Burberry in 2013, featuring Romeo Beckham, son of the former Spice Girls singer Victoria Beckham and the footballer David Beckham, was met with enthusiasm. In the brand's fashion advertisements and videos shot by Mario Testino, the then ten-year-old Beckham modeled Burberry clothing and accessories, goofing around with a big smile on his face, while adult models posed mannequin-like: still, stiff, and expressionless. Like the boys in the Tru Trussardi Junior advertisement in Figure 6.3, Beckham is represented childishly playing rather than really modeling for a fashion brand. The campaign was discussed positively in the media—it was stated, for example, that Beckham's appearance was "irresistible" and that he made a "spirited ad debut."[7] Beckham has continued to model for the brand ever since, and now he is reported to "boost" the sales of Burberry in Europe, the USA, and the Middle East[8] and earn "£45,000 for one day's work."[9]

These examples demonstrate how quickly fashion advertising featuring children have become an essential part of popular media. They engender a lot of attention, as well as strong emotions, both positive and negative, and often highly generalizing interpretations of the content of the images. The paradox seems to lie in the fact that although researchers and the market have defined children as competent players who actively generate meanings in their social environment and make their own purchase decisions, children are also seen as being particularly vulnerable. So at the same time as young children's autonomy is emphasized, the images that become public are considered problematic. The concerns related to the images overshadow discussions on the work that children must complete before the advertising can be disseminated in various media. Is that because modeling is not seen as real work? Or because the images are easier to tackle than work and working conditions?

Living Dolls

Today's living models were preceded by mannequin dolls. The *haute couture* dressmakers in Paris sent mannequins to society ladies around Europe, who would have their clothes made based on the dolls' outfits. Sounds and movements were added to the dolls thanks to technological advances in the nineteenth century, but soon they were also joined by living models who showed the clothes with robotic gestures and movements, mimicking the dolls—which is echoed in the Laura Biagiotti DOLLS advertisement in Figure 6.2. As the century wore on, the dolls were gradually relegated to children's games and the real models took their place in displaying clothes. The robotic, doll-like, expressionless, and often soulless performance of today's models is, in other words, linked to the shared history of flesh-and-blood and artificial mannequins.[10] A living model is still expected to imitate a doll, in a way: the origin of models is not in real or genuine human figures but in dummies that were made specifically for the purpose of showing clothes.

The idea can be discerned in the very concept of "model." The word can refer to an object, image, pattern, or design, based on which something is produced, reproduced, or imitated. It can also be "an exemplary person" or "a person employed to pose for an artist, sculptor, photographer, etc."[11] As a verb, "to model" means to "fashion or shape a thing" in imitation of something else, and as a noun it can refer further to a representation, archetype, image, imitation, miniature, sample, or likeness.[12] As we can see, "model" is by definition a word that refers to the act of giving abstract beauty ideals a material shape. A model is the incarnation of ideals, a kind of "exemplar" that ordinary people should aspire toward. A model is a person whose body fulfills the prevailing beauty ideals, while modeling is the work of someone who allows a company to use their face and figure in exchange for remuneration. A model does not just market commodities or embody gender-specific beauty ideals; he or she also acts as an example to consumers.[13]

The work of a model cannot really be likened to the operation of a mannequin doll, but they do share the task of giving a palpable shape to non-concrete ideals. A model is not an ideal person but a person who is turned into an ideal. It is because of their pliability that models can be people as different from each other as the curvy Marilyn Monroe and the childish, almost incorporeal Kate Moss. Both have fulfilled the ideals required of models at a specific time. These days, models are expected to have increasingly childlike features, while also being younger in age. This seems to be another important reason for the current popularity of child models.

Some of the main tools involved in the work of contemporary child models are photography and other lens-based imaging technologies. As these technologies have become more advanced, the number of child models has increased exponentially. Models first appeared on the fashion stage in the late nineteenth century, as commercial photography was starting its triumphal march. Fashion shows became spectacles of modern consumerism, in which the appearance of young women, especially, was commodified.[14] The popularity of models rose in the wake of mass production, and after the Second World War their numbers grew further thanks to radical transformations in consumption habits and the increasing penetration of advertising. As the end of the millennium approached, various visual technologies, from TV to the Internet, helped to engender supermodels, thousands of modeling agencies, the culture of the continuous search for new faces, and the visual culture of recycling models' images.

Modeling is a typical example of work in which posing is connected to photographic technology and, through that, to generating reactions and attracting and channeling attention. The better a connection the images can create with their viewers, the higher their monetary value. In the attention economy, it is essential to try to maximize the time viewers spend looking at images.[15] This means that modeling agencies, photographers, and brands spend time working out what kinds of images attract the most attention and increase sales. These days, advertisements in which children are not presented as unambiguously innocent, but in which innocence and sexuality go hand in hand, seem to awaken strong reactions and therefore garner attention. It appears that the purpose of child models is to create content in order to attract attention through specially designed technologies.

The work of a child model inseparably includes the idea of affects and their manipulation through imaging techniques. The interesting aspect of the relationship between affects and images is how technology is linked to the human body and how it can generate emotions and bodily experiences. Thanks to image manipulation technology, anybody can be given any identity, at least momentarily.[16] This is clearly present in child modeling, which is closely linked to imaging technologies (such as photography) that collect and channel attention. In this sense, the child modeling industry and visual representations of child models offer front-row seats to the affect economy.[17] Some researchers predict that technologies will change in a way that takes them away from representation and the narrative construction of subjects, and toward a direct affective impact on the body.[18] Child models and their visual representations could operate as guinea pigs for the affect economy.

A model's job as a looks-centric and emotional performance may represent the transition toward affective labour.[19] One of its main factors is the idea that modeling is a job that works beyond rationality, on a "corporal level."[20] This means that it is interlaced with corporality and the manipulation of different feelings. The popularity of child models is probably related to the fact that the figure of the innocent child crystallizes so many meanings in our culture. Merely the presence of a child in an image will most likely trigger some primitive gut reactions in the viewers. On the basis of these, viewers can form social collectives with others who feel the same way, for example, in online chat rooms or on Facebook. Various media, in turn, contribute to disseminating the information. Affective work appears to be particularly successful in children's fashion photography when they engender as much enthusiasm, confusion, and debate as possible.

The work of child models is a fascinating transitional stage or threshold. In it, the boundaries between representations and reality become blurred, as the strong reactions discussed in previous chapters demonstrate. Affect manipulation is profitable for the fashion industry when in today's era of electronic media consumers share information in a way which gives companies free publicity. Fashion companies deliberately seem to go after scandals that spread like wildfire by breaking boundaries and manipulating affects. But, contrary to what many seem to believe, the work of child models does not consist entirely of posing as sexily as possible. The cultural discourse of childhood innocence guarantees that the mere presence of a child in front of a camera will attract attention and manipulate the meanings linked to the product. The task of the child model is to imbue images with elements that cause affects in viewers, that hook people, and that provoke certain kinds of views and interpretations.

Kindergarteners in Vampy Lipstick and Stilettos

The aforementioned dimensions of modeling are not articulated when child modeling is discussed and debated in the media. Neither is the fact that children work for the fashion industry. Even though some have claimed that children lost their financial value in the nineteenth century and instead became emotionally invaluable, this is not the case when analyzing the world of child modeling.[21] And already in the early 1800s, many children were still working long days in factories, among other places, to earn money for their families.

Attention started to be paid to children's working conditions in the nineteenth century.[22] In Great Britain, for example, the first act regulating factory conditions was passed in 1802, and its objective was to protect children in cotton factories from accidents and excessively long working days. Similar regulations on the use of child labor and on their working conditions and hours were decreed throughout the century, but a law was never passed that prohibited children from working altogether.

As child labor legislation developed, children began to work less, and they acquired a new status as symbols of family unity and love. Still, as far as I can see, children never lost their financial value. Many have continued working in spite of the new childhood ideal: child labor in the fashion industry still exists outside the Western world, while in the West, children model clothing for us. The fact is that the idea of the "emotionally invaluable" child doesn't refer to just any child. It applies to Western upper- and middle-class children and the childhood ideal that centers on them. While working-class children as well as non-Western children continued going to work, playing and going to school became the privilege of Western upper- and middle-class children.

While child labor outside the Western world does raise concern in the media, modeling is apparently not considered to be the same kind of work, even though the working days of child models may be very long, when you factor in travelling to and preparing for the shoots, as well as waiting around. An interesting factor is that in the United States, for example, only the time that the child model spends in front of the camera is counted as working hours. This means that even if completing the work actually takes a child and his or her guardian eight hours, only two hours are counted, which means that the work is within the limits allowed by child labor legislation.

While the modeling work largely goes unnoticed, the same does not apply to the end products—the fashion photographs and advertising. The majority of the discussion centers on them.

One widely discussed example is a fashion editorial photographed by Sharif Hamza and published in the Christmas issue of French *Vogue* in 2011.[23] The editorial was spread across the magazine and showed several young female models, among them one of the most famous models at the time, Thylane Blondeau, daughter of the renowned French footballer Patrick Blondeau and Véronika Loubry. In the photographs she and the other girls sport visible makeup and nail polish, and wear adult women's clothing on top of children's white cotton underwear, as if suggesting a dress-up game. The clothes include, for instance, a cocktail dress made of gold-varnished leather, a leopard-print silk dressing gown, a red silk-muslin evening gown, and golden and diamond-encrusted stiletto-heeled ankle-strap sandals. The jewelry is big and heavy, featuring either golden or diamond-laced necklaces, rings, earrings, and bracelets, while the accessories include, for example, a fox fur stole and a boa made of bird-of-paradise feathers.

As can be seen in Figure 8.2, the clothes, accessories, and jewelry exude wealth and maturity, as does the model's pose and the setting: Thylane Blondeau is photographed lying on her stomach, on a tiger-skin rug, on what appears to be a bed, in front of cheetah-print wallpaper, solemnly staring at the viewer. She is wearing diamond jewelry, an asymmetrically cut red dress on top of a white cotton undershirt, and red-soled stiletto slippers decorated with leopard print, fur trim, and Swarovski crystals. While her pose and knowing look for the camera connote sophisticated adulthood, her too-big clothes and accessories make her look young and innocent. The title of the fashion editorial is Cadeaux ("Gifts"), which relates to the time of the magazine's publication, Christmas, and indicates that the products are intended for giving as presents.[24]

The editorial incited a debate about the acceptability of the images, but not about the work of little girls as models. As we can already guess, the controversy concentrated on the nature of the images and it was argued that the girls were "oversexualized."[25]

A Google search for "French Vogue Cadeaux controversy" gives over 17,000 hits and shows that these images were widely discussed in fashion blogs, newspapers, feminist blogs, and some academic blogs. Most bloggers understood that the images were purposefully controversial, but many also condemned the strategy. For example, while one blogger simply stated that

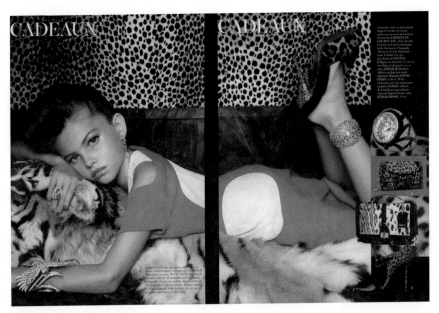

Figure 8.2 The "Cadeaux" editorial featuring the ten-year-old French child model Thylane Blondeau was condemned by the media for "oversexualizing" children. "Cadeaux", fashion editorial, *Vogue Paris*, December–January 2010–2011. Photograph by Sharif Hamza. © Vogue Paris/Condé Nast.

the images represented "kindergarteners in vampy lipstick and stilettos," languishing in bed and on a tiger-skin rug,[26] another characterized the photo series as "gross" and declared that "it never should have seen the light of day."[27] A feminist-identified blogger boldly stated that "this isn't edgy. It's inappropriate, and creepy, and I never want to see a nine-year-old girl in high-heeled leopard print bedroom slippers ever again."[28] Not everyone paid attention to the images. Many bloggers, such as Boss Lady (2011), wondered whether the then editor-in-chief of French *Vogue*, Carine Roitfeld, was fired because of these controversial images since this was the last issue of *Vogue* that she edited.

Bloggers were not the only ones to express concern. The British newspaper the *Daily Mail* reported a representative of the Mothers' Union claiming that the images represented the sexualization of children and that such "sexualisation … is one of the most pernicious ills of our era," while a spokesperson from the British CBT (Cognitive and Behavioral Therapy) & Counselling Service is reported to have said that "the images were an antithesis of what childhood in our society should be, serving solely the needs of adults and not those of children."[29] One academic blogger reported that "eight readers … alerted us to a photo spread in the December issue of French *Vogue*. The series of photographs is another piece of evidence of the adultification of young girls, an adultification that looks suspiciously like child porn."[30]

Within the context of this book, the special interest of this fashion editorial lies in that it was considered so detrimental that the chief executive of the Mothers' Union, Reg Bailey, was commissioned to carry out an independent review on the pressures faced by children. The British prime minister, David Cameron, commissioned the review, which led to the publication of the state-funded *Bailey Review* that was discussed in the previous chapter in relation to the "paedo bikini" controversy. The report has also been widely used as evidence of the commercial and sexual abuse of children, and it has been criticized by academics ever since its publication.[31]

Analysis of the debate surrounding the fashion editorial explains that the problem was not the fact that little girls had become visible as models in the fashion industry, or that fashion models were becoming ever younger. The sole focus was on the way that the girls modeled clothes using poses that did not suit their own age demographic. This disjunction generated the readings of adultification, sexualization, and exploitation. The debate went along the same lines as in the case of Calvin Klein's underwear campaign and the "paedo bikini" debate.

Evokers of Strong Emotions

What is it that gives rise to this worry again and again? One answer seems to be the persisting assumption that images have the potential to harm children, and that children and sexuality should not intersect. However, it is impossible to indicate causality between images and real actions. What we should ask is who is the victim? Is it the girl who poses in the fashion photograph? Or another girl somewhere else? If so, who is she and where does she live, and what has happened exactly? Or do the images victimize girls in general and, if so, how?

Instead of focusing on the assumed causal relationship between images and reality, attention should be directed at analyzing how and why fashion photography and fashion advertising deliberately push the boundaries of acceptability, and why and to what ends fashion marketing intentionally aims at producing emotionally charged reactions. As we have seen from previous examples, being "cutting-edge" often means challenging expected norms of middle-class propriety. The worry is therefore not only gendered; it is also class-specific, feeding the worries and anxieties of the middle class.

Furthermore, fashion photography often tends to represent its subjects — human and non-human — as desirable, inviting the viewer to visually consume the representation and hoping that this will lead to a monetary transaction or, at the very least, to the emotionally charged debate that keeps the subject matter in the public eye and gives the designer, photographer, magazine, and model much-needed free publicity. Fashion photography is an institutionalized arena constructed around the desiring gaze. It uses the language of sexuality for a purpose: to encourage viewers to desire and to purchase what they see. Gratification should be first and foremost economic, not sexual, and the child model seems to perform this job well, judging from the attention it invariably generates.

Even though modeling is hard to disconnect from the construction and dissemination of beauty ideals, it is also a job in which the model is subjected to diverse photographic techniques in hopes of eliciting various feelings and reactions. In this sense modeling is "affective labour."[32] While feelings are determined by cultural conventions and are directed toward a specific person, object, or phenomenon, affects are defined as a much more intuitive, bodily, indeterminate, and spontaneous way of reacting.[33] Affective reactions are felt deep in the body as some kind of experience of intensity, and are harder to verbalize than feelings. In other words, the task of the images is to reach the viewing subject beyond reasoning and the logical-analytical gaze. "Affective labour" thus refers to the ways in which models are intertwined with visualizing techniques in order to produce various affects in the viewing subject. It is often difficult for viewers to differentiate between the content of the images and their own, emotionally charged interpretations. The affective reaction before an image can be so strong that it makes the viewer believe that the interpretation is practically gushing out of the image while it is actually something that is created in the interaction between the viewing subject and the image.

The cultural figure of a child, especially when conceptualized as innocent, is an example of how affects and strong emotions work when viewing images, and how the producers of the images manipulate both of these as part of their work. Affect manipulation is one of the most critical objectives of fashion photography in today's visual and media-oriented information societies. Often it is impossible to put one's finger on what exactly it is about an image that awakens strong feelings. This becomes even more evident when analyzing the reactions. Whether they are about "paedo bikinis," "bulging genitals," "kindergarteners in vampy lipstick," or the "sexualization of children," the reactions seem to follow a similar logic. These are tag words or "trigger warnings,"[34] used as generalized descriptors of what is supposedly happening to children and what they should be protected from.[35]

Fashion advertisements, like any other visual representation, often draw their meanings from previous (fashion) advertisements and photographs with similar themes. A single intention or meaning of an image or a garment cannot be discerned. This is also the case with the *Vogue* fashion editorial. In fact, it is a textbook example of intertextuality. It draws its inspiration from an editorial that was published in the same magazine's December–January issue in 1978.[36]

Les Cadeaux sont un Jeu D'enfants

Les cadeaux sont un jeu d'enfants ("Gifts Are Child's Play") reads the title of a fifteen-page fashion editorial published in the December–January 1978 issue of French *Vogue*, photographed by Guy Bourdin. The title refers to the ease of buying Christmas presents, and this immediately connects the two editorials, 1978 and 2011, thematically in an intertextual reference. In contrast to many other cases, the influence of the older photographs is clearly visible here. The theme of the editorials is the same: little girls playing dress-up while modeling adult women's luxurious clothing and jewelry. Many of the arrangements in the photographs are also strikingly similar: girls hugging each other, girls standing in front of a mirror applying makeup, and a girl lying on an animal rug, as in Figure 8.3. In this editorial, the girls are also styled like miniature adults: they have heavy eye shadow, and their hair is blow-dried and elaborately coiffed. The main difference between this and the later editorial is that in these photographs, the girls do not have underwear on underneath the adult women's clothes. As a result, in some of the images, a too-big dress or dressing gown has slipped off the girl's body, revealing bare skin underneath.

The contemporary images draw from these photographs but they also reinterpret and modify them to fit the aesthetic, stylistic ideals and morals of our time. In order to see the similarities but also the crucial differences between the editorials, the concept of intertextuality is a useful tool. It helps us to remember that fashion photographs do not have a causal connection to reality and to the lives of little girls, but that they are always constructed and understood through the sedimented layers of previous images and their interpretations. Intertextuality explains how problematic, even impossible, it is to argue that representations of girls are proof of little girls' sexualization or that they constitute child pornography. In this case, as in the other examples throughout this book, a reading of an image as child pornography does not rest on an intertextual analysis between non-pornographic images such as fashion editorials and actual representations of child pornography. This is impossible for several reasons. For one, child pornography is not a legitimate image genre which would be easily available for scrutiny. It is hard, if not impossible, to obtain. A reference to child pornography is therefore a moral judgment caused by an emotional reaction, not a versed analysis of an image. "Child pornography" refers to the disturbing nature of the image rather than to the image actually being part of, or drawing from, this image genre.

Is the 2011 editorial then merely a copy of its 1978 predecessor? No, it is not. Even though the contemporary photographs are a remake, there are significant differences. With the lack of lingerie in the older editorial, the girls are depicted bare-chested. In one image, a girl stands in front of a mirror, looking at her bare and as yet undeveloped chest. In another, a girl poses together

CATHERINE AZZARO PORTE UNE ROBE DE LORIS AZZARO. PANTHERE DE ROBERT BEAULIEU. COIFFURE VALENTIN POUR J.-L. DAVID. MAQUILLAGE HEIDI MORAVETZ POUR LANCASTER.

Des fleurs pour des vases et des vases pour des fleurs

Tout ce qui vient de la Boutique Cadeaux de Christian Dior plaît,
a plu ou plaira. Le nom de Dior résonne mélodieusement à
n'importe quelle oreille, et il n'est même pas besoin d'avoir des idées
pour choisir un cadeau puisque Dior est là pour ça.
Quel soulagement! On a le choix entre les pierres dures, les assiettes
trompe-l'œil, les verres d'amitié ou de mariage, les casseroles
en cuivre rouge martelé et argent allant directement de la cuisine sur la table,
ou des vases de la ligne "autruche", en forme d'œuf cerclé de métal argenté.

Figure 8.3 The media controversy around the contemporary "Cadeaux" editorial dismissed the fact that it was an intertextual reference to an earlier editorial with the same name. Cadeaux, *Vogue Paris*, December–January 1978. © Vogue Paris 1978. Photograph by Guy Bourdin.

with another girl, wearing a silky dressing gown which has slipped off slightly, revealing her bare chest. And in the third photograph, five girls made up to look like dolls with heavy eye shadow, rouged cheeks, and red lips are tucked up in bed. They are nude from the waist up, and the bed is placed in a red room, under a sign that states, "Occupancy by more than two persons is dangerous and unlawful."[37]

The sign seems to insinuate that with five bare-chested girls occupying the bed, there is something dangerous and unlawful about the scene. In this sense, the later editorial does not play with sexuality as openly as its predecessor. Paradoxically, underclothes that made the Calvin Klein boy look like a victim of child pornography in the eyes of some viewers make the contemporary editorial seem more innocent than the 1978 one. Another possible reading, to echo John Carl Flügel, is that the girls in the older editorial are more "innocent" than in the contemporary one. As we read in previous chapters, Flügel believed that fashion changes when our conception of what is "sexy" changes. Analyzing the editorials from this perspective, the girls' bodies in the 1970s editorial were not concealed with underwear because at that time, a child's body was still regarded as asexual. The contrary applies to the contemporary editorial: the girls are dressed in undergarments because their bodies are no longer seen as asexual. The possibility of multiple, even contradictory, interpretations exposes how much the interpretation of images and clothes is affected by context.

History of the Sexual Child

The debate on the 2011 *Vogue* editorial and disputes on whether fashion and clothing sexualize children demonstrate how innocence holds a hegemonic position in the discussion on child models. The debates, like the absence of a proper visual-sartorial history of the non-heterosexual child, underline the fact that the sexual child is the "other" of innocence.

What does the history of the sexual child in fashion look like, then? So far it has not been properly researched, and I hope that this book will encourage further research and analysis on the topic. Examples can be found in *Vogue Bambini*, as I have suggested, while other examples could include risqué representations such as the adolescent, drug-consuming, and sexually active youth in Larry Clark's movies *Kids* (1995), *Bully* (2001), and *Ken Park* (2002), or the girl prostitutes played by Brooke Shields in the controversial film *Pretty Baby* (1978), directed by Louis Malle, and Jodie Foster in Martin Scorsese's *Taxi Driver* (1976), discussed by Andrew Musgrave in his book *Children in Films* (2013). A rather obvious intertextual reference to the history of the sexual girl is provided by Vladimir Nabokov's *Lolita* (1955), a name that has become a general signifier and a trope of the whole genre of the sexual(ized) girl, and a story from which many film directors and fashion photographers draw from in their work.

The visual history of the sexual girl seems much more extensive than that of the sexual boy; many representations of her figure can be found at least as far back as the nineteenth century, from photographs of Alice Liddell by Lewis Carroll in the late 1850s to Julia Margaret Cameron's sensuous photographs of girls from the 1860s–1880s, or Jock Sturges's photographs of nude girls. Perhaps the best-known contemporary examples of the sexual girl are photographs taken by the American photographer Sally Mann of her own children in the 1980s. Robert Mapplethorpe, on the other hand, has immortalized the sexual boy in his photographs of children. Both Mann and Mapplethorpe have been accused of spreading child pornography, and Mapplethorpe's photographs have also been treated as proof of his "sexual deviancy" and pedophilia.[38]

The Immaterial Value of Child Modeling

Although the most vocal reactions to child models concern the debate on children's sexualization, it should be remembered that the essence of modeling is the dissemination and marketing of various fashions, trends, and beauty ideals by evoking non-specific feelings and affects. The inclusion of deliberate trigger effects in fashion images is just as calculated as the styling of the whole image, from garments to the models and their poses.

The work of child models mostly consists of posing, which of course makes the work highly physical. But ultimately, the capability of the photograph to evoke reactions in the viewers is much more important. In the final product, the child models' physical work is dematerialized and blurred with the help of photographic technology, processing methods, image manipulation, and the presentation context, among other factors. This makes modeling an example of immaterial labor typical of post-industrial information societies.[39] "Immaterial" refers to a process in which the use of various information technologies is essential, and which comprises functions that are not understood as "labor" in the traditional meaning of the word (such as a designer's intellectual and artistic input, or the arrangement of a fashion editorial). It is work for which the outcome does not consist directly of goods or commodities, but of ideas, concepts, affective reactions, and the like.

The idea of calling a model's work immaterial may seem far-fetched: after all, a model will pose to a camera while the photographer takes pictures and the rest of the team arranges the set. But this is the very part of the work that stays "behind the scenes," so to speak—the fashion photograph effaces the physical labor needed to bring it about (e.g., standing in freezing water or posing otherwise uncomfortably), but instead highlights the importance of the model as part of constructing the intellectual, artistic, aesthetic, and immaterial content of the brand and the clothes.[40] It also accentuates symbolic meanings for which material goods—such as clothes—provide a platform.[41]

With information and (visual) symbolism having become such an indelible part of clothing, it is no longer possible to distinguish communication and information production from the product. Therefore it is no wonder that the offspring of former supermodels and Hollywood stars, as well as young movie stars in themselves, have become such important figures in selling fashionable clothes and trends. This is very effective. It shifts the focus from the physical work to discussing modeling as value and, if the model is a celebrity, to promoting the value of the product and brand. The model's renown trickles down and attaches to the clothes and brand, making the product stand out from its competitors. A well-known child makes a product special, and that is why the model almost automatically becomes a part of the product's immaterial and intellectual content and social context.

Working for the Affect Economy

The work of child models represents a new labor culture by emphasizing the performativity of work. It was suggested as early as the 1980s that the main task of some service industry employees, such as flight attendants, is to perform certain emotions, such as joy or kindness, in front of their customers.[42] Nowadays the nature of work has changed so much in some industries (fast-food restaurants, theme parks, gyms, and modeling, for example) that it can be entirely regarded as a performance that strives at producing a desired experience in the customer.

In the future, it is worth researching what kinds of traces the uncertain working conditions of the modeling world will leave on children who learn to believe that whether or not they continue to receive work depends on their own personality and their capacity to perform. Modeling does not just plant children into predetermined aesthetic molds; it also adapts them to a broader social reality. In this reality, people have increasingly started to be defined as "portfolio personalities" consisting of various projects, whose most desirable qualities are the willingness to take constant risks, adaptability, cooperation ability, and flexibility.[43]

All the examples analyzed in this book are part of a wider social process that encourages children, girls especially, to represent and see themselves as marketable products, commodities, and cunning entrepreneurs of self. In this frame of reference, the sassy styling does not represent the child as a victim, but as the neoliberal ideal: a free agent for whom self-fashioning and a sexualizing appearance are the best way of improving their personal situation.[44] A sexually alluring appearance is an essential part of the ideology of neoliberal subjectivity, which presupposes constant editing and development—but only to the end of certain predetermined subjectivity and sexuality. In this context, sexually alluring high-fashion advertising becomes an aspiration for a better life. It is a fabulous sartorial circus that is part of this new game, helping children to become assertive, powerful, and in control of their own lives and sexuality at an early age. The fashionable girl model, in particular, is represented as the stiletto-heeled post-feminist role model for any ordinary girl.

At the same time, the dual history of childhood still lives on and informs the reading of visual representations as examples of good or evil, an innocent or a sexualized childhood. Fashion media may take advantage of this dichotomy and use it quite successfully to provoke debate. The representation of the sexual child feeds into the visualized and mediatized attention economy, also defined as the "affect economy."[45] It strives at maximizing the time spent looking at and debating images. The sexual child has the job of arresting the restless gaze, to cause affects, and to channel attention. This is the central reason for the contemporary popularity of the child model.

EPILOGUE: THE RIGHT TO ONE'S OWN STYLE

> Caramel Baby & Child (where a party dress can cost up to £250) has seen sales increase by 20% for the past three years, while luxury online retailers, such as Alex and Alexa (which sells more than 9,000 items by labels including Dior, Fendi, Burberry and Ralph Lauren), are thriving.[1]

This is an excerpt from a newspaper article on the increasing popularity of children's high fashion. Even while public debate has widely concentrated on the recession in other areas of economics, the children's fashion industry is thriving. The media constantly reports on fashionable children of celebrities and royals. They have become indisputable ambassadors of style and elegance. For instance, on the birth of the first child of the duke and duchess of Cambridge, Prince George, the tabloids predicted that everything he wore would probably sell; however, it was the birth of his sister, Princess Charlotte, that was reported to be the real gift for baby boutiques, clothing stores, and fashion designers. Her birth was described as an endless marketing opportunity that would increase the sales of clothing and beauty services, and provide a role model for all the little girls who aspire to the life of a princess.

The fact that the fashions worn by royal children make the entertainment news is an excellent example of how even newborns have become important mediators of consumerism and style. After the "gay boom" of the late 1990s and early 2000s, infants and children have become the new consumer group. This book is evidence of that. When I started writing this book, children's fashion was a fairly new part of the fashion world, and most of the high-fashion advertising for children was to be found in *Vogue Bambini*. As the work draws to an end, all major high-fashion brands have kids' collections that they market online, there are several fashion blogs where ordinary parents—mothers usually—post pictures of their fashionable children, and countless online second-hand stores and Facebook groups sell children's fashions. Children have become a recognized consumer group, whose products and clothes are marketed particularly to mothers.[2]

Figure E.1 From the series *Twins*, Paris, 2012. © Heidi Lunabba.

The growth of consumption related to children tells us at least that modern capitalism is alive and well. The markets and the fashion industry are always looking for new arenas, and they turn ones that they have previously conquered into material signs that can be easily transferred to the new ones. This has clearly happened with children's fashions, which have, in many instances, become miniature versions of adult clothing, while adult clothing and fashion advertising conversely also draws inspiration from the children's world.

This book and its analysis of fashion and its visual representations demonstrate that at the beginning of the new millennium the fashion industry has thoroughly seized the concept of childhood. The focus on babies and small children demonstrates the workings of the capitalist system: it strives to turn the whole world into a production line of endless new and exchangeable commodities.[3] It also shows the effect of decreasing family sizes: as couples have fewer children, they spend increasing amounts of time and money on individual children. In this sense, the world of fashion operates as a kind of breeding system. It strives to breed increasingly perfect versions of children and babies, and to cultivate them into grown-up consumers.

Even though the news of the royal children's clothing is a continuation of the ancient royal houses' penchant for demonstrating their power by consuming luxury products, in today's culture it also has other dimensions. They bring the fashion world and brands the visibility and status they crave, and adjust ordinary consumers' views as to how their children should be dressed. Celebrity babies like George and Charlotte are tempting ambassadors and advertisers of high fashion. But they are also idols for ordinary children, and rewrite the traditional prince and princess story. Perhaps the main objective for a prince and princess is no longer to find each other and rule the kingdom, but to obtain a wardrobe filled with perfectly fitting high-fashion garments which they start collecting literally from the cradle. Fashionable clothes do not just display the privilege or good taste of royals; they also express the general view that even tiny infants have the right to their own personal style. Fashion advertising contributes to this by offering an understanding of children as cosmopolitan consumers. Their identities as global citizens will no longer be determined according to nationality but to their identification with specific brands. Despite this, the worldview that fashion represents is still very Western, even though models may come from different ethnic backgrounds. "Global citizenship" only applies to one part of the world. For example, Islamic, Indian, or Chinese fashions for children still appear in separate blogs, online stores, and YouTube channels. They have not become part of Western children's fashions, despite the assumed multiculturalism of fashion.

One of the continuing tasks of fashion studies related to children is to continue the deconstruction of the myth of innocence, and to expand analysis from the West to the other parts of the globe, critiquing the Westernization of the fashion system. Another task is to widen research from fashion magazines and their featured advertising to the internet and to the different platforms of social media that are mainly constructed around visual images, whether still or moving. Academics researching children's fashions should also be more vocal in public debates. They should add critical questions to the debate on sexualization, including that of why we consider innocence so important when it comes to clothing and visual representations of children.

NOTES

Introduction

1   Pohjala 2012, 6, 7.

2   Sommers 2012, 13.

3   http://tlc.howstuffworks.com/tv/toddlers-tiaras (accessed on December 30, 2011).

4   http://svtplay.se/v/2681935/debatt/del_1_av_18 (accessed on May 25, 2012).

5   Paasonen 2009, 3–19.

6   Millward Brown 2008.

7   Klein 2001; Quart 2003; Schor 2004. Daniel Thomas Cook (2008, 219–43), for his part, has pointed out that children are not seen in consumption-related theory.

8   Quart 2003, 151–85.

9   Schor 2004, 33, 34.

10 Lähde 2009, 36–52.

11 Ibid., 40.

12 Simpson 1994; Edwards 2006, 1997; Nixon 2003. An emphasis on male appearance also came out of reality TV series of the 1990s and early 2000s, in which gay men gave heterosexual men makeovers (Kolehmainen and Mäkinen 2009, 102–7). Sweden has seen active debates on the "beta male." The beta male is a soft family man who is simultaneously interested in his appearance and in caring for his family. The beta male is a stay-at-home dad, while his alpha female goes out to acquire an international career (Vänskä 2009a).

13 McAllister 2007, 244–58; Vänskä 2006, 40–3; Ruckenstein 2007, 100–5.

14 Lindholm 2011, 8, 9.

15 Featherstone 1982, 27.

16 Craik 2009, 215.

17 Vänskä 2007, 2–23.

18 Craik 2009, 216; Vänskä and Autio 2009, 53–69.

19 Shinkle 2008, 3.

20 http://cerosdata.bigkidlondon.com/web-assets/conde/mediakit/Italy/Vogue _Bambini.pdf (accessed on January 31, 2012).

21 Cook 2004; Schor 2004; Barber 2007.

22 Evans 2008, 17.

23 Evans 2003; Schroeder 2005.

24 Jobling 1999; Lehmann 2002; Schroeder 2005.

25 Cook 2002, 2004.

26 Of course it is also true that descriptions of everyday life are highly idealized. Thanks to Adjunct Professor Leena-Maija Rossi for pointing this out.

27 Cf., e.g., Aaltonen and Honkatukia 2002; Quart 2003; Schor 2004; Aapola et al. 2005; Anttila 2009; Paasonen 2009, 3–19; Saarikoski 2009.

28 Vänskä 2007, 2–23; Vänskä and Autio 2009, 53–69; Vänskä 2011a, 49–66, and b, 69–109.

29 Higonnet 1998; Holland 2004.

30 Banér 1994; Kincaid 1998; Sidén 2001; Frigård 2008.

31 Key 1909.

32 Similar debates have recently been seen all around the world (cf., e.g., Jyränki & Kalha 2009; Vänskä 2011b, 69–109; Angelides 2011, 102–27).

33 Giroux 2000; Rush and La Nauze 2006a.

34 Cook 2002.

35 The project was launched at the Finnish Museum of Photography in Helsinki between March 15 and May 22, 2011. After that it has toured Sweden, France, and other countries.

Chapter 1

1 Wetherell and Still 1998, 99.

2 Hacking 1999.

3 A similar pictorial constructedness has been seen in photographic art, for example in Cindy Sherman's *Film Stills* series or the staged photographs of the Finnish artist Magnus Scharmanoff.

4 Cf., e.g., Gill 1998.

5 Kress and van Leeuwen 2001.

6 Shotter 1993; Edwards et al. 1995, 25–49; Parker 1998; Burr 2003; Hibberd 2005.

7 Vivian Burr (2003, 6) points out that it is common for people not to understand the main claim of social constructionism concerning the historical and cultural specificity of knowledge, but to consider it just another way of conceptualizing the impact of the social environment on the individual. This is a poor starting point in Burr's view, because it implies that people have specific properties or characters that the environment can then affect. Social constructionism objects to the essentializing of human characteristics and identities, because it is often used for controlling people.

8 Qvortrup 2009, 28–30. Charlotte Hardman (2001, 501–17), from Britain, is one of the pioneers of studies on agency. She emphasized that children and their cultures should be researched from their own starting points.

9 E.g., Aaltonen and Honkatukia 2002; Aapola et al. 2005; Anttila 2009; Saarikoski 2009.

10 Qvortrup 2009, 25, 26.

11 Jenks 1996; Mills and Mills 1999; Kehily 2005; Qvortrup et al. 2009.

12 Qvortrup 2009, 21–3. In the seventeenth century, for example, childhood ended at the age of seven, whereas in the nineteenth it was at 13 (Lurie 1983, 37; Hendrick 1997, 33–60). Now, hardly anybody would think of considering a seven- to thirteen-year-old an adult. In the Western world, childhood ends in accordance with the United Nations Convention on the Rights of the Child, i.e., on turning eighteen.

13 E.g., Aapola 1999, 57.

14 On the blurring of girlhood and womanhood in fashion photography, see Laing 2014, 271–93.

15 Fornäs 1998, 293.

16 Hendrick 2009, 99.

17 Jenks 1996, 3; Prout 2005, 10; Honig 2009, 65.

18 Locke 1964.

19 Buck 1996, 81–4.

20 Rousseau 2011.

21 Ibid., 2. Quoted text translated by Barbara Foxley, http://www.gutenberg.org/cache/epub/5427/pg5427.html, accessed June 2015.

22 Julia V. Douthwaite (2002) describes how "child freaks" who were disabled in various ways or had been brought up as savages were submitted to very cruel human experiments with the aim of defining the boundaries between human and non-human.

23 Cunningham 2005, 44–9.

24 Ibid., 58.

25 Grylls, quoted in Heywood 2001, 24.

26 Buck 1996, 102.

27 Hendrick 1997, 33–60.

28 Ibid., 34.

29 Jensen 2007, 212.

30 Tortora and Marcketti 2015, 488.

31 Rabine and Kaiser 2006, 235–49.

32 Kapferer 1997; Klein 2001; Holt 2004; Hollis 2008.

33 Hollis 2008, 15.

34 Ariès 1962.

35 Higonnet 1998.

36 E.g., Postman 1982.

37 Pitkin 1972, 241.

38 Ibid.

39 The concept of representation as a critiquing tool has been promoted by British cultural studies derived from Neo-Marxist philosophy (Seppänen 2005, 35–40). This academic research theory was born in the industry-rich, migrant-populated city of Birmingham in western England, where the sociologist and professor of English Literature Richard Hoggart, who was originally from Leeds, established a research unit called Centre for Contemporary Cultural Studies (CCCS) in 1964. He criticized the narrow-mindedness of English Literature studies and defined a new approach: to bring English studies down from their ivory tower and into contact with the so-called real life.

40 E.g., Hall 1997.

41 Vänskä 2006; see also Viinikka 2011.

42 Austin 1990, 5, 32. In his classic *How to Do Things with Words* (1990), Austin tried to demonstrate the ways in which expressions are grammatically performative. In this context it is enough to understand it more broadly as the ability of words to be actual actions, rather than just things that lead to actions.

43 Derrida 1972, 1–23. The first two chapters of Derrida's *Of Grammatology* (1976) encourage researchers to investigate any theory in detail. In doing so, we realize that all thought structures can be deconstructed. All existing thought models can be proven to be just that—models, that is, products of certain systems of meaning rather than factual descriptions of external states.

44 www.arthur.tm.fr/#la_marque, accessed December 2011.

45 Fornäs 1998; Tomlinson 1999; Seppänen 2005; Vänskä 2006.

46 Bryson 2003, 230.

47 Buck 1996, 129.

48 Baudrillard 1998, 32–59.

49 Cf., e.g., Robertson 1992; Beck 2000; Held and McGrew 2005; Ritzer 2007. These days the term "globalization" has a rather clichéd usage, but the term in itself is not that new. It was used already in the nineteenth and early twentieth centuries in discussions of how the world was getting closer thanks to the technological advances of the industrial age. The term started to be used in academic circles in the 1960s and 1970s to refer to the growing political and economic dependence of the Western world (Held and McGrew 2005, 9).

50 Skeptics have wondered what it is that is global about globalization, when it usually seems to lead to Westernization or Americanization (Hirst 1997, 409–25).

51 Tomlinson 1999, 2, 3, *passim*.

52 Maynard 2003, 57–75.

53 Cf., e.g., Perry and Podkin 2000, 87–97.

54 Cf., e.g., Hall 1991, 19–40; Robertson 1992; Tomlinson 1999, 69, 195, 196.

55 Castañeda 2002, 102.

56 Hebdige 1979; Paasonen 2009, 9, 10.

57 Markkula and Härkönen 2009, 77–82.

58 Maffesoli 1996.

59 Muniz and O'Guinn 2001, 412–32.

Chapter 2

1 Barnard 1996, 10–12.

2 Kawamura 2005, 3, 4.

3 Baudelaire 2001.

4   Flugel 1950, 129, 130.

5   The *fashion system* is a complex institution and a network of specialized and interdependent gatekeepers—e.g., design, display, manufacturing, distribution, and sales—which has the power to transform clothing into fashion by granting it a special status and value. On the conceptual development of the fashion system, see, e.g., Barthes 1967; König 1973; Davis 1992; Entwistle 2000; Kawamura 2005.

6   Simmel 1986. See also Bruzzi and Church Gibson 2013.

7   Veblen 2002.

8   Ibid.

9   Crane 2000, 67–98; English 2007, 28–43.

10 Barthes 1990.

11 Davis 1992.

12 Kawamura 2005.

13 Brannon 2005.

14 Kawamura 2005, 73–88; Mower and Martinez 2007; Church Gibson 2012.

15 Kawamura 2005, 6.

16 Ibid., 73–88.

17 The other important properties of fashion are change, ambivalence, and novelty (Kawamura 2005, 4–6).

18 Barthes 1990.

19 Paterson 2007, 10–35.

20 Riello and McNeil 2010, 3.

21 Carlyle 2008.

22 Evans and Breward 2005.

23 The dandy was preceded by "macaroni" in the mid-seventeenth century. The macaroni were a sub-culture of English men who wore and exaggerated contemporary courtly fashions, spoke with a distinguishable dialect, and had special clubs in London (McNeil 2000, 373–404).

24 Baudelaire 2001.

25 Paoletti 2012.

26 Ibid., 24.

27 Cf., e.g., Groom 2013, 300, 301.

28 Evans 2011, 56–69.

29 Bourdieu 1984. Later research on the topic can be found, for instance, in Samil Aledin's thesis *Teenagers' Brand Relationships in Daily Life* (2009) and Elias le Grand's thesis on white working-class youths from South London who use high-fashion brands as a construction material for their own identity project (le Grand 2010).

30 Bourdieu 1984, 198–225.

31 Hebdige 1979.

32 Polhemus 1994.

33 Jobling 1999.

34 McCracken 1993, 169.

35 Corrigan 1998.

36 Ibid., 69.

37 Simmel 1986; Carlyle 2008.

38 Craik 2009, 3.

39 Lurie 1983; Barthes 1990; Davis 1992; Craik 1994.

40 Fisher 1977; Hebdige 1979; Lurie 1983; Barnard 1996.

41 Davis 1992.

42 Ibid., 5–8.

43 The idea of the importance of the materiality of clothes in forming meanings is supported, for example, by Daniel Miller, who criticizes the primary status of language in cultural studies (Miller 1987). He points out that our culture, which is dominated by linguistic and textual analysis models, has forgotten that the first experiences a baby has of the world come through material objects, not language. A parent's skin, the mother's breast, or a bedtime toy are important for children because they are points of contact with the outer world: not quite a part of the child but not separate, either (Miller 1987, 90–2). The same logic applies to clothes: they are also an interface between the body and the external world. Although clothes mean, symbolize, reference, verify, and express various things, it is also important to remember that their material properties, for example, are not completely articulated through language.

44 Barnard 1996, 29, 30.

45 Eco 1972.

46 Hall 1997.

47 Hall 1992a, 132–48.

48 Barnard 1996.

49 Perrot 1994.

50 Craik 2009. Besides modernization, the change was based on the figure of the modern dandy, who gave up excessive and colorful clothing and favored high-quality tailoring.

51 Veblen 2002.

52 Tortora and Marcketti 2015, 322.

53 Vinken 2004, 12.

54 Andrew Bolton (2003) remarks that, contrary to common understanding, the skirt is originally a non-gender-specific or a masculine garment, and it only became associated with women after the so-called Great Masculine Renunciation of the late eighteenth and early nineteenth centuries. Furthermore, men not wearing skirts is a Western phenomenon, as Middle Eastern and Asian men regularly wear skirts.

55 Hall 1992a, 132–48.

56 Davis 1992.

57 Hall 1992b, 355–80.

58 Hall 1992a, 145–8.

Chapter 3

1   Williamson 1978; Goffman 1979; Jhally 1990; Cortese 1999; Malmelin 2003; Rossi 2003; Schroeder and Zwick 2004, 21–52; Vänskä 2006; Vänskä and Autio 2009, 53–69.

2   Goffman 1979, 84.

3   Mills and Mills 1999, 10.

4   Augustine 2002.

5   Lyman 1974, 88, 89.

6   Tucker 1974, 229–57.

7   Ibid., 231.

8   Ibid., 232.

9   Cunningham 2005, 63.

10 Ariès 1962.

11 Researchers of the Middle Ages, especially, have criticized Ariès's division. According to many, children were treated with greater sensitivity in premodern times than in later centuries (Pollock 1983; Shahar 1990; Hanawalt 1993; Orme 2001). Nicholas Orme (2001, 5) suggests that "medieval people … had concepts of what childhood was, and when it began and ended. The arrival of children in the world was a notable event, and their upbringing and education were taken seriously." Harry Hendrick (2009, 101), on the other hand, has pointed out that childhood did exist as a social role in the Middle Ages, but not as a concept. In Hendrick's view, the latter would imply more than just a distinction between adults and children; it refers to childhood as an abstract idea, connected to diverse symbolic meanings.

12 Ariès 1962, 102.

13 Ibid., 106.

14 This thought is also supported by research on linguistic differences between the Middle Ages and the modern age by Mikhail Bakhtin (1995), among others. Bakhtin writes that language was used fairly freely in fifteenth-century France, but that norms were tightened significantly in the following century, widening the gap between familiar and official speech. The canon for proper speech was finally established in the seventeenth century.

15 Ariès 1962, 106–19.

16 Ibid., 137–338; Foucault 2005. Self-control meant, among other things, monitoring and restricting the sexual behavior, e.g., masturbation, of children (cf., e.g., Lacqueur 2003).

17 This is not to say that Ariès's history of childhood has not received criticism. Cf., e.g., Wilson 1980; Vann 1982; Pollock 1983.

18 Jenks 1996, 3; Prout 2005, 10; Hendrick 2009, 100.

19 There are also new age categories now between childhood and adulthood: preteen, teen, and adolescent. In today's culture, the worlds in which adults and children live have come closer together. For example, children and adults may go to the same pop concerts or wear similar clothes (Vänskä & Autio 2009, 63–5).

20 Kelynack 1910; cited in Wooldridge 2006, 23.

21 Lee Edelman (2004) writes about children as symbols of "reproductive futurism." In his view, the figure of a child signifies the continuity of humanity and the heteronormative gender order.

22 Higonnet 1998.

23 Clothes had a completely different status then. Often for poorest social classes they were their most valuable property, recycled from one generation to the next, whereas royalty and the aristocracy could demonstrate their power by changing their clothes with the fashions. There were also some fabrics and colors that could only be used by the upper classes.

24 Ariès 1962; cf. also Lurie 1983. Paoletti 2012, 21; Tortora and Marcketti 2015, 450.

25 Rousseau 2011.

26 Ibid., 210–12. Excerpt translated by Barbara Foxley, quoted from http://www.gutenberg.org/cache/epub/5427/pg5427.html, accessed June 2016.

27 Pointon 1993, 177–226; Higonnet 1998.

28 Ariès 1962, 54–62.

29 Higonnet 1998, 22–72; Heywood 2001, 25–7.

30 Higonnet and Albinson 1997, 125–7.

31 Higonnet 1998, 17.

32 Meyer 1988, 117.

33 Higonnet 1998, 51–5.

34 Higonnet and Albinson 1997, 135–7; Higonnet 1998, 27.

35 Heywood 2001, 39.

36 Ariès 1962, 56.

37 Heywood 2001, 39.

38 Gorham 1982, 42–4.

39 Sennet 1978.

40 Paoletti 2012, 87.

41 Pastoureau (2004, 140) points out that the same applied to orange and purple.

42 Garber 1997, 1; Ambjörnsson 2011. The same applies to dresses: 100 years ago, both girls and boys wore dresses, whereas these days a boy in frilly clothes is shocking for many adults.

43 Heller, 1989, 116–18; Garber 1997, 1; Pastoureau, 2004, 26–8; Koller 2008, 403.

44 Plant 1988.

45 Pastel colors were invented in the eighteenth century by mixing chalk into pigments. In today's color theory they are known as hybrid colors, in contrast to primary colors. Chemically produced hybrid colors are also known as postmodern colors, whereas pure or unblended colors are modernist (Cf. Kress & Leeuwen 2001, 356).

46 Pastoureau 2004, 82, 223.

47 The Nazis marked homosexuals with a pink triangle. In gay circles, that symbol is now used as an empowering sign. The term "pink money" was coined in the 1990s to refer to gay purchasing power.

48 Pastoureau 2004, 134.

49 Gage 1999, 2000.

50 Pastoureau 2004, 17.

51 Ibid., 32.

52 Since ancient history, the color palette had consisted of three main colors: white, red, and black. These three were the poles around which all other colors were organized: red was its own color, while yellow was assimilated into white, and green, blue, and purple belonged with black. This chromatic system led to a large number of symbolic meanings and categories. From the time of Aristotle up until Newton's day, the most common order of classifying colors was as follows: white, yellow, red, green, blue, black (Gage 1999, *passim*; Pastoureau 2004, 81).

53 Goethe was by no means the only one to highlight the color blue. It was an important color also for the other German Romantics: the blue flower of Novalis became a symbol for ideal and pure poetry (Pastoureau 2004, 140). Romanticism established the idea of blue as the color of love, melancholy, dreams, and fairy tales. The connection with melancholy still exists in the concept of "the blues."

54 Goethe 2013. Excerpt translated by R. D. Boylan, quoted from https://www .gutenberg.org/files/2527/2527-h/2527-h.htm, accessed June 2016.

55 Paoletti 2012, 87.

56 Higonnet and Albinson 1997, 133.

57 Higonnet 1998.

58 Butler 2006.

59 Jhally 1990.

60 Butler 2006, 2004.

61 Hall 1992a, 141.

62 Rose 1996, 58–66.

63 Althusser 1984, 86–143.

Chapter 4

1 Sennett 1978.

2 Ibid., 152. Thomas Carlyle's novel about dandyism, *Sartor Resartus*, contains an excellent analysis of this idea. Carlyle stresses the fact that all matter only exists in order to represent spirituality or an abstraction. This is why he placed such importance on clothes (Carlyle 2008).

3 Sennett 1978, 153.

4 Ibid., 156; cf. also Wilson 1985; Simmel 1986.

5 Foucault 1988.

6 Walkerdine 2003, 237–48.

7 The scientific thinking of the time, among others Charles Darwin's evolutionary theory and his work *The Expression of Emotion in Man and Animals* (1998), lies behind this. Darwin tried to formulate a scientific method for determining a person's character from his appearance. He believed that a person's qualities were visibly summarized in his looks. The 1800s were also the golden age of detective novels. Arthur Conan Doyle's Sherlock Holmes, for example, often determined a criminal's identity based on his or her appearance. This was inherited by classic Western movies, in which a black cowboy hat signaled a crook, for example.

8   Some of this image analysis has been previously published in the articles Vänskä 2007, 2–23; Vänskä 2009b, 205–26.

9   Cross 2004, 53, 54.

10 Sanchez-Eppeler 2005, xviii; Zelizer 1985.

11 Gage 1999; Paoletti 2012, 22.

12 Ibid., 33, 60.

13 Ibid., 89.

14 Tucker 1974, 232.

15 Kaiser and Huun 2002, 191.

16 Dyer 2010, 127.

17 Kincaid 1998. Jessica Valenti (2010) has pointed out that it is innocence in itself that makes girls sexually desirable and therefore potential victims of sex offences.

18 Higonnet 1998, 153.

19 Groom 2013, 44–51.

20 Piponnier and Mane 1997, 114–41.

21 Sennett 1978, 165.

22 Egan and Hawkes 2010.

23 Higonnet and Albinson 1997, 119–44.

24 Egan and Hawkes 2010; Kehily and Montgomery 2004, 61, 62.

25 Walkerdine 1997, 166, 167.

26 Skeggs 1997.

27 Driscoll 2002; Blank 2007.

28 Freud 1964, 193.

29 Sedgwick 1991a, 818–37; Laqueur 2003; Egan and Hawkes 2010, 33, 34.

30 McClintock 1995, 207–23.

31 Said 2011.

32 Cf., e.g., Loomba 1998.

33 Castañeda 2002.

34 The research outcomes were influenced by racial prejudices and stereotypes, and measurements were purposefully applied for reinforcing racial hierarchies (McClintock 1995).

35 Castañeda 2002, 33.

36 Talbot 1899, 102, quoted in Castañeda 2002, 36.

37 Rantonen 1997.

38 The sexologist Richard von Krafft-Ebing, for example, linked sexual perversions to racial degeneration (Krafft-Ebing 1965).

39 Boyarin 1995, 129.

40 E.g., Harrison et al. 2008, 51, 52.

41 McClintock 1995; Ahokas and Rantonen 1996, 65–8; Rantonen 1997.

42 Dyer 2002, 47.

43 Hall 1992c, 278.

44 Ibid., 279.

45 McClintock 1995; Rantonen 1997.

46 Merskin 2011, 16.

47 Cf., e.g., Mulvey 1989, 14–26; Hooks 1992; Hall 1996.

48 Honig 2009, 62.

49 Holt 2002, 70–90, 2004.

50 E.g., Spivak 1999.

51 Holt 2002, 70–90.

Chapter 5

1 Hamilton 2011.

2 Rush and La Nauze 2006a, vii.

3 Bailey 2011.

4 Ibid., 9, 14–17.

5 Ibid., 22.

6 Rush and La Nauze 2006b, 5.

7 Ibid., 6.

8 Cf., e.g., Ingrassia 1995.

9 Arnold 1999, 279–96; Akba 2006, http://www.independent.co.uk/news/uk/this-britain/photograph-that-inspired-heroin-chic-is-selected-for-ultimate-fashion-show-423542.html, accessed June 2016.

10 Newman 1999.

11 Mohr 2004, 17–30.

12 Key 1999.

13 Branson 1999.

14 Driscoll 2002.

15 Branson 1999; Business Wire 1999; Key 1999; Newman 1999. Of course one may ask what is meant by "family." Is it a safe haven or a place where children and women are exposed to violence and sexual abuse? By claiming that the campaign represented an innocent, intimate family idyll, Calvin Klein actually suggested that it could be the latter.

16 Branson 1999.

17 Attwood et al. 2012, 73. The reports have also been criticized for fetishizing innocence and taking sexualization as a given (e.g., Egan & Hawke 2008, 307–22; Faulkner 2010, 106–17; Angelides 2011, 102–27; Faulkner 2011).

18 Austin 1990; also cf. Chapter 2.

19 Attwood et al. 2012, 69–94.

20 E.g., Brundson 2000; Walkerdine et al. 2001; Gill 2003, 100–6.

21 Kincaid 2004, 3–16.

22 McNair 2002. Imogen Tyler (2008, 17–34) has analyzed the so-called chavs, i.e., lower-class, uneducated, and often unemployed English people and the hate that is directed toward them. She says that the very term is derogatory and classist. A "chav mum," for example, is a woman who reproduces without going to work and contributing to society. The distaste is seen also in the fact that the mothers' way of dressing and behaving is classed as vulgar: stereotypically a *chav mum* wears too-tight, revealing, attention-seeking clothes and drinks to get drunk.

23 E.g., Kehily 1999; Auster 2002; McRobbie 2004, 255–65; Attwood 2006, 77–94.

24 Barnard 1996.

25 The case of the two ten-year-old boys who kidnapped and tortured the two-year-old James Bulger in Liverpool in 1993 is often brought up as an example of worries concerning boys' behavior. The end result is the same as in the sexualization debate: according to the general consensus, the case proves that the golden age of childhood is over and innocence has been corrupted (Davis & Bourhill 1997, 46–74).

26 The media discourse that has led to revelations, for example, of cases of pedophilia among Catholic priests may have changed views.

27 Vänskä 2011c, 36–41.

28 Steele 1985.

29 Ribeiro 2003.

30 There is a growing body of research analyzing the intertwining of religious faith and fashion. It concentrates on Islam and the role of the veil (see Lewis 2007). Linda Duits and Liesbet van Zoonen (2006) created controversy by drawing a parallel between Muslim veils and the so-called porno-chic clothing.

31 Ribeiro 2003, 43–58.

32 Anti-luxury laws were in place to regulate the use of colors and fabrics. They clearly specified which were to be used by what social group. Therefore fabrics and colors could be used to determine a person's social status and profession. Pastoureau (2004, 91–3) points out that the main differentiations were between Christians and Jews, Muslims and other non-Christians. Additionally, there were distinctions between classes.

33 See the previous chapter.

34 Skeggs 1997, 99, emphasis in the original.

35 Davis 1992, 83.

36 E.g., Steele 1985; Wilson 1985.

37 Davis 1992.

38 Jameson 1984, 51–92; Tséelon 1992, 115–28; Gergen 1999.

39 Kincaid 1998; Faulkner 2011.

40 Gamman and Makinen 1995, 41.

41 See Chapter 2

42 Entwistle 2000, 181.

43 Bordo 1999.

44 Arnold 1999, 279–96.

45 Barnard 1996, 145–6.

46 Malcolm Barnard (1996, 147) cites certain female pop stars as typical examples of the kinderwhore look: the British PJ Harvey and the American Courtney Love (the singer in the band Hole), among others. Britney Spears, who was at one time known for her pigtails, school uniform, long socks, and childish voice, could be added to the list.

47 Phelps 2015.

48 Elliott 1995.

49 Tucker 1998, 141–57.

50 E.g., James and Prout 1990; Jenks 1996; James et al. 1998.

51 Levine 2003, 29.

52 Ibid., 29, 30. The forms of enjoyment of young working-class girls, such as dancing and flirting, went against the Victorians' religious and moral codes. The fact that many girls ended up as prostitutes was also a factor in the suffragettes' demands for socioeconomic changes for factory workers and women.

53 Foucault 1988; cf. also Weeks 1981.

54 Rubin 1984, 280, 281, 293.

55 Ibid., 267–93.

56 Foucault 1988, 276.

57 Hocquenghem, quoted by Foucault (1988, 277).

58 Allyn 2000.

59 Rubin 1984, 283.

60 Foucault 1988, 277.

61 Castañeda 2002, 47; Bray 2009, 177.

62 Thanks to Marco Pecorari for translating the excerpts from Italian into English.

63 Ibid.

64 Duggan and Hunter 1995.

65 Brownmiller 1976; Dworkin 1979; Miller 1984; Dworkin and MacKinnon 1988; MacKinnon 1993.

66 Freud 1981a, 143–56, 1981b, 157–85, 1981c, 189–221.

67 Freud 1981c, 189–221.

68 Ibid., 192, 193.

69 Laplanche and Pontalis 1968, 1–18.

70 DeMause 1974. DeMause criticizes Philippe Ariès's (1962) description of the history of childhood. Whereas Ariès claims that childhood as we know it did not exist before the seventeenth century, DeMause's view is that what Ariès describes as miniature adulthood is pure exploitation. See the chapter "Innocent Children."

71 Kempe et al. 1985, 143–54; Jenks 1996, 90–3; Helfer et al. 1997.

72 Jenks 1996, 94, 95.

73 Herman and Hirschman 1977, 741; cf. also Herman 1981.

74 Alcoff 1996, 133.

75 de Lauretis 1984.

76 Laplance and Pontalis 1968, 1–17.

77 Lacan 1977, 1–7.

78 De Lauretis 1984, 1987, 1994a, 2007.

79 De Lauretis 1984, 37–70, *passim*, 2004, 139–68, 2007, 122–5. Teresa de Lauretis writes about "imaging" especially in her book *Alice Doesn't* (1984, 37, 38, 84–6).

80 De Lauretis 2007, 122, 123.

81 Mulvey 1989, 14–26.

82 Ibid., 18.

83 Ibid., 19–21. In her later text, "Afterthoughts on 'Visual Pleasure and Narrative Cinema' Inspired by King Vidor's *Duel in the Sun* (1946)," from 1981, however, Mulvey expands on her thoughts and states that the viewer does not have to be male. The active role of a female viewer requires *cross-identification*; in other words, a woman must look at things like a man to avoid adopting a masochistic viewing position. (For critiques on the female gaze, cf. Vänskä 2006, 123–40.)

84 Mohr 2004, 17–30. For discussion on the changes in the cultural and political meanings related to child abusers, see Philip Jenkins, *Moral Panic* (2004).

85 Ibid., 20.

86 Walkerdine 1997; Bordo 1999.

87 Sender 2004.

Chapter 6

1   Vänskä and Autio 2009, 53–69.

2   Jhally 1990, 134.

3   Wilson 1985, 117.

4   Cf. also Entwistle 2000, 140–2.

5   Goffman 1979.

6   Butler 1993.

7   Warner 1991, 3–17; Rossi 2006, 19–28.

8   Rossi 2006, 19. The fact that they are common does not mean that all forms of heterosexuality are normative.

9   Althusser 1984.

10 Jhally 1990, 135, 136; Rossi 2003, 11. cf. also Vänskä 2007, 2–23.

11 De Lauretis 1984, 37, 38

12 De Lauretis 2004, 35–7.

13 Bertilsson 1986, 19–35; Luhmann 1983.

14 Illouz 1997. According to Georg Simmel (1984, 161), erotic love is a form of communication with a clear functional purpose: the survival of the species.

15 Aubert 1965.

16 Jaggar 1974, 275–91.

17 Vänskä 2006, 95–105.

18 Laurent Berlant and Michael Warner (2000, 312, 316–18) write very aptly about how heterosexuality is the opposite of other sexualities. By this they mean that heterosexuals do not need to do anything to be understood as representatives of their sexuality. A homosexual person, on the other hand, continuously comes up against everyday situations where they have to prove their sexuality.

19 Kincaid 1998; Egan and Hawkes 2010; Mancini 2010.

20 Gay 2006.

21 Schwartz 1999.

22 Sophocles 1988.

23 Carl Gustav Jung suggested the name of Electra complex to the female Oedipus complex in 1913. According to Jung, the myth of Electra reveals the psychosexual conflict between mother and daughter. In Greek mythology, Electra and her brother Orestes took revenge for the murder of their father Agamemnon by killing their mother Clytemnestra and their stepfather Aegisthus (Sophocles 1955). Freud rejected Jung's suggestion, however, and spoke of the "feminine Oedipus attitude" (Scott 2005, 8).

24 Freud 1964, 177, 178.

25 Otto Rank (1959) and Erich Fromm (1980) have pointed out that Freud's theory must be interpreted against the background of the gender theory of his time. Freud had grown up in a patriarchal culture that emphasized the status of the father, so it is no wonder that he ended up interpreting the Oedipal myth as hatred by Oedipus toward his father. Some authors claim that Freud rejected any point of view that threatened the power of authoritarian fathers (Efron 1977). The feminist criticism of Freud's theories is mostly based on the same arguments (Millett 1989).

26 Cf., e.g., Cacciatore 2007; Korteniemi-Poikela and Cacciatore 2010; WHO 2010.

27 Korteniemi-Poikela and Cacciatore 2010.

28 Ojanen 2011; Oinas 2011, 305–42.

29 E.g., Mallon and DeCrescenzo 2006; Drescher and Byne 2014.

30 E.g., Time staff 2014; Grinberg 2015.

31 Bond Stockton 2004, 277–315, 2009; Edelman 2004.

32 Leiss et al. 2005, 15–19.

33 Kekki 2006b, 128.

Chapter 7

1 Durham 2009; Levin and Kilbourne 2009; Orenstein 2011.

2 "Cisgender" refers to those who identify with the gender they have been assigned at birth. The term is also now used as an assumption of normative gender and its invisible status in contrast to expressions and embodiments of the gender of those who do not conform with the gender they have been assigned at birth, most often with transgender people. Cf., e.g., Schilt and Westbrook 2009.

3   Jagose 1998, 38.

4   The idea of coming out of the closet is related to the ideology of the gay and lesbian liberation movement of the 1960s and 1970s, whose aim was to destroy the conventions and institutions that led to traditional concepts of the gender dichotomy between men and women and sexual desire between genders. Their aim was to liberate not only those who desired people of the same sex but also the whole of society, including heterosexuals.

5   Bond Stockton 2004, 283.

6   Naturally, there has been debate on equal human rights, too. Many believe, for example, that excluding gays from the institution of marriage is a human rights violation.

7   Kekki 2006b, 127, 128.

8   Kilodavis 2011.

9   Freud 1971, 103, 104.

10 Ibid., 95.

11 Butler 1990, 274. See also Butler 1993.

12 Barad 2003.

13 Barad 2015, 399.

14 Stryker and Sullivan 2009.

15 de Lauretis 1991, iii–xviii.

16 Sedgwick 1997. See also Sedgwick 1991b.

17 Angelides 2004, 163.

18 de Lauretis 1999, 48.

19 Warner 2000.

20 Ellis 1900; Vinken 2004 12; Freud 2006, 535–67; Vänskä 2006, 115; Mancini 2010, 65–8.

21 Non-heterosexuals are experts at this kind of suggestion. In the days when their sexuality was still considered criminal, they had to communicate their orientation to others through their clothes. Unlike heterosexuals, gays and lesbians had to hide their sexuality for a long time, which led to a culture of concealment and euphemisms (Hekanaho 2006, 22). What could not be spoken out loud had to be expressed in other ways. This is why the LGBT community has learnt to present their sexuality visually, through clothes and body language.

22 Ambjörnsson 2011.

23 Vänskä 2006, 111–16.

24 Vänskä forthcoming. Suffragettes had worn trousers since Amelia Bloomer introduced the "bloomer costume," an ensemble of the knee-length dress over full trousers, in the 1850s.

25 Krafft-Ebing 1965; Ellis 1900.

26 Cf., e.g., Herdt 1994.

27 Freud 1964, 510.

28 Vänskä 2006, 132–5.

29 Ibid., 106–22; Dittmar 1998, 319–39.

30 Saarikoski 2009.

31 Lewis and Rolley 1996, 178–90.

32 Cf., e.g., Faderman 2001, 63–144.

33 Vänskä 2006, 123–40; Rossi 2003.

34 Kekki 2006b, 127, 128.

35 Freud 1971, 107.

36 Connell 2000, 6, 7, 1995, 8–21.

37 Connell 1995, 8.

38 Ibid., 11.

39 Carrigan et al. 1985, 592.

40 Jokinen 2000, 215.

41 Ibid., 213. Jokinen (2000, 68–70) speaks of the rites of passage in which boys reach manhood only by enduring physical and mental pain. These rites are thought to prove a man's "masculine fitness."

42 Jokinen 2003, 12–15, 2000, 214, 215.

43 Jokinen 2003, 18.

44 Jokinen 2000, 224.

45 Hoikkala 1993, 365, 366.

46 Sedgwick 1985.

47 Ibid., 3, 4.

48 Ibid., 21.

49 The French philosopher Luce Irigaray wrote of homosociality between men in the 1980s. She did not distinguish homosexuality from homosociality, but classified them both as concepts that shut women out and emphasize sameness (Irigaray 1996).

50 Craik 2005, 29–33, *passim*; Craik 2005, 21–50; Peoples 2014.

51 Freud 1971, 55–152.

52 Craik 2009, 59.

53 Craik 2005, 224–7.

54 Mann 1985.

55 Mort 1988, 193–224; Vänskä 2006, 93–106.

56 Mort 1996, 32.

57 Cf., e.g., Gluckman and Reed 1997, 3–10.

58 Puustinen 2008.

59 Sender 2004, 1.

60 Cf., e.g., Rossi 2007, 122–36.

61 Cole 2000.

62 Walters 2001, 9, 10.

63 Clark 1993, 186–201.

64 Breward and Evans 2005.

65 Carlyle 2008.

66 Barthes 2005, 60–4.

67 McNeil 2000, 2013.

68 Sender 2004.

69 Ibid.

Chapter 8

1 E.g., Skeggs 2004; Lair et. al. 2005; Walkerdine et. al. 2012.

2 Lindholm 2011.

3 This did not happen with Kate Moss, however. Although companies including Hennes & Mauritz, Chanel and Burberry cancelled their contracts with Moss in 2005, after the model was caught using cocaine, many people, including Alexander McQueen, supported her. McQueen organized a whole fashion show around her and wore a T-shirt with the slogan "We love you Kate."

4 Church-Gibson 2012.

5 BBC News, http://www.bbc.co.uk/newsbeat/article/32603741/irresponsible-prada-miu-miu-advert-banned-for-sexualising-a-model.

6 uk.eonline.com/news/hailee_steinfelds_miu_miu_ad_banned_in/277045 (accessed on December 15, 2011).

7 Nudd 2013, n.p.

8 Farrell 2015, https://www.theguardian.com/business/2015/jan/14/romeo-beckham-boosts-burberry-sales.

9 Pocklington 2014.

10 Evans 2003, 165–75. The word "mannequin" now applies to both human models and dummies.

11 Evans 2013.

12 Ibid., 2013.

13 Wissinger 2015.

14 Evans 2001, 271, 272.

15 Wissinger 2007a, 235; see also Wissinger 2015.

16 Ibid., 231.

17 Ibid., 232.

18 Clough 2007.

19 Hardt 1999.

20 Ibid., 96.

21 Zelizer 1985.

22 E.g., Heywood 2001, 121–44; Cunningham 2005, 140–5.

23 A preliminary version of this sub-chapter was published in *Journal of Girlhood Studies*. See Vänskä 2015.

24 I made every effort to obtain permission to publish some of the images from this series, but without success; permission was either denied or proved too expensive to be viable. I urge the reader to look at the photographs online: http://trendland.com/cadeaux-by-sharif-hamza-for-vogue-paris/.

25 Mark 2014, http://www.theukfashionspot.co.uk/runway-news/450991-controversial
    -vogue-images-ever-published/5/.

26 O'Connor 2011, n.p.

27 Tom and Lorenzo 2011, n.p.

28 Angyal 2011, n.p.

29 Daily Mail 2011, n.p.

30 Wade 2011, n.p.

31 Cf. Attwood et al. 2012; Barker and Duchinsky 2012; Gill 2012; Duchinsky and
    Barker 2013.

32 Wissinger 2007a, 231–60 and 2007b, 250–69. Wissinger bases her thoughts on the
    definition of affects as gut reactions given by the media researcher Brian Massumi.
    See also Wissinger 2015.

33 Massumi 2002.

34 "Trigger warning" is a concept that has become widely used on the Internet and in
    academia. Its aim is to warn people of the possibility of disturbing media content,
    so that they know to either avoid the content or encounter it knowing they may be
    "triggered." There is also a growing pro/con discussion around the use of trigger
    warnings; see a summary of these debates in Kyrölä, 2015.

35 Paasonen 2011, 241.

36 I am grateful to one of my sharp-eyed students for finding this series of earlier
    images.

37 The photographs in question can be viewed online: http://www.guybourdin.net/
    beauty_pages/girl_in_mirror.html and http://www.guybourdin.net/beauty_pages/
    girls_in_bed.html.

38 Higonnet 1998, 182–5.

39 Lazzarrato 1996, 132–46.

40 Ibid., 133.

41 Lash and Urry 1994.

42 Hochchild 1983.

43 Naskali 2010, 251–68.

44 McRobbie 2004.

45 Ahmed 2004.

Epilogue

1   Craik 2015, http://www.theguardian.com/fashion/2015/feb/15/childrenswear
    -childrens-fashion-prince-george-suri-cruise-harper-beckham.

2   Andersen et al. 2007, 94–8.

3   Marx 1992; Bruun et al. 2009.

SOURCES
AND BIBLIOGRAPHY

Aaltonen, Sanna & Päivi Honkatukia (eds.) (2002). *Tulkintoja tytöistä*. Nuorisotutkimusseuran julkaisuja 27, Tietolipas 187. Helsinki: Finnish Literature Society.

Aapola, Sinikka (1999). *Murrosikä ja sukupuoli. Julkiset ja yksityiset ikämäärittelyt*. Helsinki: Finnish Literature Society.

Aapola, Sinikka (2002). "Pikkutyttöjä vai pikkuaikuisia? Tytöt, vanhemmat ja kontrolli." In Sanna Aaltonen & Päivi Honkatukia (eds.), *Tulkintoja tytöistä*. Helsinki: Finnish Literature Society, 129–47.

Aapola, Sinikka, Marnina Gonick, & Anita Harris (eds.) (2005). *Young Femininity. Girlhood, Power and Social Change*. New York: Palgrave.

Ahokas, Pirjo & Eila Rantonen (1996). "Feminismin muukalaiset. Rodun ja etnisyyden haasteet." In Päivi Kosonen (ed.), *Naissubjekti ja postmoderni*. Helsinki: Gaudeamus, 65–88.

Ahmed, Sara (2004). "Affective Economies." *Social Text* 79, 117–39.

Ahmed, Sara (2010). "Creating Disturbance: Feminism, Happiness and Affective Differences." In Marianne Liljeström & Susanna Paasonen (eds.), *Working with Affect in Feminist Readings: Disturbing Differences*. London: Routledge, 33–46.

Akba, Arifa (2006). "Photograph that inspired 'heroin chic' is selected for ultimate fashion show," *The Independent*, November 9, 2006. http://www.independent.co.uk/news/uk/this-britain/photograph-that-inspired-heroin-chic-is-selected-for-ultimate-fashion-show-423542.html (accessed February 16, 2016).

Alcoff, Linda Martin (1996). "Dangerous Pleasures: Foucault and the Politics of Pedophilia." In Susan J. Hekman (ed.), *Feminist Interpretations of Foucault*. Pennsylvania: Pennsylvania University Press, 99–136.

Aledin, Samil (2009). *Teenagers' Brand Relationships in Daily Life. A Qualitative Study of Brand Meanings and Their Motivational Ground among Teenagers in Helsinki and London Metropolitan Areas*. Turku: Turku School of Economics.

Allyn, David (2000). *Make Love, Not War: The Sexual Revolution: An Unfettered History*. London and New York: Routledge.

Althusser, Louis (1984). *Ideologiset valtiokoneistot*. Finnish translation by Leevi Lehto & Hannu Sivenius. Tampere and Helsinki: Vastapaino & Kansankulttuuri (original in French published in 1976).

Ambjörnsson, Fanny (2011). *Rosa: den farliga färgen*. Stockholm: Ordfront.

Andersen, Lars Pynt, Elin Sorensen, & Marianne Babiel Kjaer (2007). "Not Too Conspicuous, Mothers' Consumption of Baby Clothing." In Stefania Borghini, Mary Ann McGrath, & Cele Otnes (eds.), *European Advances in Consumer Research*, Volume 8. Duluth, MN: Association for Consumer Research, 94–8.

Angelides, Steven (2004). "Feminism, Child Sexual Abuse, and the Erasure of Child Sexuality." *GLQ: A Journal of Lesbian and Gay Studies* 2, 141–77.

Angelides, Steven (2011). "What's Behind Child Sex Panics? The Bill Henson Scandal." *Lambda Nordica* 2–3, 102–27.

Angyal, Chloe (2011). "French *Vogue* Fashion Spread Features Sexy Children." *Feministing*. http://feministing.com/2011/01/05/french-vogue-fashion-spread-features-sexy-sexy-children/ (accessed January 23, 2015).

Anttila, Anna (2009). *Leikin asia. Näkökulmia varhaisnuorten romanttiseen seurustelukulttuuriin*. Helsinki: Yliopistopaino.

Ariès, Philippe (1962). *Centuries of Childhood: A Social History of Family Life*. Translated by Robert Baldick. London: Jonathan Cape (original in French published in 1960).

Arnold, Rebecca (1999). "Heroin Chic." *Fashion Theory* 3:3, 279–96.

Arthur (2016). "The Brand". http://www.boutique-arthur.com/en/p-the-brand.html (accessed December 23, 2016).

Attwood, Feona (2006). "Sexed Up: Theorizing the Sexualization of Culture." *Sexualities* 9:1, 77–94.

Attwood, Feona et al. (2012). "Engaging with the Bailey Review: Blogging, Academia and Authenticity." *Psychology and Sexuality* 3:1, 69–94.

Aubert, Wilhelm (1965). *The Hidden Society*. Totowa, NJ: Bedminster Press.

Augustine, Saint (2002). *The Confessions of Saint Augustine (Confessiones)*. Translated by E. B. Pusey (Edward Bouverie). Project Gutenberg (original in Latin published in 401).

Auster, Albert (2002). "*Sex and the City*: New Television Images of Women." *Television Quarterly* 32:4, 52–5.

Austin, J. L. (1990). *How to Do Things with Words*. Harvard: Harvard University Press (first published in 1962).

Bailey, Reg (2011). *Letting Children Be Children. Report of an Independent Review of the Commercialisation and Sexualisation of Childhood*. London: Department of Education.

Bakhtin, Mikhail (1995). *François Rabelais—Keskiajan ja renessanssin nauru*. Finnish translation by Tapani Laine & Paula Nieminen. Helsinki: Kustannus Oy Taifuuni (original in Russian published in 1965).

Banér, Anne (1994). *Bilden av barnet: från antiken till 1900*. Stockholm: Bergh.

Barad, Karen (2003). "Posthumanist Performativity: Toward an Understanding of How Matter Comes to Matter." *Signs: Journal of Women in Culture and Society* 28:3, 801–31.

Barad, Karen (2015). "Transmaterialities: Trans*/Matter/Realities and Queer Political Imaginings." *GLQ: A Journal of Lesbian and Gay Studies* 21:2–3, 387–422.

Barber, Benjamin R. (2007). *Consumed: How Markets Corrupt Children, Infantilize Adults, and Swallow Citizens Whole*. New York and London: W. W. Norton & Company.

Barker, Meg, and Robbie Duchinsky. (2012). "Sexualisation's Four Faces: Sexualisation and Gender Stereotyping in the Bailey Review." *Gender and Education* 24:3, 303–10.

Barnard, Malcolm (1996). *Fashion as Communication*. London and New York: Routledge.

Barthes, Roland (1990). *The Fashion System*. Translated by M. Ward & R. Howard. Berkeley: University of California Press (original in French published in 1967).

Barthes, Roland (2005). "Dandyism and Fashion." In Andy Stafford & Michael Carter (eds.), *The Language of Fashion*. Translated by Andy Stafford. Oxford: Berg (original in French published in 1962).

Baudelaire, Charles (2001). *Modernin elämän maalari ja muita kirjoituksia*. Finnish translation by Antti Nylén. Helsinki: Desura (original in French published in 1863).

Baudrillard, Jean (1998). "Simulacra and simulations." In M. Poster (ed.), *Jean Baudrillard. Selected Writings*. Second extended edition. Cambridge and Oxford: Polity, 169–87 (original in French published in 1981).

BBC Online (2015). "'Irresponsible' Prada Miu Miu advert banned for 'sexualising a model.'" http://www.bbc.co.uk/newsbeat/article/32603741/irresponsible-prada-miu-miu-advert-banned-for-sexualising-a-model (accessed February 19, 2016).

Beck, Ulrich (2000). *What Is Globalization?* Oxford: Polity Press.

Berger, Peter & Thomas Luckmann (1966). *The Social Construction of Reality. A Treatise in the Sociology of Knowledge*. New York: Irvington Publishers Inc.

Berlant, Lauren & Michael Warner (2000). "Sex in Public." In Lauren Berlant (ed.), *Intimacy*. Chicago: Chicago University Press, 311–30.

Bertilsson, Margareta (1986). "Love's Labour Lost? A Sociological View." *Theory Culture Society* 3:2, 19–35.

Blank, Hanne (2007). *Virgin: The Untouched History*. New York: Bloomsbury.

Bolton, Andrew (2003). *Bravehearts. Men in Skirts*. London: V & A Publications.

Bond Stockton, Kathryn (2004). "Growing Sideways, or Versions of the Queer Child: The Ghost, the Homosexual, the Freudian, the Innocent, and the Interval of Animal." In Steven Bruhm & Natasha Hurley (eds.), *Curiouser. On the Queerness of Children*. Minneapolis and London: Minnesota University Press, 277–316.

Bond Stockton, Kathryn (2009). *The Queer Child, or Growing Sideways in the Twentieth Century*. Durham and London: Duke University Press.

Bordo, Susan (1999). *The Male Body: A New Look at Men in Public and in Private*. New York, NY: Farrar, Straus & Giroux.

Boss, Lady (2011). "Has French VOGUE Taken Child Models Too Far?" *DrJay's.com*, January 6, 2011. http://live.drjays.com/index.php/2011/01/06/has-french-vogue-taken-child-models-too-far/ (accessed January 23, 2015).

Bourdieu, Pierre (1977). *Outline of a Theory of a Practice*. Cambridge: Cambridge University Press.

Bourdieu, Pierre (1984). *Distinction—A Social Critique of the Judgement of Taste*. Cambridge: Harvard University Press (original in French published in 1979).

Bourdin, Guy (Photographer) (1978). "Les Cadeaux Sont un Jeu d'Enfants." *French Vogue* Decembre 1977–Janvier 1978:582, 204–21.

Boyarin, David (1995). "Freud's Baby, Fliess's Maybe. Homophobia, Anti-Semitism, and the Invention of Oedipus." *GLQ* 2, 115–47.

Brannon, Evelyn L. (2005). *Fashion Forecasting*. New York: Fairchild Publications.

Branson, Louise (1999). "Calvin Klein Advert 'Pedophile Porn.'" *The Scotsman* 2, 19.

Bray, Abigail (2009). "Governing The Gaze." *Feminist Media Studies* 9:2, 173–91.

Breward, Christopher & Caroline Evans (eds.) (2005). *Fashion and Modernity*. Oxford: Berg.

Brownmiller, Susan (1976). *Against Our Will: Men, Women and Rape*. Harmondsworth: Penguin.

Brunsdon, Charlotte (2000). "Post-Feminism and Shopping Films." In Joanne Hollows, Peter Hutchings, & Mark Jancovich (eds.), *The Film Studies Reader*. New York: Oxford University Press, 289–99.

Bruun, Otto, Teppo Eskelinen, Ilkka Kauppinen, & Hanna Kuusela (eds.) (2009). *Immateriaalitalous: kapitalismin uusin muoto*. Helsinki: Gaudeamus.

Bruzzi, Stella and Pamela Church Gibson (eds.) (2013). *Fashion Cultures Revisited: Theories, Explorations and Analysis*. New York and London: Routledge.

Buck, Anne (1996). *Clothes and the Child. A Handbook of Children's Dress in England 1500–1900*. Carlton, Bedford: Ruth Bean Publishers.

Burgin, Victor, James Donald, & Cora Kaplan (eds.) (1989). *Formations of Fantasy*. London: Methuen.

Burr, Vivien (2003). *Social Constructionism*. New York and London: Routledge.

Butler, Judith (1990). "Performative Acts and Gender Constitution: An Essay in Phenomenology and Feminist Theory." In Sue-Ellen Case (ed.), *Performing Feminisms: Feminist Critical Theory and Theatre*. Baltimore: Johns Hopkins University Press.

Butler, Judith (1993). *Bodies that Matter: On the Discursive Limits of "Sex."* New York and London: Routledge.

Butler, Judith (2004) *Undoing Gender*. New York and London: Routledge.

Butler, Judith (2006). *Hankala sukupuoli: Feminismi ja identiteetin kumous*. Finnish translation by Tuija Pulkkinen & Leena-Maija Rossi. Helsinki: Gaudeamus (original in English [Gender Trouble: Feminism and the Subversion of Identity] published in 1990).

Bryman, Alan (2004). *The Disneyization of Society*. London: Sage.

Bryson, Norman (2003). "Visual Culture and the Dearth of Images." *Journal of Visual Culture* 2:2, 229–32.

Cacciatore, Raisa (2007) *Huomenna pannaan pussauskoppiin: eväitä tyttönä ja poikana kasvamisen haasteisiin syntymästä murrosikään*. Helsinki: WSOY.

"Calvin Klein Introduces Designer Underwear for Kids." *Business Wire*, February 17, 1999.

Carlyle, Thomas (2008). *Sartor Resartus*. Oxford: Oxford University Press (first published in 1831).

Carrigan, Tim, Raewyn Connell, & John Lee (1985). Toward a New Sociology of Masculinity. *Theory and Society* 14:5, 551–604.

Castañeda, Claudia (2002). *Figurations. Child, Bodies, Worlds*. Durham and London: Duke University Press.

Church Gibson, Pamela (2012). *Fashion and Celebrity Culture*. London and New York: Berg.

Clark, Danae (1993). "Commodity Lesbianism." In Henry Abelove, Michèle Aina Barale, & David M. Halperin (eds.), *The Lesbian and Gay Studies Reader*. New York and London: Routledge, 186–201.

Clough, Patricia Ticineto (2007). "Introduction." In Patricia Ticineto Clough & Jean Halley (eds.), *The Affective Turn. Theorizing the Social*. Durham and London: Duke University Press, 1–33.

Cole, Shaun (2000). *"Don We Now Our Gay Apparel": Gay Men's Dress in the Twentieth Century*. Oxford: Berg.

Connell, Raewyn (1995). *Masculinities*. Cambridge: Polity Press.

Connell, Raewyn (2000). *The Men and the Boys*. Cambridge: Polity Press.

Cook, Daniel Thomas (ed.) (2002). *Symbolic Childhood*. New York: Peter Lang.

Cook, Daniel Thomas (2004). *The Commodification of Childhood. The Children's Clothing Industry and the Rise of the Child Consumer*. Durham and London: Duke University Press.

Cook, Daniel Thomas (2008). "The Missing Child in Consumption Theory." *Journal of Consumer Culture* 8:2, 219–43.

Corrigan, Peter (1998). *The Sociology of Consumption: An Introduction*. London: Sage.

Cortese, Anthony (1999). *Provocateur: Images of Women and Minorities in Advertising*. Lanham, MD: Rowman & Littlefield.

Cowie, Elizabeth (1993). "From Fantasia." In Anthony Easthope (ed.), *Contemporary Film Theory*. New York: Longman, 147–61.

Craik, Jennifer (1994). *The Face of Fashion: Cultural Studies in Fashion*. New York and London: Routledge.

Craik, Jennifer (2005). *Uniforms Exposed: From Conformity to Transgression*. Oxford: Berg.

Craik, Jennifer (2009). *Fashion. The Key Concepts*. Oxford: Berg.

Craik, Laura (2015). "Children's fashion: Small people, big business." *The Observer,* February 15. http://www.theguardian.com/fashion/2015/feb/15/childrenswear-childrens-fashion-prince-george-suri-cruise-harper-beckham (accessed February 19, 2016).

Crane, Diana (2000). *Fashion and Its Social Agendas. Class, Gender, and Identity in Clothing*. Chicago and London: The University of Chicago Press.

Cross, Gary (2004). *The Cute and the Cool: Wondrous Innocence and Modern American Children's Relationships*. London: Routledge.

Cunningham, Hugh (2005). *Children and Childhood in Western Society since 1500*. London: Longman.

Darwin, Charles (1998). *The Expression of Emotion in Man and Animal*. Third edition. New York: Oxford University Press (first published in 1872).

Davis, Fred (1992). *Fashion, Culture and Identity*. Chicago and London: Chicago University Press.

Davis, Howard & Marc Bourhill (1997). "Crisis: The Demonization of Children and Young People." In Phil Scraton (ed.), *Childhood in Crisis?* Florence, KY: Routledge, 46–74.

Dean, Deborah (2005). "Recruiting a Self: Women Performers and Aesthetic Labour." *Work, Employment & Society* 19:4, 761–74.

DeMause, Lloyd (1974). *The History of Childhood*. London: Souvenir Press.

Derrida, Jacques (1972). *Limited Inc*. Evanston, IL: Northwestern University Press.

Derrida, Jacques (1976). *Of Grammatology*. Translated by Gayatri Chakravorty Spivak. Baltimore and London: Johns Hopkins University Press (original in French published in 1967).

Dittmar, Linda (1998). "The Straight Goods. Lesbian Chic and Identity Capital on Not-so-Queer Planet." In Deborah Bright (ed.), *The Passionate Camera. Photography and Bodies of Desire*. London and New York: Routledge, 319–39.

Douthwaite, Julia (2002). *The Wild Girl, Natural Man and the Monster. Dangerous Experiments in the Age of Enlightenment*. Chicago: The University of Chicago Press.

Drescher, Jack & Byne William (eds.) (2014). *Treating Transgender Children and Adolescents: An Interdisciplinary Discussion*. New York and London: Routledge.

Driscoll, Catherine (2002). *Girls: Feminine Adolescence in Popular Culture and Cultural Theory*. New York: Columbia University Press.

Duchinsky, Robbie & Meg Barker (2013). "Doing the Möbius Strip: The Politics of the Bailey Review." *Sexualities* 16:5–6, 730–42.

Duggan, Lisa & Nan D. Hunter (eds.) (1995). *Sex Wars: Sexual Dissent and Political Culture*. New York: Routledge.

Duits, Linda & Liesbet van Zoonen (2006). "Headscarves and Porno-Chic: Disciplining Girls' Bodies in the Multicultural Society." *European Journal of Women's Studies* 13:2, 103–17.

Durham, Gigi (2009). *The Lolita Effect: The Media Sexualization of Young Girls*. New York: The Overlook Press.

Dworkin, Andrea (1979). *Pornography: Men Possessing Women*. London: Women's Press.

Dworkin, Andrea & Katherine MacKinnon (1988). *Pornography and Civil Rights: A New Day for Women's Equality*. Organizing Against Pornography, a resource center for education and action based in Minneapolis. Permanent link: http://www.nostatusquo.com/ACLU/dworkin/other/ordinance/newday/TOC.htm (accessed October 13, 2016).

Dyer, Richard (2002). *Älä katso! Seksuaalisuus ja rotu viihteen kuvastossa*. ed. Martti Lahti. Tampere: Vastapaino.

Dyer, Richard (2010). *White: Essays on Race and Culture*. London and New York: Routledge.

Eco, Umberto (1972). "Social Life as a Sign System." In Don Robey (ed.), *Structuralism. The Wolfson College Lectures 1972*. London: Jonathan Cape, 57–72.

Edelman, Lee (2004). *No Future. Queer Theory and the Death Drive*. Durham and London: Duke University Press.

Edwards, Derek, Malcolm Ashmore, & Jonathan Potter (1995). "Death and Furniture: The Rhetoric, Politics and Theology of Bottom Line Arguments against Relativism." *History of the Human Sciences* 8, 25–49.

Edwards, Tim (1997). *Man in the Mirror. Men's Fashion, Masculinity and Consumer Society*. London and Herndon, VA: Cassell.

Edwards, Tim (2006). *Cultures of masculinity*. London: Routledge.

Efron, Arthur (1977). "Freud's Self-Analysis and the Nature of Psychoanalytic Criticism." *International Review of Psycho-Analysis* 4, 253–80.

Egan, R. Danielle & Gail Hawkes (2008). "Girls, Sexuality and the Strange Carnalities of Advertisements: Deconstructing the Discourse of Corporate Paedophilia." *Australian Feminist Studies* 23:57, 307–22.

Egan, R. Danielle & Gail Hawkes (2010). *Theorizing the Sexual Child in Modernity*. New York: Palgrave Macmillan.

Elliott, Stuart (1995). "Calvin Klein to Withdraw Child Jean Ads." *New York Times*, August 28. http://www.nytimes.com/1995/08/28/business/the-media-business-advertising-calvin-klein-to-withdraw-child-jean-ads.html (accessed February 16, 2016).

Ellis, Havelock (1900). *Studies in the Psychology of Sex*. New York: Random House (first published in 1895).

English, Bonnie (2007). *A Cultural History of Fashion in the 20th Century. From the Catwalk to the Sidewalk*. Oxford and New York: Berg.

Entwistle, Joanne (2000). *The Fashioned Body. Fashion, Dress and Modern Social Theory*. Cambridge: Polity Press.

Entwistle, Joanne (2009). *The Aesthetic Economy of Fashion. Markets and Values in Clothing and Modelling*. Oxford and New York: Berg.

Entwistle, Joanne & Elizabeth Wissinger (2006). "Keeping Up Appearances: Aesthetic Labour in the Fashion Modelling Industries of London and New York." *The Sociological Review* 54:4, 775–94.

Evans, Caroline (2001). "The Enchanted Spectacle." *Fashion Theory* 5:3, 271–310.

Evans, Caroline (2003). *Fashion at the Edge: Spectacle, Modernity, and Deathliness*. New Haven and London: Yale University Press.

Evans, Caroline (2008). "A Shop of Images and Signs." In Eugénie Shinkle (ed.), *Fashion as Photograph: Viewing and Reviewing Images of Fashion*. London and New York: I. B. Tauris & Co, 17–28.

Evans, Caroline (2011). "The Ontology of the Fashion Model." *AA Files* 63:2011, 56–69.

Evans, Caroline (2013). *The Mechanical Smile. Modernism and the First Fashion Shows in France and America, 1900–1929*. New Haven and London: Yale University Press.

Evans, Caroline & Christopher Breward (eds.) (2005). *Fashion and Modernity*. Oxford: Berg.

Evans, Caroline & Minna Thornton (1989). *Women and Fashion: A New Look*. London and New York: Quartet Books.

Faderman, Lillian (2001). *Surpassing the Love of Men. Romantic Friendship & Love between Women from the Renaissance to the Present*. New York: Perennial. An Imprint of HarperCollins Publishers (first published in 1981).

Farrell, Sean (2015). "Romeo Beckham Boosts Burberry Sales." *The Guardian*, January 14. http://www.theguardian.com/business/2015/jan/14/romeo-beckham-boosts-burberry-sales (accessed October 13, 2016).

Faulkner, Joanne (2010). "The Innocence Fetish: The Commodification and Sexualisation of Children in the Media and Popular Culture." *Media International Australia* 135:5, 106–17.

Faulkner, Joanne (2011). *The Importance of Being Innocent: Why We Worry about Children*. Cambridge: Cambridge University Press.

Featherstone, Mike (1982). "The Body in Consumer Culture." *Theory Culture Society* 1, 18–33.

Feldman, Jenny (2008). *Barbie Gets Her Own Runway Show*. www.glamour.com/fashion/blogs/slaves-to-fashion/2008/11/barbie-gets-her-own-runway-sho.html (accessed February 9, 2010).

Fisher, Hal (1977). *Gay Semiotics. A Photographic Study of Visual Coding among Homosexual Men*. San Francisco: NFS Press.

Flugel, J. C. (1950). *The Psychology of Clothes*. London: The Hogarth Press and The Institute of Psycho-Analysis (first published in 1930).

Fornäs, Johan (1998). *Kulttuuriteoria. Myöhäismodernin ulottuvuuksia*. Finnish translation by Mikko Lehtonen, Kaarina Hazard, Virpi Blom, & Juha Herkman. Tampere: Vastapaino (original in English [Cultural Theory and Late Modernity] published in 1995).

Foucault, Michel (1988). "Technologies of the Self: A Seminar with Michel Foucault." In Luther H. Martin, Huck Gutman, & Patrick H. Hutton (eds.), *Technologies of the Self*. London: Tavistock, 16–49.

Foucault, Michel (2005). *Tarkkailla ja rangaista*. Finnish edition translated by Eevi Nivanka and proofread by Jukka Kemppinen. Helsinki: Otava (original in French published in 1976).

Freud, Sigmund (1964). "The Taboo of Virginity." In James Strachey (ed.), *The Standard Edition of the Complete Psychological Works of Sigmund Freud. Vol. 11. Five lectures on Psycho-Analysis, Leonardo Da Vinci and Other Works*. Translated by James Strachey. London: The Hogarth Press, 193–208 (original in German published in 1918).

Freud, Sigmund (1966). "Extracts from the Fliess Papers." In James Strachey (ed.), *The Standard Edition of the Complete Psychological Works of Sigmund Freud. Vol. 1 (1886–1899), Pre-Psycho-Analytic Publications and Unpublished Drafts*. Translated by James Strachey. London: The Hogarth Press (original in German published in 1892–1899).

Freud, Sigmund (1971). "Kolme seksuaaliteoreettista tutkielmaa." In *Seksuaaliteoria*. Finnish translation by Erkki Puranen. Jyväskylä: Gummerus, 55–152 (original in German published in 1904–1905).

Freud, Sigmund (1981a). "Heredity and the Aetiology of the Neuroses." In James Strachey (ed.), *The Standard Edition of the Complete Psychological Works of Sigmund Freud. Vol. 3 (1893–1899), Early Psycho-Analytic Publications*. Translated by James Strachey. London: The Hogarth Press, 143–56 (original in German published in 1896).

Freud, Sigmund (1981b). "Further Remarks on the Neuro-Psychoses of Defense." In James Strachey (ed.), *The Standard Edition of the Complete Psychological Works of Sigmund Freud. Vol. 3 (1893–1899), Early Psycho-Analytic Publications*. Translated by James Strachey. London: The Hogarth Press and The Institute of Psycho-Analysis, 157–85 (original in German published in 1896).

Freud, Sigmund (1981c). "The Aetiology of Hysteria." In James Strachey (ed.), *The Standard Edition of the Complete Psychological Works of Sigmund Freud. Vol. 3 (1893–1899), Early Psycho-Analytic Publications*. Translated by James Strachey. London: The Hogarth Press, 189–221 (original in German published in 1896).

Freud, Sigmund (2001). *Unien tulkinta*. Finnish translation by Erkki Puranen. Helsinki: Gummerus/Loisto (original in German published in 1900).

Freud, Sigmund (2006). "Erään naisen homoseksuaalisuuden psykogeneesistä. Homoseksuaalinen nainen." In *Tapauskertomukset*. Finnish translation by Seppo Hyrkäs. Helsinki: Teos, 535–67 (original in German published in 1920).

Frigård, Johanna (2008). *Alastomuuden oikeutus: julkistettujen alastonkuvien moderneja ideaaleja Suomessa 1900–1940*. Helsinki: Finnish Literature Society.

Fromm, Erich (1980). *Freud ja freudilaisuus*. Finnish translation by Marja-Leena Närhi. Helsinki: Kirjayhtymä (original in German published in 1979).

Fuss, Diana (1992). "Fashion and the Homospectatorial Look." *Critical Inquiry* 18, 713–37.

Gage, John (1999). *Color and Culture: Practice and Meaning from Antiquity to Abstraction*. Berkeley: University of California Press.

Gage, John (2000). *Color and Meaning: Art, Science, and Symbolism*. Berkeley: University of California Press.

Gamman, Lorrainen & Merja Mäkinen (1995). *Female Fetishism*. New York: New York University Press.

Garber, Marjorie (1997). *Vested Interests. Cross-Dressing and Cultural Anxiety*. New York: HarperCollins Publishers.

Gay, Peter (2006). *Freud: A Life for Our Time*. New York: W. W. Norton & Company.

Genet, Jean (2002). *Querelle*. Finnish translation by Päivi Malinen. Helsinki: Like (original in French published in 1947).

Gergen, Kenneth J. (1999). *An Invitation to Social Construction*. London: Sage.

Gill, Alison (1998). "Deconstruction Fashion: The Making of Unfinished, Decomposing and Re-assembled Clothes." *Fashion Theory* 2:1, 25–50.

Gill, Rosalind (2003). "From Sexual Objectification to Sexual Subjectification: The Resexualisation of Women's Bodies in the Media." *Feminist Media Studies* 3:1, 100–6.

Gill, Rosalind (2012). "Media, Empowerment and the 'Sexualization of Culture' Debates." *Sex Roles* 66, 736–45.

Giroux, Henry (2000). *Stealing Innocence: Youth, Corporate Power, and the Politics of Culture*. New York: St. Martin's Press.

Gluckman, Amy & Betsy Reed (eds.) (1997). *Homo Economics: Capitalism, Community, and Lesbian and Gay Life*. London and New York: Routledge.

Goethe, Johann Wolfgang von (2013). *The Sorrows of Young Werther*. Translated by R. D. Boylan. Project Gutenberg eBook. http://www.gutenberg.org/files/2527/2527-h/2527-h.htm (accessed October 13, 2016) (original in German published in 1774).

Goffman, Erwing (1979). *Gender Advertisements*. Cambridge, MA: Harvard University Press.

Gorham, Deborah (1982). *The Victorian Girl and the Feminine Ideal*. London: Croom Helm.

le Grand, Elias (2010). *Class, Place and Identity in a Satellite Town*. Stockholm: Acta Universitatis Stockholmiensis.

Grinberg, Emanuella (2015). "Why transgender teen Jazz Jennings is everywhere." CNN, March 19. http://edition.cnn.com/2015/03/16/living/feat-transgender-teen-jazz-jennings/ (accessed February 17, 2016).

Groom, Gloria (2013). "Claude Monet: Camille." In Gloria Groom (ed.), *Impressionism, Fashion, & Modernity*. New Haven and London: Yale University Press, 44–51.

Groom, Gloria (2013). "Fashion Plates." In Gloria Groom (ed.), *Impressionism, Fashion, & Modernity*. New Haven and London: Yale University Press, 300, 301.

Hacking, Ian (1999). *The Social Construction of What?* Harvard: Harvard University Press.

Hall, Stuart (1991). "The Local and Global: Globalization and Ethnicity." In Anthony D. King (ed.), *Cultural, Globalization and the World-System: Contemporary Conditions for the Representation of Identity*. Binghamton: State University of New York, 19–40.

Hall, Stuart (1992a). "Sisäänkoodaus/uloskoodaus." In Juha Koivisto, Mikko Lehtonen, Timo Uusitupa, & Lawrence Grossberg (eds.), *Kulttuurin ja politiikan murroksia*. Tampere: Vastapaino, 132–48 (engl. alkuteksti 1973).

Hall, Stuart (1992b). "Postmodernismista ja artikulaatiosta." In Juha Koivisto, Mikko Lehtonen, Timo Uusitupa, & Lawrence Grossberg (eds.), *Kulttuurin ja politiikan murroksia*. Tampere: Vastapaino, 355–80 (engl. alkuteksti 1986).

Hall, Stuart (1992c). "Kulttuurin ja politiikan murroksia." In Juha Koivisto, Mikko Lehtonen, Timo Uusitupa, & Lawrence Grossberg (eds.), *Kulttuurin ja politiikan murroksia*. Tampere: Vastapaino.

Hall, Stuart (1996). *Identiteetti*. Translated into Finnish and edited by Mikko Lehtonen & Juha Herkman. Tampere: Vastapaino.

Hall, Stuart (ed.) (1997). *Representation. Cultural Representations and Signifying Practices*. London: Sage.

Haller, John M. (1995). *Outcasts from Evolution: Scientific Attitudes of Racial Inferiority, 1895–1900*. Urbana: University of Illinois Press (first published in 1971).

Hamilton, Jane (2011). "Paedo bikini banned." *The Sun*. http://www.thesun.co.uk/sol/homepage/news/2931327/Primarks-padded-bikini-tops-for-kids-condemned.html (accessed January 12, 2011).

Hamza, Sharif (Photographer) (2011). "Cadeaux." *French Vogue*, no. 913.

Hanawalt, Barbara A. (1993). *Growing Up in Medieval London: The Experience of Childhood in History*. New York and Oxford: Oxford University Press.

Haraway, Donna (2007). *When Species Meet*. Minneapolis: University of Minnesota Press.

Hardman, Charlotte (2001). "Can There Be an Anthropology of Children?" *Childhood* 11:8, 501–17 (first published in 1973).

Hardt, Michael (1999). "Affective Labor." *Boundary* 226:2, 89–100.

Harrison, Mathew S., Wendy Reynolds-Dobbs, & Kecia M. Thomas (2008). "Skin Color Bias in the Workplace: The Media's Role and Implications towards Preference." In Ronald E. Hall (ed.), *Racism in the 21st Century: An Empirical Analysis of Skin Color*. New York: Springer, 47–62.

Heath, Stephen (1980). *Questions of Cinema*. Bloomington: Indiana University Press.

Hebdige, Dick (1979). *Subculture: The Meaning of Style*. London: Methuen.

Hekanaho, Pia Livia (2006). *Yhden äänen muotokuvia: queer-luentoja Marguerite Yourcenarin teoksista*. Helsinki: Yliopistopaino.

Held, David & Anthony McGrew (2005). *Globalisaatio. Puolesta ja vastaan*. Tampere: Vastapaino.

Helfer, Mary Edna, Ruth S. Kempe, & Richard D. Krugman (eds.) (1997). *The Battered Child*. Chicago: University of Chicago Press (first published in 1968).

Heller, Eva (1989). *Wie Farben wirken: Farbpsychologie, Farbsymbolik, kreative Farbgestaltung*. Reinbek: Rowohlt.

Hendrick, Harry (1997). "Constructions and Reconstructions of British Childhood: An Interpretative Survey, 1800 to the Present." In Allison James & James Prout (eds.), *Constructing and Reconstructing Childhood: Contemporary Issues in the Sociological Study of Childhood*. New York and London: Routledge, 33–60.

Hendrick, Harry (2009). "The Evolution of Childhood in Western Europe c.1400–c.1750." In Jens Qvortrup, William A. Corsaro, & Michael-Sebastian Honig (eds.), *The Palgrave Handbook of Childhood Studies*. Houndmills, Basingstoke, Hampshire: Palgrave Macmillan, 99–113.

Herdt Gilbert (ed.) (1994). *Third Sex, Third Gender: Beyond Sexual Dimorphism in Culture and History*. New York: Zone Books.

Herman, Judith Lewis (1981). *Father-Daughter Incest*. Cambridge, MA: Harvard University Press.

Herman, Judith Lewis & Lisa Hirschman (1977). "Father-Daughter Incest." *Signs: Journal of Women in Culture and Society* 2:4, 735–56.

Heywood, Colin (2001). *A History of Childhood: Children and Childhood in the West from Medieval to Modern Times*. Cambridge: Polity.

Hibberd, Fiona J. (2005). *Unfolding Social Constructionism*. New York: Springer.

Higonnet, Anne (1998). *Pictures of Innocence. The History and Crisis of Ideal Childhood*. New York: Thames and Hudson.

Higonnet, Anne & Cassi Albinson (1997). "Clothing the Child's Body." *Fashion Theory* 1:2, 119–44.

Hirst Paul (1997). "The Global Economy: Myths and Realities." *International Affairs* 73:3, 409–25.

Hochchild, Arlie Russell (2003). *The Managed Heart: Commercialization of Human Feeling*. Twentieth Anniversary Edition, with a New Afterword. Berkeley: University of California Press (first published in 1983).

Hoikkala, Tommi (1993). *Katoaako kasvatus, himmeneekö aikuisuus? Aikuistumisen puhe ja kulttuurimallit*. Helsinki: Gaudeamus.

Holland, Patricia (2004). *Picturing Childhood: The Myth of the Child in Popular Imagery*. London: I. B. Tauris.

Hollis, Nigel (2008). *The Global Brand: How to Create and Develop Lasting Brand Value in the World Market*. London: Palgrave Macmillan.

Holt, Douglas B. (2002). "Why Do Brands Cause Trouble? A Dialectical Theory of Consumer Culture and Branding." *Journal of Consumer Research* 29:1, 70–90.

Holt, Douglas B. (2004). *How Brands Become Icons. The Principles of Cultural Branding*. Boston, MA: Harvard Business School Press.

Honig, Michael-Sebastian (2009). "How Is the Child Constituted in Childhood Studies?" In Jens Qvortrup, William A. Corsaro, & Michael-Sebastian Honig (eds.), *The Palgrave Handbook of Childhood Studies*. Houndmills, Basingstoke, Hampshire: Palgrave Macmillan, 62–77.

hooks, bell (1992). *Black Looks: Race and Representation*. Boston, MA: South End Press.

Illouz, Eva (1997). *Consuming the Romantic Utopia. Love and the Cultural Contradictions of Capitalism*. Berkeley, Los Angeles, Oxford: University of California Press.

Iltalehti (2012). "Näin söpön lahjan Niinistö antoi Estellelle!" April 18, 2012. http://www.iltalehti.fi/kuninkaalliset/2012041815469117_kg.shtml (accessed October 19, 2015).

Ingrassia, Michele (1995). "Calvin Klein on 'Kiddie Porn' Advertisements." *Newsweek* September 11, 1995. http://europe.newsweek.com/calvin-klein-kiddie-porn-advertisements-182964?rm=eu (accessed February 15, 2016).

Irigaray, Luce (1996). *Sukupuolieron etiikka*. Finnish translation by Pia Sivenius. Helsinki: Gaudeamus (original in French published in 1984).

Itkonen, Erkki, Maritta Pesonen, & Olli Syväoja (eds.) (1987). *Suomen kielen etymologinen sanakirja*. Helsinki: Finno-Ugrian Society.

Jaggar, Alison (1974). "On Sexual Equality." *Ethics* 84:4, 275–91.

Jagose, Annamarie (1998). *Queer Theory: An Introduction*. New York: New York University Press.

James, Allison & Alan Prout (eds.) (1990). *Constructing and Reconstructing Childhood*. London: Falmer Press.

James, Allison, Chris Jenks, & Alan Prout (1998). *Theorizing Childhood*. Cambridge: Polity Press.

Jameson, Fredric (1984). "Postmodernism, or the Cultural Logic of Late Capitalism." *New Left Review* 146, 51–92.

Jenkins, Philip (2004). *Moral Panic: Changing Concepts of the Child Molester in Modern America*. New Heaven: Yale University Press.

Jenks, Chris (1996). *Childhood*. London and New York: Routledge.

Jensen, Ole B. (2007). "Culture Stories: Understanding Cultural Urban Branding." *Planning Theory* 6:3, 211–36.

Jhally, Sut (1990). *The Codes of Advertising: Fetishism and the Political Economy of Meaning in the Consumer Society*. New York and London: Routledge.

Jobling, Paul (1999). *Fashion Spreads: World and Image in Fashion Photography since 1980*. Oxford: Berg.

Jokinen, Arto (2000). *Panssaroitu maskuliinisuus: mies, väkivalta ja kulttuuri*. Tampere: Tampereen yliopisto.

Jokinen, Arto (ed.) (2003). *Yhdestä puusta: maskuliinisuuksien rakentuminen populaarikulttuureissa*. Tampere: Tampereen yliopisto.

Jyränki, Juulia & Harri Kalha (2009). *Tapaus Neitsythuorakirkko*. Tampere: Vastapaino.

Kaiser, Susan B. & Kathleen Huun (2002). "Fashioning Innocence and Anxiety: Clothing, Gender, and Symbolic Childhood." In Daniel Thomas Cook (ed.), *Symbolic Childhood*. New York: Peter Lang, 183–210.

Kapferer, Jean-Noel (1997). *Strategic Brand Management*. Second edition. London: Kogan Page.

Kawamura, Yuniya (2005). *Fashion-ology. An Introduction to Fashion Studies*. Oxford: Berg.

Kehily, Mary-Jane (1999). "More Sugar? Teenage Magazines, Gender Displays and Sexual Learning." *European Journal of Cultural Studies* 2:1, 65–89.

Kehily, Mary-Jane (ed.) (2005). *An Introduction to Childhood Studies*. Berkshire: Open University Press.

Kehily, Mary-Jane & Heather Montgomery (2004). "Innocence and Experience: A Historical Approach to Childhood and Sexuality." In Mary-Jane Kehily (ed.), *Introduction to Childhood Studies*. Maidenhead: Open University Press/McGraw Hill, 57–74.

Kekki, Lasse (2006a). "Pervon puolustus." *Kulttuurintutkimus* 3:23, 3–18.

Kekki, Lasse (2006b). "Pervolapsen häpeä ja toivo." In Taina Kinnunen & Anne Puuronen (eds.), *Seksuaalinen ruumis*. Helsinki: Gaudeamus, 127–42.

Kempe, Henry C. et al. (1985). "The Battered-Child Syndrome." *Child Abuse & Neglect* 9, 143–54 (first published in 1962).

Key, Ellen (1909). *The Century of the Child*. New York and London: G. P. Putnam's Sons (first published in 1900).

Key, Ivor (1999). "Has Calvin Klein Gone Too Far in New Underwear Ads Campaign?" *Daily Mail* (London), February 18, 1999.

Kilodavis, Cheryl (2011). *My Princess Boy*. New York: Simon & Schuster.

Kincaid, James R. (1998). *Erotic Innocence: The Culture of Child Molesting*. Durham: Duke University Press.

Kincaid, James R. (2004). "Producing Erotic Children." In Steven Bruhm & Natasha Hurley (eds.), *Curiouser. On the Queerness of Children*. Minneapolis and London: Minnesota University Press, 3–16.

Kismaric, Susan & Eva Respini (2008). "Fashioning Fiction in Photography since 1990." In Eugénie Shinkle (ed.), *Fashion as Photograph: Viewing and Reviewing Images of Fashion*. London and New York: I. B. Tauris & Co, 29–45.

Klein, Naomi (2001). *No Logo. Tähtäimessä brändivaltiaat*. Finnish translation by Liisa Laaksonen & Maarit Tillman. Helsinki: WSOY (original in English [No Logo: Taking Aim at the Brand Bullies] published in 2000).

Koivunen, Anu (1995). *Isänmaan moninaiset äidinkasvot: sotavuosien suomalainen naisten elokuva sukupuoliteknologiana*. Turku: Finnish Society for Cinema Studies.

Kolehmainen, Marjo & Katariina Mäkinen (2009). "Seksuaalisen eron tuottaminen visuaalisessa kulutuskulttuurissa." *Nuorisotutkimus* 27:4, 102–7.

Koller, Veronika (2008). "'Not Just a Colour': Pink as a Gender and Sexuality Marker in Visual Communication." *Visual Communication* 7:4, 395–423.

König, René (1973). *The Restless Image: A Sociology of Fashion*. Translated by F. Bradley. London: George Allen & Unwin.

Korteniemi-Poikela, Erja & Raisa Cacciatore (2010). *Portaita pitkin. Lapsen ja nuoren seksuaalisuuden kehittyminen*. Helsinki: WSOY.

Krafft-Ebing, Richard von (1965). *Psychopathia Sexualis: With Special Reference to the Antipathic Sexual Instinct: A Medico-Forensic Study*. Translated by Franklin S. Klaf. New York: Stein and Day (original in German published in 1886).

Kress, Gunther & Theo van Leeuwen (2001). *Reading Images: The Grammar of Visual Design*. London: Routledge.

Kyrölä, Katariina (2015). "Toward a Contextual Pedagogy of Pain: Trigger Warnings and the Value of Sometimes Feeling Really, Really Bad." *lambda nordica*, 1/2015, 126–44. http://www.lambdanordica.se/artikelarkiv_sokresultat. php?lang=en&fields%5B0%5D=art_id&arkivsok=511 (accessed February 27, 2016).

Lacan, Jacques (1977). "The Mirror Stage as Formative of the Function of the I as Revealed in Psychoanalytic Experience." In Jacques Lacan (ed.), *Écrits: A Selection*. Translated by Alan Sheridan. New York: W. W. Norton, 1–7 (original in French published in 1949).

Lacqueur, Thomas (2003). *Solitary Sex: A History of Masturbation*. New York: Zone Books.

Lähde, Miia (2009). "Lasten itseymmärrys kulutuskulttuurissa: ulkonäkösuhteen muotoutuminen alakoululaisten kirjoituksissa." *Nuorisotutkimus* 27:4, 37–54.

Laing, Morna (2014). "The Lula Girl as 'Sublime and Childlike': Nostalgic Investments in Contemporary Fashion Magazines." *Critical Studies in Fashion and Beauty* 5:2, 271–93.

Lair, Daniel J., Katie Sullivan, & George Cheney (2005). "Marketization and the Recasting of the Professional Self. The Rhetoric and Ethics of Personal Branding." *Management Communication Quarterly* 18:3, 307–43.

Langer, Beryl (2004). "The Business of Branded Enchantment: Ambivalence and Disjuncture in the Global Children's Culture Industry." *Journal of Consumer Culture* 4:2, 251–77.

Laplanche, Jean & Jean-Bertrand Pontalis (1968). "Fantasy and the Origins of Sexuality." *International Journal of Psycho-Analysis* 49, 1–18.

Laqueur, Thomas Walter (2003). *Solitary Sex: A History of Masturbation*. New York: Zone Books.

Lash, Scott & John Urry (1994). *Economies of Signs and Space*. London: Sage.

de Lauretis, Teresa (1984). *Alice Doesn't: Feminism, Semiotics, Cinema*. Bloomington: Indiana University Press.

de Lauretis, Teresa (1987). *Technologies of Gender: Essays on Theory, Film, and Fiction*. Basingstoke: Macmillan.

de Lauretis, Teresa (1991). "Queer Theory: Lesbian and Gay Sexualities." *Differences: A Journal of Feminist Cultural Studies* 3:2, iii–xviii.

de Lauretis, Teresa (1994). *The Practice of Love. Lesbian Sexuality and Perverse Desire*. Bloomington and Indianapolis: Indiana University Press.

de Lauretis, Teresa (1999). "Letter to an Unknown Woman." In Ronnie C. Lesser & Erica Schoenberg (ed.), *That Obscure Subject of Desire: Freud's Female Homosexual Revisited*. New York and London: Routledge, 37–53.

de Lauretis, Teresa (2004). *Itsepäinen vietti. Kirjoituksia sukupuolesta, elokuvasta ja seksuaalisuudesta*. ed. Anu Koivunen. Finnish translation by Tutta Palin & Kaisa Sivenius. Tampere: Vastapaino.

de Lauretis, Teresa (2007). *Figures of Resistance. Essays in Film and Theory*. Urbana and Chicago: University of Illinois Press.

Lazzarato, Maurizio (1996). "Immaterial Labour." In Paolo Virno & Michael Hardt (eds.), *Radical Thought in Italy*. Translated by Paul Colilli & Ed Emory. Minneapolis: University of Minnesota Press, 132–46.

Lehmann, Ulrich (2002). "Fashion Photography." In Ulrich Lehmann & Gilles Lipovetsky (eds.), *Chick Clicks: Creativity in Contemporary Fashion Photography*. Ostfildern-Ruit: Hatje Cantz Publishers.

Lehtonen, Mikko (1994). *Kyklooppi ja kojootti. Subjekti 1600–1900-lukujen kulttuuri- ja kirjallisuusteorioissa*. Tampere: Vastapaino.

Leiss, William, Stephen Kline, Sut Jhally, & Jackie Botterill (2005). *Social Communication in Advertising: Consumption in the Mediated Marketplace*. London and New York: Routledge.

Levin, Diane E. & Jean Kilbourne (2009). *Too Sexy Too Soon? The New Sexualized Childhood and What Parents Can Do to Protect*. New York: Ballantine Books.

Levine, Judith (2003). *Harmful to Minors: The Perils of Protecting Children from Sex*. Minnesota: Minnesota University Press.

Lewis, Reina (2007). "Veils and Sales: Muslims and the Spaces of Postcolonial Fashion Retail." *Fashion Theory* 11:4, 432–42.

Lewis, Reina & Katrina Rolley (1996). "(Ad)dressing the Dyke: Lesbian Looks and Lesbians Looking." In Peter Horne & Reina Lewis (eds.), *Outlooks: Lesbian and Gay Sexualities and Visual Cultures*. New York and London: Routledge, 178–90.

Lindholm, Maria (2011). "Flickan är den nya modeikonen." *Dagens Nyheter*. May 8, 2011, 8, 9.

Lipovetsky, Gilles (1994). *The Empire of Fashion. Dressing Modern Democracy*. Princeton: Princeton University Press.

Locke, John (1964). *Some Thoughts Concerning Education*. Abridged and edited with an introduction and commentary by F. W. Garforth. London: Heinemann (first published in 1693).

Lomrantz, Tracey (2009). "Barbie Gets a Makeover: 50 Designers Do Clothes for Our Favorite Doll." http://www.glamour.com/fashion/blogs/slaves-to-fashion/2009/02/barbie-gets-a-makeover-50-desi.html (accessed May 5, 2011).

Loomba, Ania (1998). *Colonialism—Postcolonialism*. London: Routledge.

Luhmann, Niklas (1983). *Liebe als Passion. Zur Codierung von Intimität*. Frankfurt: Schurkamp.

Lurie, Alison (1983). *The Language of Clothes*. New York: Random House.

Lury, Celia (1996). *Consumer Culture*. Oxford: Blackwell.

Lyman, Richard B. (1974). "Barbarism and Religion: Late Roman and Early Medieval Childhood." In Lloyd deMause (ed.), *History of Childhood*. London: Souvenir Press, 75–100.

MacKinnon, Catherine (1993). *Only Words*. Cambridge, MA: Harvard University Press.

Mail Foreign Service (2011). "Far Too Much, Far Too Young: Outrage over Shocking Images of the 10-Year-Old Model Who Has Graced the Pages of *Vogue*." *Daily Mail*, August 10. http://www.dailymail.co.uk/femail/article-2022305/Thylane-Lena-Rose-Blondeau-Shocking-images-10-YEAR-OLD-Vogue-model.html#ixzz3iKaoclgR (accessed January 23, 2015).

Mallon, Gerald & Teresa DeCrescenzo (2006). "Transgender Children and Youth: A Child Welfare Practice Perspective." *Child Welfare* 85.2 (Mar/Apr 2006), 215–41.

Maffesoli, Michel (1996). *The Contemplation of the World: Figures of Community Style*. Translated by Susan Emanuel. Minneapolis, MN: Minnesota University Press.

Malmelin, Nando (2003). *Mainonnan lukutaito. Mainonnan viestinnällistä luonnetta ymmärtämässä*. Helsinki: Gaudeamus.

Mancini, Elena (2010). *Magnus Hirschfeld and the Quest for Sexual Freedom: A History of the First International Sexual Freedom Movement*. New York: Palgrave Macmillan.

Mann, Thomas (1985). *Kuolema Venetsiassa ja muita kertomuksia*. Finnish translation by Oili Suominen. Helsinki: Tammi (original in German published in 1912).

Mark, E. (2014). "The 5 Most Controversial Vogue Images Ever Published." http://www.theukfashionspot.co.uk/runway-news/450991-controversial-vogue-images-ever-published/5/ (accessed February 19, 2016).

Markkula, Annu & Susanna Härkönen (2009). "Kuluttajuus muotiblogeissa: netnografista tarkastelua." *Nuorisotutkimus* 27:4, 77–82.

Marx, Karl (1992). *Capital: A Critique of Political Economy*. Volume 1. Translated by B. Fowkes. London: Penguin Books (original in German published in 1867).

Massumi, Brian (2002). *Parables of the Virtual: Movement, Affect, Sensation*. Durham: Duke University Press.

Maynard, Michael (2003). "From Global to Glocal: How Gillette's Sensor Excel Accommodates to Japan." *Keio Communication Review* 25, 57–75.

McAllister, Matthew P. (2007). "'Girls with a Passion for Fashion.' The Bratz Brand as Integrated Spectacular Consumption." *Journal of Children and Media* 1:3, 244–58.

McClintock, Anne (1995). *Imperial Leather: Race, Gender, and Sexuality in the Colonial Contest*. New York and London: Routledge.

McCracken, Ellen (1993). *Decoding Women's Magazines: From Mademoiselle to Ms*. Basingstoke: Macmillan.

McCracken, Grant (1988). *Culture and Consumption: New Approaches to the Symbolic Character of Consumer Goods and Activities*. Bloomington, IN: Indiana University Press.

McNair, Brian (2002). *Striptease Culture: Sex, Media and the Democratization of Desire*. London and New York: Routledge.

McNeil, Peter (2000). "Macaroni Masculinities." *Fashion Theory* 4:4, 373–404.

McNeil, Peter (2013). "Conspicuous Waist: Queer Dress in the 'Long Eighteenth Century.'" In Valerie Steele (ed.), *A Queer History of Fashion: From the Closet to the Catwalk*. New Haven and London in association with the Fashion Institute of Technology. New York: Yale University Press.

McRobbie, Angela (2004). "Post-Feminism and Popular Culture." *Feminist Media Studies* 4:3, 255–65.

Merskin, Debra (2011). *Media, Minorities and Meaning. A Critical Introduction*. New York: Peter Lang Publishing.

Meyer, Susan E. (1988). *A Treasury of the Great Children's Book Illustrators*. New York: Abrams.

Miller, Alice (1984). *For Your Own Good: Hidden Cruelty in Child-Rearing and the Roots of Violence*. New York: Farrar, Straus, Giroux.

Miller, Daniel (1987). *Material Culture and Mass Consumption*. Oxford and New York: Basil Blackwell.

Millett, Kate (1989). *Sexual Politics*. London: Virago Press.

Mills, Richar W. & Jean Mills (1999). *Childhood Studies: A Reader in Perspectives of Childhood*. New York and London: Routledge.

Millward Brown, K. (2008). *Demi raportti 2008*. Helsinki: A-lehdet Oy/Demi.

Missy (2011). "French Vogue Controversial Toddler Edition PHOTOS." *Bitten & Bound*, January 8, 2011. http://www.bittenandbound.com/2011/01/08/french-vogue-controversial-toddler-edition-photos/ (accessed January 23, 2015).

Mohr, Richard D. (2004). "The pedophilia of everyday life." In Steven Bruhm & Natasha Hurley (ed.), *Curiouser. On the Queerness of Children*. Minneapolis and London: University of Minnesota Press, 17–30.

Moore, Christopher M. & Grete Birtwistle (2004). "The Burberry Business Model: Creating an International Luxury Fashion Brand." *International Journal of Retail & Distribution Management* 32:8, 412–22.

Mort, Frank (1988). "Boy's Own? Masculinity, Style and Popular Culture." In Rowena Chapman & Jonathan Rutherford (ed.), *Male Order. Unwrapping Masculinity*. London: Lawrence & Wishart, 193–224.

Mort, Frank (1996). *Cultures of Consumption: Masculinities and Social Space in Late-Twentieth Century Britain*. London and New York: Routledge.

Mower, Sarah & Raúl Martínez (2007). *Stylist: The Interpreters of Fashion*. New York: Style.com in association with Rizzoli.

Mulvey, Laura (1989). "Visual Pleasure and Narrative Cinema." In *Visual and Other Pleasures*. Hampshire and New York: Palgrave: 14–26 (first published in 1975).

Mulvey, Laura (1989). "Afterthoughts on 'Visual Pleasure and Narrative Cinema' Inspired by King Vidor's *Duel in the Sun* (1946)." In Laura Mulvey (ed.), *Visual and Other Pleasures*. Hampshire and New York: Palgrave, 29–38 (first published in 1981).

Muniz Albert M. Jr. & Thomas C. O'Guinn (2001). Brand Community. *Journal of Consumer Research* 27:3, 412–32.

Musgrave, Andrew (2013). *Children in Films: Volumes 1 to 8*. S.l.: Lightship Guides and Publications.

Nabokov, Vladimir (1956). *Lolita*. Helsinki: WSOY.

Naskali, Päivi (2010). "Toistoa ja vastarintaa. Yliopisto-opiskelijat ja yrittäjyyskasvatus." In Katri Komulainen, Seija Keskitalo-Foley, Maija Korhonen, & Sirpa Lappalainen (eds.), *Yrittäjyyskasvatus hallintana*. Tampere: Vastapaino, 251–68.

Newman, Andy (1999). "Calvin Klein Cancels Ads with Children Amid Criticism." *The New York Times*, February 17,1999.

Nietzsche, Friedrich (2004). *Iloinen tiede*. Finnish translation by J. A. Hollo; poetry translated by Aarno Peromies & Toivo Lyy. Helsinki: Otava (original in German published in 1882).

Nixon, Sean (2003). *Hard Looks: Masculinities, Spectatorship and Contemporary Consumption*. London: Routledge.

Nudd, Tim (2013). "Romeo Beckham, 10, Makes Spirited Ad Debut for Burberry." *Adweek*, January 13. http://www.adweek.com/adfreak/romeo-beckham-10-makes-spirited-ad-debut-burberry-146251 (accessed October 5, 2015).

O'Connor, Maureen. (2011). "French Vogue Grooms Its Youngest Models Yet." *Gawker*, January 5, 2011. http://gawker.com/5725620/french-vogue-grooms-its-youngest-models-yet/ (accessed January 23, 2015).

Oinas, Elina (2011). "Tyttötutkimuksen näkökulmia ruumiillisuuteen." In Karoliina Ojanen, Heta Mulari, & Sanna Aaltonen (eds.), *Entäs tytöt. Johdatus tyttötutkimukseen*. Tampere: Vastapaino & Helsinki: Finnish Youth Research Society, 305–42.

Ojanen, Karoliina (2011). *Tyttöjen toinen koti: etnografinen tutkimus tyttökulttuurista ratsastustalleilla*. Helsinki: The Finnish Literature Society.

Orenstein, Peggy (2011). *Cinderella Ate My Daughter: Dispatches from the Front Lines of the New Girlie-Girl Culture*. New York: HarperCollins Publishers.

Orme, Nicholas (2001). *Medieval Children*. New Haven and London: Yale University Press.

Paasonen, Susanna (2009). "Affektiivisia miniatyyrimaailmoja: tytöt ja muotinuket brändiyhteisöissä." *Nuorisotutkimus* 27:4, 3–19.

Paasonen, Susanna (2011). *Carnal Resonance*. Cambridge, MA and London: MIT Press.

Paoletti, Jo B. (2012). *Pink and Blue: Telling the Boys from the Girls in America*. Bloomington, IN: Indiana University Press.

Papadopoulos, Linda. (2010). *Sexualisation of Young People Review*. London: Home Office Publication. http://webarchive.nationalarchives.gov.uk/20130128103514/ http://homeoffice.gov.uk/documents/sexualisation-young-people.html (accessed June 28, 2015).

Parker, Ian (ed.) (1998). *Social Constructionism, Discourse and Realism*. London: SAGE.

Pastoureau, Michel (2004). *Blue: The History of a Color*. Princeton: Princeton University Press.

Paterson, Mark (2007). *Consumption and Everyday Life*. London and New York: Routledge.

Peoples, Sharon (2014). "Embodying the Military: Uniforms." *Critical Studies in Men's Fashion* 1:1, 7–21.

Perrot, Philippe (1994). *Fashioning the Bourgeoisie: A History of Clothing in the Nineteenth Century*. Princeton, NJ: Princeton University Press.

Perry, Monica & Charles Bodkin (2000). "Content analysis of Fortune 100 Company Web Sites." *Corporate Communications: An International Journal* 5:2, 87–97.

Petersson, Torbjörn (2012). "Barnbristen blir Japans nästa kris." *Dagens Nyheter*, March 14, 2012, 14, 15.

Phelps, Nicole (2015). "Sex Sells: Calvin Klein's 1990s Ads Stirred Libidos and Controversies in Equal Measure." *Vogue*, September 1. http://www.vogue.com/13297709/calvin-klein-jeans-90s-ads-kate-moss-mark-wahlberg-controversy/ (accessed February 16, 2016).

Piaget, Jean (2002). *The Principles of Genetic Epistemology*. London and New York: Routledge (original in French published in 1970).

Piponnier, Françoise & Perrine Mane (1997). *Dress in the Middle Ages*. Translated by Caroline Beamish. New Haven and London: Yale University Press.

Pitkin, Hanna Fenichel (1972). *The Concept of Representation*. Berkley: University of California Press.

Plant, Richard (1988). *The Pink Triangle: The Nazi War against Homosexuals*. New York: Holt Paperbacks.

Pocklington, Rebecca (2014). "Romeo Beckham, 12, 'Paid £45,000' for One Day's Work on New Burberry Campaign." *Mirror*, November 10. http://www.mirror.co.uk/3am/celebrity-news/romeo-beckham-12-paid-45000-4604033 (accessed October 5, 2015).

Pohjala, Heidi (2012). "Shortsit kiellettiin!" *Ilta-Sanomat*, June 5, 2012, 6, 7.

Pointon, Marcia (1993). "The State of the Child." In Marcia Pointon: *Hanging the Head. Portraiture and Social Formation in Eighteenth-Century England*. New Haven and London: Yale University Press, 177–226.

Polhemus, Ted (1978/2011). *Fashion and Anti-Fashion. Exploring Adornment and Dress from an Anthropological Perspective*. London: Thames & Hudson.

Polhemus, Ted (1994). *Street Style. From the Sidewalk to the Catwalk*. London: Thames & Hudson.

Pollock, Linda (1983). *Forgotten Children: Parent-Child Relations from 1500–1900*. New York: Cambridge University Press.

Postman, Neil (1982). *Lyhenevä lapsuus*. Finnish translation by Ilkka Rekiarvo. Helsinki: WSOY (original in English [The Disapperance of Childhood] published in 1982).

Prout, James (2005). *The Future of Childhood: Towards the Interdisciplinary Study of Children*. London: RoutledgeFalmer.

"Pukeutumisleikkejä." *Elle* 1/2011, 48.

Puustinen, Liina (2008). *Kuluttajamuotti: kuluttajuuden tuottamisesta mainonnan instituutioissa*. Helsinki: Gaudeamus.

Quart, Alissa (2003). *Brändätyt: Ostetaan ja myydään nuoria*. Finnish translation by Taina Juvala. Helsinki: Like.

Qvortrup, Jens (2009). "Childhood as a Structural Form." In Jens Qvortrup, William A. Corsaro, & Michael-Sebastian Honig (eds.), *The Palgrave Handbook of Childhood Studies*. Houndmills, Basingstoke and Hampshire: Palgrave Macmillan, 21–33.

Qvortrup, Jens, William A. Corsaro, & Michael-Sebastian Honig (eds.) (2009). *The Palgrave Handbook of Childhood Studies*. Houndmills, Basingstoke, Hamshire: Palgrave Macmillan.

Rabine, Leslie W. & Susan Kaiser (2006). "Sewing Machines and Dream Machines in Los Angeles and San Francisco: The Case of the Blue Jean." In Christopher Breward & David Gilbert (eds.), *Fashion's World Cities*. Oxford and New York: Berg, 235–49.

Rank, Otto (1959). "Forms of Kinship and the Individual's Role in the Family." In P. Freund (ed.), *The Myth of the Birth of the Hero and Other Writings*. New York: Vintage Books (original in German published in 1932).

Rantonen, Eila (1997). Muukalaisnaiset materiana eli huomioita geosukupuoli-politiikasta. *Niin & Näin* 3. http://www.netn.fi/397/netn_397_rant.html (accessed October 13, 2016).

Ribeiro, Aileen (2003). *Dress and Morality*. Oxford: Berg (first published in 1986).

Riello, Giorgio and McNeil, Peter (eds.) (2010). *The Fashion History Reader. Global Perspectives*. London and New York: Routledge.

Ritzer, George (ed.) (2007). *The Blackwell Companion to Globalization*. Malden, Oxford and Carlton: Blackwell Publishing.

Robertson, Roland (1992). *Globalization: Social Theory and Global Culture*. London: Sage.

Robertson, Roland (1995). "Glocalization: Time-Space and Homogeneity-Heterogeneity." In Mike Featherstone, Scott Lash, & Roland Robertson (eds.), *Global Modernities*. London: Sage, 23–44.

Rose, Jacqueline (1996). *States of Fantasy*. Oxford: Clarendon Press.

Rossi, Leena-Maija (2003). *Heterotehdas. Televisiomainonta sukupuolituotantona*. Helsinki: Gaudeamus.

Rossi, Leena-Maija (2006). "Heteronormatiivisuus. Käsitteen elämää ja kummastelua." *Kulttuurintutkimus* 23:3, 19–28.

Rossi, Leena-Maija (2007). "Queer TV? Kumouksellisten representaatioiden politiikasta ja ehdoista." In Leena-Maija Rossi & Anita Seppä (eds.), *Tarkemmin katsoen. Visuaalisen kulttuurin lukukirja*. Helsinki: Gaudeamus, 122–36.

Rousseau, Jean-Jacques (2011). *Émile*. Translated by Barbara Foxley. Project Gutenberg eBook. http://www.gutenberg.org/cache/epub/5427/pg5427-images.html (original in French published in 1762).

Rubin, Gayle (1984). "Thinking Sex: Notes for a Radical Theory of the Politics of Sexuality." In Carole S. Vance (ed.), *Pleasure and Danger: Exploring Female Sexuality*. Boston: Routledge and Kegan Paul, 267–93.

Ruckenstein, Minna (2007). "Viattomien lasten suojelusta tyttöjen kulutukseen: kiistelty Bratz-nukke." *Nuorisotutkimus* 26:3, 100–5.

Rush, Emma & Andrea La Nauze (2006a). "Corporate Paedophilia: Sexualisation of Children in Australia." Discussion Paper no. 90/2006.

Rush, Emma & Andrea La Nauze (2006b). "Letting Children Be Children: Stopping the Sexualisation of Children in Australia." Discussion Paper no. 93/2006.

Ryle, Gilbert (1963). *The Concept of the Mind*. Harmondsworth: Penguin.

Saarenmaa, Laura (2010). *Intiimin äänet. Julkisuuskulttuurin muutos suomalaisissa ajanvietelehdissä 1961–1975*. Tampere: University of Tampere.

Saarikoski, Helena (2009). *Nuoren naisellisuuden koreografioita. Spice Girlsin fanit tyttöyden tekijöinä*. Helsinki: SKS.

Sadeniemi, Matti, Jouko Vesikansa, Kaisa Häkkinen, & Harri Jäppinen (1978). *Nykysuomen sanakirja*. Helsinki: WSOY.

Said, Edward (2011). *Orientalismi*. Finnish translation by Kati Pitkänen. Helsinki: Gaudeamus (original in English [Orientalism] published in 1978).

Salo, Irmeli (2011). "Aller lanseeraa muotilehden 6-12-vuotiaille tytöille." *Talouselämä*. http://www.talouselama.fi/uutiset/article575257.ece (accessed February 8, 2011).

Sanchez-Eppeler, Karen (2005). *Dependent State: The Child's Part in Nineteenth-Century American Culture*. Chicago: Chicago University Press.

Sauers, Jenna. (2011). "French Vogue's Sexy Kiddie Spread Is Misunderstood." *Jezebell*, January 5, 2011. http://jezebel.com/5725707/french-vogues-sexy-kiddie-spread-is-misunderstood/ (accessed September 3, 2015).

Schilt, Kristen and Westbrook, Laurel (2009). "Doing Gender, Doing Heteronormativity: 'Gender Normals,' Transgender People, and the Social Maintenance of Heterosexuality." *Gender & Society* 23:4, 440–64.

Schor, Juliet (2004). *Born to Buy: the Commercialized Child and the New Consumer Culture*. New York: Scribner.

Schroeder, Jonathan E. (2005). *Visual Consumption*. London and New York: Routledge.

Schroeder, Jonathan E. & Detlev Zwick (2004). "Mirrors of Masculinity: Representation and Identity in Advertising Images." *Consumption, Markets and Culture* 7:1, 21–52.

Schwartz, Joseph (1999). *Cassandra's Daughter: A History of Psychoanalysis*. London: Viking Penguin, a member of Penguin Putnam Inc.

Scott, Jill (2005). *Electra after Freud: Myth and Culture*. Ithaca: Cornell University Press.

Sedgwick, Eve Kosofsky (1985). *Between Men: English Literature and Male Homosocial Desire*. New York: Duke University Press.

Sedgwick, Eve Kosofsky (1991a). "Jane Austen and the Masturbating Girl." *Critical Inquiry* 17:4, 818–37.

Sedgwick, Eve Kosofsky (1991b). *Epistemology of the Closet*. New York: Harvester Wheatsheaf.

Sedgwick, Eve Kosofsky (1997). "Paranoid Reading and Reparative Reading, or, You're So Paranoid, You Probably Think This Introduction Is about You." In Eve Kosofsky Sedgwick (ed.), *Novel Gazing: Queer Readings in Fiction*. Durham and London: Duke University Press, 1–37.

Sender, Katherine (2004). *Business, Not Politics: The Making of the Gay Market*. New York: Columbia University Press.

Sennett, Richard (1978). *The Fall of Public Man*. London: Faber.

Seppänen, Janne (2005). *Visuaalinen kulttuuri. Teoriaa ja metodeja mediakuvan tulkitsijalle*. Tampere: Vastapaino.

Shahar, Sulamith (1990). *Childhood in the Middle Ages*. London and New York: Routledge.

Shinkle, Eugénie (ed.) (2008). *Fashion as Photograph: Viewing and Reviewing Images of Fashion*. London and New York: I. B. Tauris & Co.

Shotter, John (1993). *Cultural Politics of Everyday Life: Social Constructionism, Rhetoric and Knowing of the Third Kind*. Toronto: University of Toronto Press.

Sidén, Karin (2001). *Den ideala barndomen: studier i det stormaktstida barnporträttets ikonografi och funktion*. Stockholm: Raster.

Simmel, Georg (1984). *On Women, Sexuality and Love*. Translated and edited by Guy Oakes. New Haven: Yale University Press.

Simmel, Georg (1986). *Muodin filosofia*. Finnish translation by Antti Alanen. Helsinki: Odessa (original in German published in 1904).

Simmel, Georg (2005). "The Metropolis and Mental Life." In Jan Lin & Christopher Mele (ed.), *The Urban Sociology Reader*. London and New York: Routledge, 25–31 (original in German published in 1903).

Simmel, Georg (2010). "The Metropolis and Mental Life." In Gary Bridge & Sophie Watson (ed.), *The Blackwell City Reader*. Malden, Oxford, Chichester: Wiley-Blackwell (original in German published in 1903).

Simpson, Mark (1994). "Here Come the Mirror Men: Why The Future Is Metrosexual." *The Independent*, November 15.

Skeggs, Beverley (1997). *Formations of Class and Gender*. Sage: London.

Skeggs, Beverley (2004). *Class, Self, Culture*. London and New York: Routledge.

Sommers, Sanna (2012). "Ne todelliset syyt." *Me Naiset* 24, June 14, 2012, 13.

Sophocles (1955). *Elektra*. Finnish translation by Emil Zilliacus. Schildt: Helsingfors.

Sophocles (1988). *Kuningas Oidipus*. Otava: Keuruu.

Spillers, Hortense (1987). "Mama's Baby, Papa's Maybe: An American Grammar Book." *Diacritics* 17:2, 65–81.

Spivak, Gayatri Chakravorty (1999). *A Critique of Postcolonial Reason: Toward a History of the Vanishing Present*. Cambridge, MA: Harvard University Press.

Steele, Valerie (1985). *Fashion and Eroticism: Ideals of Feminine Beauty from the Victorian Era to the Jazz Age*. New York: Oxford University Press.

Stryker, Susan & Nikki Sullivan (2009). "King's Member, Queen's Body: Transsexual Surgery, Self-Demand Amputation, and the Somatechnics of Sovereign Power." In Nikki Sullivan & Samantha Murray (eds.), *Somatechnics: Queering the Technologisation of Bodies*. Farnham: Ashgate.

Time Staff (2014). "The 25 Most Influential Teens of 2014." *The Time Magazine*, October 13 (accessed February 17, 2016).

Tom & Lorenzo. (2011). "Vogue Paris: Cadeaux." http://tomandlorenzo2.blogspot.fi/2011/01/vogue-paris-cadeaux.html (accessed January 23, 2015).

Tomlinson, John (1999). *Globalization and Culture*. Chicago: University of Chicago Press.

Tortora, Phyllis G. & Sara B. Marcketti (1989/2015). *Survey of Historic Costume*. London and New York: Bloomsbury Publishing.

Tséelon, Efrat (1992). "Is the Presented Self Sincere? Goffman, Impression Management and the Postmodern Self." *Theory, Culture &. Society* 9, 115–28.

Tucker, Lauren R. (1998). "The Framing of Calvin Klein: A Frame Analysis of Media Discourse about the August 1995 Calvin Klein Jeans Advertising Campaign." *Critical Studies in Mass Communication* 15, 141–57.

Tucker, M. J. (1974). "The Child as Beginning and End: Fifteenth and Sixteenth Century English Childhood." In Lloyd deMause (ed.), *History of Childhood*. London: Souvenir Press, 229–57.

Tyler, Imogen (2008). "Chav Mum Chav Scum." *Feminist Media Studies* 8:1, 17–34.

Utula, Katri (2012). "Estelle pukeutuu vain huippumuotiin: Takin arvo 230 euroa." *Ilta-Sanomat*, May 10, 2012. http://www.iltasanomat.fi/kuninkaalliset/art-1288468260248.html?ref=hs-tf-promo5 (accessed May 10, 2012).

Valenti, Jessica (2010). *The Purity Myth. How America's Obsession with Virginity Is Hurting Young Women*. Berkeley: Seal Press.

Vann, Richard (1982). "The Youth of Centuries Childhood." *History and Theory* 21:2, 279–98.

Vänskä, Annamari (2006). *Vikuroivia vilkaisuja. Ruumis, sukupuoli, seksuaalisuus ja visuaalisen kulttuurin tutkimus*. Taidehistoriallisia tutkimuksia, vol. 35. Helsinki: The Society for Art History in Finland.

Vänskä, Annamari (2007). "Isona minusta tulee palomies! Eli kuinka lapsia heteroseksualisoidaan Vogue Bambinin mainonnassa." *Nuorisotutkimus* 26:3, 2–23.

Vänskä, Annamari (2009a). "Betaurokset tulevat." *Dooris*, 4/2009. www.doorislehti.fi/uusin-lehti/97-betaurokset-tulevat (accessed January 31, 2012).

Vänskä, Annamari (2009b). "Kuviteltu lapsuus. Pohdintaa kuvallisuuden kietoutumisesta kuluttamiseen." In Minna Lammi, Mari Niva, & Johanna Varjonen (eds.), *Kulutuksen liikkeet. Kuluttajatutkimuskeskuksen vuosikirja 2009*. Helsinki: Consumer Society Research Centre, 205–26.

Vänskä, Annamari (2011a). "Virginal Innocence and Corporeal Sensuality. Reading Meanings of Childhood in Contemporary Fashion Advertising." *Barn* 1, 49–66.

Vänskä, Annamari (2011b). "Seducing Children?" *Lambda Nordica* 2–3, 69–109.

Vänskä, Annamari (2011c). "Erään skandaalin anatomia. Tapaus Ulla Karttunen." In Susanne Dahlgren, Sari Kivistö, & Susanna Paasonen (eds.), *Skandaali! Suomalaisen taiteen ja politiikan mediakohut*. Helsinki: Helsinki-kirjat, 21–50.

Vänskä, Annamari (2015). "Kindergarteners in Vampy Lipstick and Stilettos? On the Sexualization of Little Girls in *French Vogue*." *Journal of Girlhood Studies* 8:3, 56–72.

Vänskä, Annamari & Minna Autio (2009). "Aikuisia lapsia ja lapsiaikuisia—symbolinen lapsuus visualisoituvassa kulutuskulttuurissa." *Nuorisotutkimus* 27:4, 53–69.

Vänskä, Annamari (forthcoming). "Gender and Sexuality, 1920–2000s." In Alexandra Palmer (ed.), *Bloomsbury Series on Cultural History of Fashion & Dress, Vol 6: Fashion in the Modern Age (1920–2000)*. London and New York: Bloomsbury Publishing.

Veblen, Thorstein (2002). *Joutilas luokka*. Finnish translation by Tiina Arppe & Sulevi Riukulehto. Helsinki: Art House. (original in English [*The Theory of the Leisure Class*] published in 1899).

Viinikka, Jenni (2011). *Kuoleman kielissä*. Pro gradu thesis. Department of Finnish, Finno-Ugrian and Scandinavian Studies of the University of Helsinki.

Vinken, Barbara (2004). *Fashion Zeitgeist: Trends and Cycles in the Fashion System*. Oxford: Berg.

Vogue, Bambini (2011). cerosdata.bigkidlondon.com/web-assets/conde/mediakit/Italy/Vogue_Bambini.pdf

Wade, Lisa (2011). "Adultification & Sexualization of Girls in French *Vogue*." *Sociological Images*, January 8. http://thesocietypages.org/socimages/2011/01/08/adultification-and-sexualization-of-girls-in-french-vogue/ (accessed January 23, 2015).

Walkerdine, Valerie (1997). *Daddy's Girl: Young Girls and Popular Culture*. Basingstoke: Macmillan.

Walkerdine, Valerie (2003). "Reclassifying Upward Mobility: Femininity and the Neo-Liberal Subject." *Gender and Education*, 15:3, 237–48.

Walkerdine, Valerie, Helen Luceyn, & June Melody (2001). *Growing Up Girl: Psychosocial Explorations of Gender and Class*. Basingstoke: Palgrave.

Walkerdine, Valerie & Luis Jimenez (2012). *Gender, Work and Community after De-Industrialisation. A Psychosocial Approach to Affect*. Houndmills, Basingstoke and Hampshire: Palgrave Macmillan.

Walters, Suzanna Danuta (2001). *All the Rage: The Story of Gay Visibility in America*. Chicago: The Chicago University Press.

Warhurst, Chris, Dennis Nickson, Anne Witz, & Anne Culle (2000). "Aesthetic Labour in Interactive Service Work: Some Case Study Evidence from the 'New' Glasgow." *The Service Industries Journal* 20:3, 1–18.

Warner, Michael (1991). "Introduction: Fear of a Queer Planet." *Social Text* 9:4 [29], 3–17.

Warner, Michael (2000). *The Trouble with Normal: Sex, Politics and the Ethics of Queer Life*. Cambridge, MA: Harvard University Press.

Weeks, Jeffrey (1981). *Sex, Politics and Society. The Regulation of Sexuality since 1800*. London: Longman.

Wetherell, Margaret & Arthur Still (1998). "Realism and Relativism." In Roger Sapsford, Arthur Still, Margaret Wetherell, Dorothy Miell, & Richard Stevens (eds.), *Theory and Social Psychology*. London: Sage, 99–114.

WHO (2010). *Standards for Sexuality Education in Europe. A Framework for Policy Makers, Educational and Health Authorities and Specialists*. Federal Centre for Health Education, BZgA Cologne. www.oif.ac.at/fileadmin/OEIF/andere_Publikationen/WHO_BZgA_Standards.pdf (accessed October 13, 2016).

Williamson, Judith (1978). *Decoding Advertisements: Ideology and Meaning in Advertising*. London: Boyars.

Wilson, Adrian (1980). "The Infancy of Childhood: An Appraisal of Philippe Ariès." *History and Theory* 19:2, 132–53.

Wilson, Elisabeth (1985). *Adorned in Dreams: Fashion and Modernity*. London: Virago.

Wissinger, Elizabeth (2007a). "Always on Display: Affective Production in the Modeling Industry." In Patricia Ticineto Clough & Jean Halley (eds.), *The Affective Turn. Theorizing the Social*. Durham and London: Duke University Press, 231–60.

Wissinger, Elizabeth (2007b). "Modelling a Way of Life: Immaterial and Affective Labour in the Fashion Modelling Industry." *Ephemera* 7:1, 250–69.

Wissinger, Elizabeth (2009). "Modeling Consumption: Fashion Modeling Work in Contemporary Society." *Journal of Consumer Culture* 9:2, 273–96.

Wissinger, Elizabeth (2015). *This Year's Model: Fashion, Media, and the Making of Glamour*. New York and London: New York University Press.

Witz, Anne, Chris Warhurst, & Dennis Nickson (2003). "The Labour of Aesthetics and the Aesthetics of Organization." *Organization* 10:1, 33–54.

Wooldridge, Adrian (2006). *Measuring the Mind: Education and Psychology in England c.1860-c.1990*. Cambridge: Cambridge University Press.

Yleissopimus lapsen oikeuksista (2011). http://www.unicef.fi/Lapsen_oikeuksien_sopimus_koko (accessed October 13, 2016).

Zelizer, Viviana (1985). *Pricing the Priceless Child: The Changing Social Value of Children*. New York: Basic Books.

Research Materials

Issues of *Vogue Bambini* from 1973–2010.

INDEX